# TRANSITION IN AFRICA

# TRANSITION
# IN AFRICA

## FROM DIRECT RULE
## TO INDEPENDENCE

A Memoir by
### SIR JAMES ROBERTSON

With a foreword by
### MARGERY PERHAM

LONDON
### C. HURST & COMPANY

First published in the United Kingdom by
C. Hurst & Company (Publishers) Ltd., London

© 1974 by Sir James Robertson

ISBN 0-903983-06-0

Printed in Great Britain by
Billing & Sons Ltd., Guildford and London

# CONTENTS

# PLATES

# MAPS

# AUTHOR'S NOTE

This book was started in order to give my family some account of my service in Africa, first in the Sudan and then in Nigeria. It has been written almost entirely from memory with the aid of a few sketchy diaries and some papers which I have never destroyed. As memory is by no means reliable after many years, there are bound to be some mistakes and, furthermore, one's ideas of the past are often influenced by hindsight. However, I feel confident that the main aspects of my work in Africa are described with reasonable correctness, and that the opinions mentioned are those which I held at the relative times. I hope that I have not sounded too altruistic in emphasising the aims that most British overseas officers held towards the people whom they were administering and with whom they very largely identified themselves, whatever the official attitudes of the British Government at any particular time might be. It is true that the assumptions on which we worked were based on a paternalistic outlook towards the peoples we ruled, and the changes that we sought for them were what we, and not they, thought were good. The achievements of our work up to the time of the final hand-over were there for all to see, and it is my belief that we need not be ashamed of them.

When I look back on these years in Africa, I think of a few people as those who influenced me most: my first provincial Governor, Arthur Huddleston, and later Douglas Newbold, Governor of Kordofan and Civil Secretary in the Sudan, and in Nigeria the Colonial Secretary Alan Lennox-Boyd (now Lord Boyd). Over the years Dame Margery Perham was a constant friend and adviser, who was a great inspiration in my work and to whom I am deeply in debt. Without the wise, patient and courageous help and support of my wife I could not have managed nearly so well, and any success I may have had was undoubtedly her achievement as much as mine.

My grateful thanks are due to Peter Woodward of Reading University who took my long rambling narrative and put it into shape, pruning and editing, cutting out repetitious and unnecessary deviations from the main theme. He has succeeded in this without altering my language or changing the sense of my first draft. He has no responsibility for anything I have said about individuals or for the historical accuracy of my account.

I also wish to thank Mr. Christopher Hurst, the publisher, for his consideration, his help and his courtesy.

Dame Margery Perham has put me further in her debt by writing a foreword, for which I am most grateful.

J. W. R.

# FOREWORD

The rapid dissolution of Britain's immense colonial empire was largely due to the effects of the Second World War both in arousing the ambitions of the ruled and weakening the power and self-confidence of the rulers. The dissolution resulted from no single over-all decision by Britain herself and no concerted movement among the ruled. In Africa each of the states which gained their independence in the twelve years between 1956 and 1968 followed their own paths to freedom at different dates. The achievement of independence seems to have been followed by a tendency both in the former rulers and in the ruled, though for different reasons, to turn their attention away from the colonial period and the process by which it was terminated. On the African side this was due partly to an unacknowledged but natural distaste to dwell upon the fact of their subjection and upon the British side by the desire to concentrate more upon new opportunities than upon the loss of imperial power and prestige. The time, however, is likely to come, and is perhaps even now coming, when there will be an increasing interest, especially upon the British side, in reviewing the imperial record partly, perhaps, in order to test our impression that there is little in it of which we need, by any relative moral standard, to be ashamed.

Perhaps the most important evidence for this re-assessment is that which can be provided by the men who carried the highest responsibilities of power in ipmerial government and who handled its termination. They need to choose the time when their past work can be seen in perspective yet before, with increasing age, the scene becomes dim or is suffused with too roseate a light. This book is proof enough that Sir James Robertson has chosen his time well. We are fortunate, too, in gaining from him a double record of the process of colonial emancipation in the Sudan and in Nigeria and of his having, therefore, served under both the Foreign Office and the Colonial Office.

Sir James' first chapters bring out the peculiar features of the Sudan, so striking to anyone studying the country after working in Colonial Office territories. Among these was the high degree both of the autonomy of the British staff, working under a somewhat inattentive and uninstructed Foreign Office, and also of its unity, that of men sharing together a working lifetime and being drawn largely from the same social and educational source. It was a well-known comment that the Sudan was 'a country of Blacks ruled by Blues'. One enthusiastic foreign observer, intending, it seems, a compliment, referred to the Sudan administrators as the British Samurai.

The picture given of the Sudan during Sir James' period as a district and provincial officer are of peaceful developments. The steadiness and loyal co-operation of the Sudanese during the war of 1939–46, in a region set between areas of active war, were tributes to Sudanese confidence in their British rulers. Among them he rightly names his friend, the Civil Secretary, Sir Douglas Newbold, one of the finest and most humane men, using the word in its fullest sense, ever sent from Britain to rule in Africa. Yet, with so much to admire in the administration of the Sudan, the student of the rest of British Africa is obliged to remark the relative delay in the Sudan in developing the first elements of self-government. But he will also remark the speed with which, as Sir James' record shows, the omission was made good.

Some of the most interesting pages in the book deal with the almost frenzied struggle that was carried on in Khartoum, Cairo, London and New York to insure that the Sudanese should not emerge from British control to fall under that of Egypt. This struggle, in which Sir James worked successfully with his Governor-General, Sir Hubert Huddleston, was perhaps the finest hour of his long service to the Sudan.

He makes no attempt to explain away the tragic side of the emancipation of the Sudan, the fate which befell the tribes in the south when they rejected union with the north and brought upon themselves the years of conflict, depopulation and dispersal which have only recently ended in a settlement which, we must hope, will bring unity, restoration and re-settlement to these unhappy tribes. Sir James' explanation of the Sudan Government's 'southern policy', that of keeping the southern provinces largely separate from the north, raises issues which take us back to the original establishment of the condominium which combined the Muslim Arabs of the north with the pagan tribes they had so long raided for slaves. As with many other problems in ex-colonial Africa, in seeking reasons for the troubles which have followed African emancipations, the British can claim that their policies were overtaken by the unexpected speed with which the political leaders, within those arbitiarily designed states, attained their independence.

Sir James' appointment in 1955 as Governor-General of Nigeria meant that he was assigned the task of bringing the most populous of African colonial dependencies to independence, a task accomplished within five years. It would be a mistake to regard his work as a mere presidency over a formal stage towards independence. There were still many large problems to be settled. Moreover, Sir James was dealing with three political leaders of the three main regions who were highly differentiated characters, often as much interested in their position within their own regions as in the constitution of the new central government. The only part of Nigeria in any way comparable with the Sudan was the Muslim north, and not the whole of that, while the situation he had known in the Sudan was reversed in Nigeria in that the southern pagan and Christian states were in most ways far more politically developed and ambitious than the northern Muslims.

To watch Sir James in this new setting, among the able and assertive political leaders, was to recognize what valuable qualities he brought to his new task, dignity and imperturbability combined with a sense of humour and of proportion. He was like a charioteer whose task was not to choose the course or the winning post but to keep his three highly spirited horses running in unison. It was a task which needed his detachment from the intensities of Nigeria's recent political history; other assets were his calm manner, his common sense and a massive stature. Most valuable was the friendship and respect which quickly developed between himself and Sir Abubakar Tafawa Balewa, the grave and upright northerner who became the first federal prime minister. Their deep mutual respect made up as far as possible for the difficulties caused by the decision of the most active and obvious leader of the north, Sir Ahmadu Bello, to remain as premier of the vast northern region but to claim at the same time to manipulate the ex-schoolmaster who had become the federal prime minister.* Sir James also managed to deal with the strong, markedly different personalities of the western and eastern leaders, Awolowo and Azikiwe.

So, as Sir James describes, with royal visits to Nigeria, meetings of the young regional legislatures and of the new central council, with constructive conferences in the stately setting of Lancaster House, the six years' tenure of the last governor came to its appointed end. How much serious controversy went on behind the political stage will be revealed with the opening of the Colonial Office archives. I doubt whether historians will find any dramatic revelations. The last stages are described by Sir James in this book. These were conducted with the dignity and completeness which befitted such a large and historic

* To underline the remarkable development of this man from isolated and humble beginnings into a statesman of world-wide stature it might be interesting to record a fact I learned after his death, that I was the first white woman he saw. This must have been when I spent a year working in Nigeria in 1931 and called in at the rural school in Bauchi where he was teaching, a brief encounter of which I have no recollection. What I most remember of him was a remark he made at the time of independence, when we were discussing his difficulties with other politicians, some of whom were not always as honourable as himself. 'I do not believe that any man is wholly evil.'

enfranchisement. It is easy to understand that Sir James was much moved by the final ceremony on the night of 30 September in the crowded Lagos racecourse, when the Union Jack was hauled down and the Nigerian flag went up. It was impossible at that moment not to look back over the complex history of our relations with Nigeria, first in its several parts and later in its totality. For me the memory of Lord Lugard, with those four interventions into Nigerian history which had caused me years of deeply interesting study, was dominant in my mind.

Any record of Sir James Robertson's work would be incomplete if it did not refer to an aspect which it might have been difficult for him to include, the contribution to his work made by his wife. I know well from my travels over many years how much, as a lesser queen beside the gubernatorial representative of the British crown, the wife could help to make or mar her husband's work in the highly sensitive setting of a British dependency. All who have known Lady Robertson in her public life will endorse my opinion that, with her intelligence, wit and humanity, she has been the ideal partner.

One final observation. The question may be asked whether Britain, in the person of her chief representative during the final phases of en-franchisement, bears any responsibility for the assassinations and the destructive civil war which stained Nigeria's independence six years after its achievement. It may be well to remind ourselves that the people of the Eastern Region who tried to break away had been the most eager to achieve Nigerian unification and had, perhaps the most to gain from it. In considering the post-independence tragedies of both the Southern Sudan and of south-eastern Nigeria, it must be accepted that no British administration, handling the tense, final process of colonial emancipation, could have re-made situations which resulted from hasty frontier-making in the malleable Africa of the preceding century. We can only hope that in both countries the settlements which have followed the tragic post-independence bloodshed will be constructive and final.

MARGERY PERHAM

# PART ONE

# THE SUDAN: SERVICE IN THE PROVINCES

# CHAPTER I

# THE WAY TO THE SUDAN

Successive generations of young people find themselves with the choice of different kinds of careers; new doors are opening, but old ones may also close. Those of us who went to serve in Africa in the years following the First World War were among the last to have the opportunity of a life-time's service in the British administration of the continent. The Africa which we knew was changing rapidly, moving from trusteeship to independence, and all British staff were in some way caught up in the political evolution; between 1922 and 1960 I was to have a closer view of this process than most. In my case, the choice of an overseas career was encouraged by the long connection of my family with India.

Grandfather Robertson had been in business in India with the Borneo Company and was still there when my father went out to Calcutta in 1867. He in turn spent twenty years in the jute business, before returning to his native Scotland and buying a jute mill in Dundee. My father was a shrewd practical businessman with few pretensions to learning, but my mother came from a very different background. She was the daughter of a Scottish schoolmaster named Adam Wilson, the head classics teacher at Dundee High School, and her grandfather, Dr. John Rankine, had been Moderator of the United Presbyterian Church. At the time of my parents' marriage when father returned from India, he was forty-nine and my mother thirty years younger.

Their marriage produced six children, three girls and three boys, of whom I was the eldest. In 1909, on father's retirement, the family moved to Edinburgh, and after preparatory school I entered the upper school of Merchiston Castle in 1913, where I remained until called up for the army in April 1918. By that time I had become captain of school and played for both the rugby and cricket teams, as well as winning a number of school prizes. My army training was at the 14th Officers' Cadet Battalion at Romford in Essex, but as the war was approaching an end, my batch did not go to our regiments but remained at Romford until demobilised in January 1919. So instead of going to war, I went up to Balliol College, Oxford, and was there until the end of the summer term in 1922. Like most people I thoroughly enjoyed my time at Oxford and made many good friends. I came down after taking my B.A. with third-class honours in Classical 'Moderations' and second-class in 'Greats' and with a Blue for rugby football in 1921.

As the time to leave Oxford approached I began to consider my future. Ever since I was quite young my father had hoped that I would enter the Indian Civil Service, and I had been encouraged to think of that service as the best in the world. My tutor at Balliol, Sandy Lindsay* thought that I would need to do a year's special cramming to be sure of passing the I.C.S. examinations well, and this in some ways seemed attractive as I could then have had another year at Oxford and perhaps played again for the Varsity XV. On the other hand conditions in India seemed very unsettled, with the papers full of the Amritsar affair and other disturbances. I listened also to men I knew who had gone to the Sudan Political Service and the Colonial Service, and who spoke well of both those careers. My father did not press me to decide on India, and in the end I put my name down for the Sudan and the colonies, thinking that if neither accepted me I could stay another year and try for the I.C.S.

There were no written examinations for the Sudan and I was interviewed by two representatives of the Sudan Government at Hertford College on their preliminary selection visit to Oxford. I was not sure what impression I made at this interview, for on opening the door I fell down the two steps into the room, cursing volubly, and on looking up found myself facing the two laughing officials. However, it can't have done me much harm for I was asked to attend a final selection board in London. In later years I was to sit on many boards where four or five members of the Political Service informally interviewed the hopeful applicants. I do not remember much of what I was asked, but the members of the board were friendly, and I know we had some discussion about the game of bridge.

I was selected before my university results were known, and asked to start a language course at the School of Oriental Studies, then a small institution at Finsbury Circus in London. Wider studies such as anthropology and law were later added to the syllabus, but in my time we confined ourselves to Arabic, under the tuition of Professor H. A. R. Gibb,† assisted by an Egyptian sheikh. The course was composed of written Arabic, and the colloquial Arabic spoken in the Sudan was not covered. At this course I got to know the men who had been selected with me, none of whom I had met previously. We were eight in all, two from Cambridge and six from Oxford. In the course of our service we grew to know each other well, and although our meetings

---

* A. D. (*Sandy*) *Lindsay*. Tutor in Classics and Philosophy, Balliol College, Oxford. 1906–22. Master of Balliol 1924–49. Lord Lindsay of Birker. Died 1952.

† *H. A. R. Gibb (Sir Hamilton Gibb)*. Lecturer, School of Oriental Studies, London University 1921. Professor of Arabic, London University 1930.

are now infrequent, they remain a source of great pleasure fifty years later.

During these weeks too I read a lot about the country to which I was going and acquired a broad, rudimentary knowledge of it. The Sudan is a vast plain of nearly 1,000,000 square miles, through which flow the Blue and White Niles until they join at Khartoum and then run northwards into Egypt. The plain has outcrops of hills, the largest of which are the central Nuba mountains, the volcanic Jebel Marra range in the western province of Darfur, and in the east the Red Sea Hills. The people are very varied. In the north there is a strong Arab element, reflected in the dominant language and religion of the region. Most of the north is very arid. Between Khartoum and Egypt few people live away from the riverain lands, where primitive water wheels and buckets are often all that irrigate the scant crops, which – together with the dates on the palms – constitute the main source of food. Arab influence is also strong in the agriculturally productive central belt of the country. Here large quantities of grain are produced on rain-watered lands, and the sap of the acacia tree provides the valuable export of gum arabic. There are also large herds of camel, cattle, sheep and goats whose owners are usually semi-nomadic, moving from north to south in search of water and grass. Further south, where the rainfall becomes heavier, the green countryside is wooded and more tropical. The cattle-owning tribes of the central area give way to peoples of purely African descent; generally less sophisticated than the northern peoples, they live by extremely primitive subsistence agriculture.

Politically the international status of the Sudan was peculiar. After Lord Kitchener's reconquest of the country in 1898 on behalf of the Egyptian and British Governments, an agreement was reached between the two countries under which the Sudan was to be administered by a Governor-General on behalf of them both. The Condominium, as it was called, was intended to recognise the fact that although Egypt had colonised the Sudan in the early nineteenth century, the Egyptians had been driven out by the Mahdist uprising in the 1880s and were only able to return with British assistance. The right of Egyptian involvement in the Sudan was unquestioned, but from the start their role was deliberately made less than that of the British. The Egyptian flag, however, flew over all government buildings beside the Union Jack. The Sudan was thus not officially a colony and from the British standpoint was the responsibility of the Foreign rather than the Colonial office.

It was with such limited knowledge as this that I sailed from Tilbury on 10 November 1922, together with the other seven Sudan probationers. Our trip out, the first of many such journeys, was uneventful until we reached Egypt. In Cairo we broke our travelling for a few days before setting off on the journey to Khartoum. We saw the sights of the city – the citadel, the Pyramids, the Mouski and the Gezira Club, and were introduced to the Sudan Agent, by whom we were taken to 'touch our topees' to Lord Allenby, the British High Commissioner. He talked to us kindly about our new jobs, but I remember him as a big awe-inspiring man. I did not much like Cairo then, and subsequent visits over the years failed to make it any more palatable. The flies and the dust, the beggars and noise in the streets, the barely disguised dislike of the British, and the obvious contrast between rich pashas and poor fellahin made Cairo an unhappy place. I was, of course, to visit it many times in the future, at first on journeys to and from leave and after the war as Civil Secretary, when I went annually to meet the British authorities in the Embassy, see the Sudan Agency and talk to members of the Egyptian Government about Sudanese affairs. But I never understood the attraction which Cairo had for so many British people or the affection which they felt for it.

Our train journey to the Sudan began in the evening in sleeping cars which went as far as Luxor, where next morning we changed and boarded a narrow-gauge train, which took us on to Shellal just above the Aswan Dam. This train went very slowly and was extremely hot, dusty and uncomfortable, so that it was a real relief to get out and board the river steamer which took us to Wadi Halfa. The cabins were clean, the ship spotless, and the Sudanese servants seemed charmingly polite after the Egyptians; but I remember being rather shaken when I was shown into the bathroom and found the bathwater the dark brown silty colour of the Nile flood. Experience soon showed this to be the normal sort of bath that I would have in several of my stations for the next few years.

There were a number of Sudan officials on board returning from leave, as well the two sisters of Sir Charles Lyall,* the Civil Secretary. They all showed great kindness to the young probationers. The trip on the river was a wonderful experience as we slowly chugged upstream past villages, temples, palm groves and the little bits of green cultivation along the banks; the highlight of the journey was the view of Abu Simbel. After two days we arrived at Wadi Halfa in the Sudan and felt that we had almost reached our destination. Wadi Halfa was a clean, well-planned little town, but we did not see much of it, as we were put on the mail train almost as soon as we arrived, and soon set

* *Sir Charles Lyall*. Sudan Political Service 1901. Governor Kassala Province 1917–21. Civil Secretary 1921–6. Died 1942.

off on the journey across the desert. The railway, built by Lord Kitchener during 1897 and 1898 for the reconquest of the Sudan, runs over the desert for about 240 miles from Wadi Halfa to Abu Hamed, cutting across the great bend of the Nile. It is one of the most desolate stretches of desert I have seen; nothing but sand, broken only occasionally by a desolate little rocky hill. In the dawn and in the evenings it has great beauty with the colour brought out by the rising or setting sun, but for most of the day it is dry, parched, dusty and dreary. There are ten stations, with no names – just numbered one to ten – at two or three of which water is pumped up from deep wells. A few station staff, dependent for life itself on the passing trains, spend lonely months there – as I was to appreciate nearly thirty years later when I had to deal with strikes of the railway staff. Eventually we reached Abu Hamed on the Nile, went along the river through Berber and Atbara, and after one more night in the train we chugged across the Blue Nile Bridge and into Khartoum station.

Khartoum in 1922 was a much smaller place than in 1953 when I finished my service in the Sudan. The town had not spread across the railway past the station away to the south. Beyond the line there were only a few native houses, which later expanded into large suburbs, but even within the semicircle of the railway there were big empty spaces, especially to the south-east, where bungalows for officials were soon to appear. Among the buildings in the middle of the town there were further areas which were soon filled up, and the market and commercial part of the town was far smaller and less busy than a few years later. The most senior officials lived along the riverside in houses which are now largely government offices.

We were accommodated in the Grand Hotel, and as was customary for young probationers, spent about three weeks in Khartoum before going out to the provinces. During that time we were introduced to senior officials, shown something of the way in which the country was administered, and bought kit and stores for our new life. We visited the main Government offices and spent a day in Omdurman with the District Commissioner seeing how he dealt with the various problems which came to him. We also visited the Agricultural Department research station at Shambat, and had lectures from departmental officials and from the Deputy Governor of Khartoum – Robin Baily* – who told us that we should model our behaviour on that of a 'genial baron'. We were instructed in our responsibilities for tax assessment and collection, district accounts and budgets, and our duty to see that

* *R. E. H. Baily*. Sudan Political Service 1909. Deputy Governor Khartoum 1921–5. Governor Kassala Province 1926–33. Retired 1933.

government money was kept securely in the town treasuries and checked by us at frequent intervals.

We were summoned to the Palace to meet the Governor-General, Sir Lee Stack, a friendly, quiet, wise man, who talked to us about our future work and about the provinces to which we were to be posted. I met him again about a year later on a Friday morning when I was preparing to shoot sand-grouse at Butri in my district, and he and a shooting party arrived from Khartoum. He was very kind and put a shy and embarrassed young officer at his ease by inviting me to join his party.

Fortunately we found a number of horses, whose owners were on leave, which required exercising; on these we explored the environs of Khartoum in the mornings and evenings, not without some contretemps when we met the steam trams and the horses bolted. We were entertained by the 'high-ups' to dinner and bridge parties – I was anxious when I won 26 piastres from MacMic – Harold MacMichael,* the Deputy Civil Secretary. We attended a dance at the Civil Secretary's house, which Sir Charles Lyall gave at the behest of his sisters. But after about three weeks in Khartoum we were despatched to our provinces, and three of us set off for Blue Nile.

It is difficult to recapture after fifty years the feelings I then had towards the country in which I was to spend most of my career. I had of course read of Gordon's death at Khartoum in 1885 and Kitchener's reconquest of the Sudan thirteen years later, and I felt proud to have been selected to follow the pioneers who had opened up the country and brought peace and orderly government to its peoples. I felt little concern for my personal future, health, security or salary. Perhaps there was a doubt in my mind whether I would be able to live up to the challenge, but I had no doubt that the task was an altruistic one. We were to work for the benefit of the people in accordance with the traditions we had inherited and absorbed, and expected to learn more of what this meant in practice when we got down to the task. I have often been asked in later years whether in 1922 we were made conscious of an intention to lead the Sudan to self-government in the future, and I have always had to say that I do not remember this goal being put before us. What was, however, made abundantly clear to us was that we were servants of the Sudanese, appointed by the Governor-General and the Sudan Government, to which our loyalty was given;

* *Sir Harold MacMichael.* Sudan Political Service 1905. Sub-Governor Darfur 1917–18. Assistant Civil Secretary 1919–25. Civil Secretary 1926–34. Governor Tanganyika 1933–7. High Commissioner Palestine 1939–44. Constitutional Commissioner Malta 1946. Died 1969.

we were not there to forward British aims, except in so far as they accorded with the welfare of the Sudanese. Our duty in our districts was to keep the peace, to see that fair dealing was meted out to the people, and that the Sudanese were not sacrificed to foreign enterprise or foreign development. In my first few years there was great searching of heart among administrative officers about the morality of the Gezira scheme, the Kassala Cotton Company in the Gash Delta, and similar development projects, which altered the hereditary customs, land-holding and livelihood of the people. I well remember heated arguments with those developing the cotton-growing Gezira scheme whether their work was for the good of the local people or for the benefit of Lancashire. 'Have you done a good day's work for Lancashire?' was a question which did not get a very polite answer in 1923 from an officer working on the Gezira to whom it was put.

Gradually, however, we came to see that social advances, economic development and the raising of living standards were important aspects of our work for the wefare of the Sudanese, just as, on the political and administrative side, the delegation of authority to local and national bodies became, from about 1927 onwards, one of the main preoccupations of the Political Service.

# THE ANGLO-EGYPTIAN SUDAN

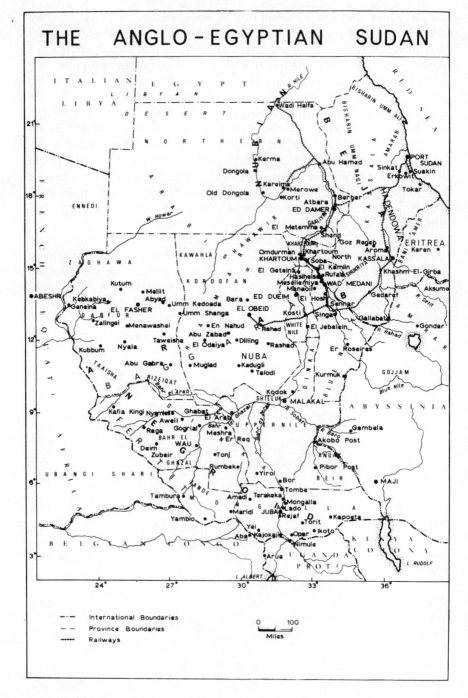

--- International Boundaries
-- Province Boundaries
++++ Railways

0 ____ 100
Miles

# CHAPTER II

# SERVICE ON THE BLUE NILE
## KAMLIN 1922–1925

The Blue Nile flows swiftly through a massive gorge from its source in Lake Tana, in Ethiopia, until it reaches the plains of the Sudan. Once there it slows a little and turns north and slightly west on its course to Khartoum and its meeting with the White Nile. As the crow flies the distance from the Ethiopian border to Khartoum is approximately 300 miles, and both the country and the people vary as one travels along the river. The actual Blue Nile Province changed its boundaries twice between the wars, but for most of my time in the Sudan it consisted of a broad area of the country on both sides of the river. I little realised, when I was first posted to the province in 1922 that I would be spending much of my provincial career there and become acquainted with the river and its peoples right up to the Ethiopian border.

The first sight I had of the province was very different from that of later years. The huge Gezira scheme, which has proved to be the backbone of the Sudan economy, was then only beginning. The dam across the Blue Nile was under construction at Sennar, and work on canalisation had started; but the canals had not yet reached the northern parts of the Gezira plain and instead of the green fields of cotton and other crops which are now to be seen, the country appeared simply as a flat and very dusty plain.

The 120-mile train journey from Khartoum to Wad Medani, the site of the provincial headquarters, took us from 8 a.m. until 2 p.m. with frequent lengthy stops. We alighted after our slow journey, hoping to be taken to lunch by some kindly person. Instead, we were escorted to the *muderiah* – the province headquarters – where, after the introductions, the Governor immediately packed us into his car, and we were driven off to see the pilot irrigation scheme at Hosh. This scheme made use of pumped water until the Sennar dam was completed, but I don't think that we appreciated the merits of the Hosh experiment very much that afternoon, as the Governor drove us fast in his Model 'T' Ford over banks and bumps for an hour and a half. Luncheon at 4 p.m. was very welcome to three boys who had breakfasted at 7 a.m. before leaving Khartoum. This was my first introduc-

tion to the Governor, Arthur Huddleston,* under whom I was to work
in the coming years. A newcomer could be greatly influenced by his
provincial governor, for it was to him that the District Commissioner
was directly responsible. I saw a lot of Huddleston during my early
days in the Sudan, and developed a great admiration for him. He was
immensely keen on his job, sparing neither himself nor his staff; but
he was at the same time always ready to help juniors like me to find
their way around, and he could relax and make us feel at home in spite
of his seniority – which seemed immense to us, though he was only
forty-two. I learned a great deal from him about the details of district
work, the mysteries of finance, forms and procedure, as well as from his
attitude to the work and to the people. During the years when I was in
Kamlin, I had several visits from him on his way to Khartoum. He
would arrive in the afternoon, examine the state of the office, and then
spend the night in my uncomfortable and poorly furnished house.
He had a good appetite, and so long as there was enough to eat and
drink it fortunately did not seem to matter whether the meat was
tough and the cooking pretty second-rate.

We had arrived in Wad Medani just before Christmas and were
naturally called on to help with decorations and other preparations.
There were tennis and polo tournaments, and on Christmas Day a
morning service and a big evening party at the Governor's house
where everybody turned up after dinner. It was to be my last opportunity for such diversions for some while, as two days later I left to take
up the post to which Huddleston had allocated me. I was to be the
Assistant Commissioner in the Rufa'a and Hassaheissa District, which
lay to the north of Wad Medani.

    With my District Commissioner, S. G. Budgett,† I set off for Hassa-
heissa, a station on the railway line to Khartoum. There we crossed
the river and rode the four miles to Rufa'a, a town on the east bank
of the Nile where our house was situated. There was no motor transport
then, and this was my first experience on a camel. The journey soon
became routine for we had an office in both towns so that one or the
other of us went over to Hassaheissa two or three times a week. We
usually rode over in the early light, preceded by a cook who produced
breakfast in Hassaheissa, and after a morning's work in the office

* *Arthur Huddleston.* Joined Sudan Political Service 1904. Governor, Khartoum
1920-2, Blue Nile 1922-7. Financial Secretary 1928-31. Director Royal Technical
College, Glasgow 1933-45. Died 1948.

    † *S. G. Budgett.* Joined Sudan Political Service 1920. War service 1914-19.
District Officer 1920-9. Retired 1929. Headmaster and teacher at Sandgate School,
Esher, Felsted and Stowe. Ordained as priest 1946.

lunched there before riding back to Rufa'a in the afternoon, some-times dallying on the way to shoot a pigeon or two, or duck if we could find them.

I was by now acquiring some experience of the organisation of the Sudan Government. I had already met the Governor-General, who was at the time of my arrival also *Sirdar* – Commander-in-Chief – of the Egyptian army. (After Sir Lee Stack's assassination in 1924 this joint position was discontinued.)* Under him were the Civil, Legal and Financial Secretaries and below them the Province Governors. These posts, together with those of District Commissioner and Assistant, were all held by British staff. The lower rungs were filled by Egyptian army officers who were seconded to work in junior administrative posts and were known as *mamurs* and sub-*mamurs*; a few such posts were also occupied by Sudanese. Many of the Egyptians had had long experience of service in the Sudan and some of them were very useful. They were, however, in a very difficult position for technically they were junior to the youngest British administrators, in addition to which many of them disliked the Sudan and had the reputation, unjustly in most cases, of lining their pockets at the expense of the local people. The political situation also put them in an awkward dilemma. If they were loyal to the Sudan Government, they were acting against general sentiment in Egypt which was deeply opposed to the British presence in the Sudan. We had Egyptian officials in both Rufa'a and Hassahe-issa and, as I was a new boy, they gave me much help and good advice – both of which I needed greatly in those early days. I was to renew my acquaintance with the *mamur* at Hassaheissa, Ahmed Atia, when he later became Minister of War in the Egyptian Government.

Traditional Sudanese structures were also utilised for administra-tive purposes. Each district was divided into a number of *khuts* under an appointed head. The *khuts* were further split into two or three *omadias* and each of these comprised several sheikhships, or headships of sub-tribes. The successive Egyptian and Mahdist Governments had seriously disrupted traditional authority, especially in the riverain areas, and when I first arrived, administration of the people was pretty direct. None of our local sheikhs had the power of trying cases, nor of assessing or collecting taxes on their own, although duties of this kind devolved upon them increasingly during the inter-war years. How-ever, their ability to make compromise suggestions and interim deci-sions was useful, and certainly approved of by us as officials. Un-

* *Sir Lee Stack.* Seconded from Egyptian Army to Sudan Government 1904. Private Secretary to Governor-General 1904–7. Sudan Agent in Cairo 1908–14. Civil Secretary 1914. Governor-General and *Sirdar* 1919–24. Assassinated in Cairo 1924.

fortunately, Khartoum was not always so amenable, and I remember one case of a man, who had run amuck and killed about twenty sheep belonging to someone he disliked. He was shut up by the local sheikh to be cured of his madness, but escaped to Khartoum where he appealed to the Chief Justice for wrongful imprisonment. After considerable correspondence with the Chief Justice, I was told that I must try the sheikh for wrongfully arresting and detaining the complainant. This I thought too much, and replied that I would do so if the Chief Justice would arrange for his client to be sent to a lunatic asylum. As there was no such institution in the Sudan at that time, I heard no more of the matter.

The period as an Assistant District Commissioner was essentially one of learning through experience following the introduction which we had received in England and Khartoum. Life in Rufa'a with Budgett was certainly a useful education for the tasks ahead. The officers' house at Rufa'a was small – three rooms and verandah – and I always thought it was very gentlemanly of Budgett to let me share it with him instead of sending me to live in the government rest house. He was a cheerful and charming companion with whom I very much enjoyed serving. During the First War he had been in the Air Force and had some bad crashes; in one of these his aircraft had dived straight into the ground, and Budgett had a favourite photograph of it standing on its nose. He had some original and odd ideas. On tour he carried with him a small army of toy soldiers with which he amused himself, the small boys, and sometimes venerable white-bearded sheikhs. It was also a common practice of his to fly a kite so that the people should know the whereabouts of their D.C. He had, however, one habit which I did not always appreciate. Any Sudanese could meet their D.C. by buying a petition for three piastres – the equivalent of three new pence – and having the petition-writer state their complaint on it for another two piastres. Budgett adopted the unusual practice of daily filling the office with all the petitioners before he began the hearings in order that all should know what was being done in every case; the scene may be left to the imagination. It was also his intention that by so doing he prevented the office door-keeper from taking small bribes to facilitate early entry to the D.C. Some months later, when I had been transferred to the neighbouring district of Kamlin, rather scruffy men, usually well known as troublesome litigants, used to turn up with little notes addressed to me by Budgett saying, 'Dear J. W., this charming old gentleman has a case he wishes to put before you. I am sure you will help him.' Budgett was musical and artistic, and we both had some good gramophone records which afforded us much enjoyment. He was also a keen horseman and gave me much good advice on the subject as well as introducing me to knocking a polo ball about in the evenings; he had even constructed a sandy golf course at Rufa'a where we played in the morning on Friday, our day of rest.

He also initiated me into the arts of trekking in the hinterland of the district. We rose with the sun and rode for three or four hours on our camels before halting at a particular village. There we would meet the sheikh and the notables and hear complaints and cases until it was time to move off again for a shorter journey in the evening, when a similar programme was carried out. The rides in the early morning as the sun climbed above the flat desert country were always pleasant, and compensated for the more arduous treks in the heat of the afternoon sun.

As well as gaining general experience there were more precise lessons to be learned. The instruction in Arabic we had received in London did not really help us to understand the Sudanese colloquial dialect, though I discovered after two or three months how to co-ordinate it with the purer written Arabic and grammar we had been taught. At Rufa'a there was only one English-speaking clerk, and he had plenty to do dealing with the correspondence, as well as finding and translating relevant papers, without being continually at the beck and call of the non-Arabic speaker. From the start I had to attempt to work without a translator, and after some months I found I could at least understand and make myself understood fairly easily. Language was essential for our position as magistrates, since all evidence was delivered in Arabic. Fortunately a second-class magistrate had pretty restricted powers, and there was always the right of appeal to the Governor, so that the administration of justice was not too arbitrary.

After a year's experience I went in January 1924 to sit the examination in Arabic and law. All probationers in the political service had to pass the higher standard Arabic exam before they were confirmed in their appointments and received an increase in pay, while without the necessary legal qualification they could not be first-class magistrates. It was not difficult to mug up enough law from the codes and ordinances – Budgett used to chant the definitions of various crimes in his bath to well-known psalm tunes – but it was not so easy to learn written Arabic in an outstation. I found that dictation was the one paper in the exam for which proper tuition was a real benefit. While I was at Kamlin the headmaster of the elementary school, Sheikh Abu Bakr el Meleik, was kind enough to help me. Although he spoke no English, he was a good enough teacher to get through to me. He had a long career in primary education, and when he retired in about 1948,

founded a private girls' secondary school in Omdurman, which was
still flourishing when I visited it in 1962. The gathering at the exams
was most enjoyable as all my contemporaries turned up, as well as one
or two friends who had failed the previous year. We had much to
discuss and argue about, and it made a pleasant break from the ordinary routine. The examinations were conducted somewhat casually,
and in my year one of the examiners complained that a good deal of
co-operation seemed to be going on. But there were dangers in collaboration, for one of the candidates seeking help mistook a whispered
'war drum' for 'wardrobe' and had great difficulty fitting it into the
rest of the translation. I managed to scrape through both subjects at
the first attempt, and was thus confirmed in my appointment and
created a first-class magistrate.

It was not long after I had arrived at Rufa'a that I first found myself
left alone to cope with the district. Budgett had to go to Wad Medani
hospital with a bout of fever, and I felt very much at sea left with all
the mail and local business. To add to my troubles I had to contend
with a couple of unnerving incidents. The first concerned an eclipse
of the moon. I did not know that such a phenomenon was greeted
locally with drum beating, singing and loud noises, or that the people
put out saucers of food before their houses to appease the devils who
were 'eating up the moon'. When the crescendo of noise built up I
feared a dangerous incident was developing and wondered if it was
the result of some unwise action of mine! It was not only the local people
who caused concern to a newcomer – the senior British staff too seemed
daunting figures. The Province Judge, Charles Holford, arrived to try
civil cases in Rufa'a. He seemed on that first visit a testy, peppery little
man to whom nothing was ever right. The transport to carry him from
the ferry was late in arriving, the rest house was insanitary, and some
cases could not be tried because witnesses had not been properly summoned. As the officer in charge, all the blame properly fell on me,
though he was good enough to tell me how bad my staff was!
    It seemed a major responsibility running one district single-handed
so soon after my arrival. But I found before long that the problems of
sickness, and the annual leave that all British staff enjoyed, left me
running the neighbouring district of Kamlin as well; to make matters
worse this happened during the rainy season when travel was difficult,
so that I had to utilise the official *felucca*, or sailing boat. This craft was
stationed at Kamlin and the crew had to pull it upstream against the
rapidly rising floodwater of the Blue Nile – a task which took them
several days. I then embarked at Rufa'a and travelled rapidly back
down river, making my presence known to the riverside villagers.

My contact with Kamlin became more than an interim measure, for in October I was sent to take permanent charge of the district, and I remained there for two happy years. The district covered a wide area on both sides of the Blue Nile and stretched up very close to Khartoum. From the rudimentary knowledge I had already acquired, I knew that one of the first tasks was to learn about the local people and meet influential personages. One of the most important villages in the district was at Um Dubban on the east bank of the river. Sudanese Islam has always placed great importance on the role of individual holy men, and a number were buried in Um Dubban. As was the custom, their bodies lay in round, pointed buildings known as *gubbas*. It was thus a holy centre for the neighbourhood, and was looked after by Sheikh Hassab el Rasul wad Bedr who also ran a *mezgid*, or religious school for boys. His family was influential, and his brother Sheikh Tayeb Mohamed Bedr was a Sheikh of *khut* as well as being a local trader. A nephew, Sir el Khitim Abbas wad Bedr, was in charge of all the Messelamia sheikhships. I very much enjoyed travelling among the Messelamia and the Battahin, semi-nomadic peoples who lived on the eastern bank of the river. It was when on trek among these peoples, sixty miles from Kamlin, that I received by police messenger an urgent telegram in code. We had a letter code which was really very simple to use but required knowledge of the code word. I had forgotten the word, which was locked up in the office safe in Kamlin. So I broke camp and went off as hard as I could by camel to Kamlin, and after a hard sixty-mile ride got to my office, undid the code telegram and found that all it contained was information that the price of sugar – a government monopoly – was to be put up in a few days time!

As well as learning about the locals, I had to get to know the junior officials. There was an Egyptian *mamur* named Hanafi Ali, a short, fat, unctuous little man whom I disliked. This seemed to be a general reaction for he was unpopular with the people, and quarrelled with the sub-*mamur*, a tall, thin Sudanese named Amer Beshir. Amer's father had served as camelman to the Khalifa Abdullahi, the ruler of the Sudan, during the Mahdia. His son, Mohamed Amer Beshir, was then at Gordon College and I used to lend him English books when he came to Kamlin during vacations. He later did good work as translator in the Legislative Assembly, where we saw a lot more of each other. Amer Beshir had been transferred to Kamlin from En Nahud in Kordofan, and shortly after his arrival I received a number of orders for distraint on his property to meet judgement debts which he had incurred to shopkeepers in En Nahud. Normally action in such a case would be taken by a clerk from the office, but I thought it would be less derogatory to the sub-*mamur*'s reputation if I sent the *mamur* to distrain on his property. I was astonished when the *mamur*, pale and sweating, dashed into my office saying that Amer had met him at the door of his house with a drawn sword in his hand, swearing that he would not let him in. I had to go and do this chore myself.

District life was nothing if not varied and I soon settled down to the many tasks that confronted me. One of the most complex jobs was the collection of taxes, a problem with which I had already become acquainted in Rufa'a. It was necessary to make a regular check on the herd tax lists. These were prepared by the local sheikhs who were supposed to list all the animals belonging to their people – camels, horses, donkeys, cattle, sheep and goats. The job of checking entailed finding the herds, getting them divided up between their various owners and then seeing whether they had all been included in the lists.

In dealing with sedentary villagers the task was relatively easy, as in the early morning their herds were gathered before going out to graze, and the owners were simply asked to point out their own animals, which I then checked against the list. Usually a considerable number of apparently ownerless animals were left at the end. Some were immature and not liable for tax, but others had simply not been listed and then one either fined their owners on the spot and added the animals to the list, or if they belonged to the old or infirm, remitted the fines. In the event of failure to pay fines, the animals were immediately driven off for sale at the local market.

To find and compare the nomad herds with the lists was not nearly so easy, and involved long rides at night to the watering places where the nomads were rumoured to be. I still remember my excitement at finding a flock of 400 sheep some thirty miles away from a second flock of about the same number in the same owner's name, and thus I was sure that he had nearer 800 animals rather than the 400 that he claimed. All my instincts told me that he could not have driven 400 sheep some thirty miles in twenty-four hours. Even after the checking the job was not finished, for my first task in Kamlin involved dealing with the appeals – over 1,400 of them.

In addition to herds, the grain crops – mainly sorghum – were also liable for tax. These cereals, which grew in the wadis of the east bank and on the plains of the Gezira between the Blue and White Niles, were listed and assessed by boards of elders, and we officials had then to check their reckoning. This meant riding through the crops roughly assessing the acreage, and as a sample, measuring a few areas and beating out some of the grain to estimate the size of the yield. We tried to see a tenth of the fields on any one list and, from our own assessment, estimate the accuracy of the figures provided by the local boards. I think we always erred on the light side in order to not overtax the people, but I have no doubt that the local boards and the *mamurs*, who also assisted, sometimes made a good deal of money on this exercise. I disliked this work very much, for the pollen gave me bad attacks of hay fever.

Crimes, robbery and affray made regular demands on my time, and in Kamlin I became involved with a regular network of camel theft. There was indeed every incentive to engage in this trade, for the price of a camel, perhaps £15, made it easy to win a bride. It was not difficult to steal a camel from the grazing areas around Rufa'a and drive it north through Kamlin district and on to the riverside market towns of Shendi or Ed Damer in the north. The journey was not a long one, and it was possible for the animal to be sold before the owner knew it was missing. Authorities in three districts became involved in trying to track down the robber, and correspondence was naturally slow. I made strenuous efforts to put down these activities, and as a mark of success was nicknamed *Timsah el haramyia* – crocodile of the thieves. It was amusing to be addressed as *Ya Timsah* – 'Oh Crocodile'!

The Battahin tribe were particularly active in camel stealing and it required joint efforts with officers from the neighbouring Kassala province to try and limit their activities. I went up once to meet the Governor of Kassala and two of his D.C.s at Abu Deleig. The Battahin sheikhs were also assembled to hear the riot act read, and after this, as a visual lesson, the Eastern Arab Corps used machine-guns to demolish a mud brick wall. The lesson seemed pretty ineffective, for in my two years there was little reduction in camel theft – most of which was the work of the Battahin.

There was also a great deal of litigation about land to be dealt with. The wadis – small valleys – on the east bank were very fertile land when dry; and when there were heavy rains, the water flowing down them often overflowed its banks, irrigating the neighbouring land. But the wadis used to change course due to the force of the water and the softness of the sandy land, and when that happened the disagreements began. I used to go out to the scene of the dispute and hear the evidence on the spot, sometimes making the plaintiff walk along the boundary he claimed, carrying the Koran on his head. A shouting crowd accompanied him, composed of supporters and opponents, and he often had to be restrained by his friends from perjuring himself. The changing nature of the land led to constant review of some cases, and we had several dedicated litigants. One little man, Ahmed

B

el Garoad, had a leather bag filled with papers – summonses, decisions and letters from the Chief Justice and others. If a case went against him he would be petitioning the C.J. within a couple of days: hence his nickname, '*el Garoad*' – the sprinter.

A local activity which interested me was education. Five of the small riverside towns had elementary schools where boys aged between roughly six and fourteen years of age were taught the 'three Rs', received instruction in the Koran, and were encouraged to play association football. Academic standards were not high and only a small percentage went on to the one secondary school – the Gordon College in Khartoum. The teaching was old-fashioned, with a good deal of rote learning and strict discipline. I discovered as I travelled around that the schools were not full, and at the towns of Hillalia and Eilafun we tried by cajolery and threats to get more children to attend. I suppose that in the country districts fathers found their boys useful on the land and with the animals, and they had not yet learned that education was the gateway to more highly-paid jobs. Girls' education was, of course, far behind boys', but in Rufa'a there was an exceptional school. Sheikh Babikr Bedri, a wonderful man, had started teaching his daughters and those of his friends some years before, and this school had continued to flourish although he had now moved to Omdurman. In later years, when Sudanese politicians and journalists complained of the Sudan Government's neglect of education, I used to remind them how difficult it was to get children to attend school in 1923.

Trouble from an unlikely source was provided by the Intelligence Department in Khartoum. They employed Sudanese agents who toured the country ostensibly to see that peace was being maintained, justice being done and nobody plotting against the Government. These agents in many cases used their position to blackmail influential or wealthy local people with the threat of a damaging report to the Director of Intelligence. I heard many such stories and asked for the Governor's advice. The answer was simple. The agents had no obvious means of livelihood and could not admit officially that they were intelligence agents; nor would that department acknowledge them. They could therefore be arrested as vagabonds. I often wondered what my dossier at Intelligence H.Q. was like after I had dealt with a few of these men in this way.

It was in 1924, in Kamlin, that I first met Sayed Abdel Rahman, the son of the Mahdi, whom I was often to see later when he became one of the leading political figures in the country. Sayed Abdel Rahman

was the Mahdi's only surviving son and had lived quietly and impe-
cuniously in Omdurman until the First World War. Great Britain was
then at war with Turkey, and the authorities in the Sudan were
anxious lest the leaders of the Khatmia sect, led by Sayed Ali Mirghani,
who at that time was the unrivalled religious leader in the Sudan,
might sympathise with the Turks as fellow-Muslims. They therefore
built up Sayed Abdel Rahman, who still had a considerable following,
because Mahdism was historically anti-Turkish. When I first met him
he had begun to develop his power, but he had not yet amassed
the wealth he later acquired. He was a tall, good-looking man of fine
bearing, always beautifully dressed. He was also intelligent, with a
pleasant voice and charming manner. On the occasion of this first
meeting he was visiting some of his relatives among the Danagla population of Kamlin. He flew a Union Jack above the house in which he was
living, and my Egyptian *mamur* protested that this was surely wrong
and that he was not permitted to fly the British flag alone but should
hoist the Egyptian one as well. I replied that he could fly whatever
flags he liked on a private house, and that it was only on public buildings
that both flags had to be flown. I have often wondered what my attitude
would have been if S.A.R. had flown only the Egyptian flag.

The most serious disturbances during my early years occurred
while I was stationed in Kamlin, and the Egyptian flag – or lack of it –
figured in these events as well. In the years after the First World War
the Egyptians gained their independence from the protectorate under
which Britain had placed the country in 1914. Egyptian politicians
then began their long series of claims to the Sudan, which had been an
Egyptian colony before the uprising of the Mahdi in 1882 had driven
them out. The main tactics open to the Egyptians were negotiations
with the British Government and the encouragement of unrest in the
Sudan. The position of Egyptian administrators has already been
seen, but there were also a considerable number of Egyptian officers
serving in the army. The senior officers in the Egyptian army, including
the Sirdar – who was also Governor-General of the Sudan – were
British, and the rank and file of the soldiers were mostly Sudanese.
However, the majority of the junior officers were Egyptians, and with
the admistrators they comprised a network of potential Egyptian
influence throughout the country.

Anglo-Egyptian relations were deteriorating in 1924 and I soon
found myself involved in developments. While in Cairo on the way back
from leave I watched a big parade of British troops in the Opera Square
following rioting in the city; and after these incidents a colleague and
I were issued with revolvers and given the diplomatic mail to guard
on the way to Khartoum; fortunately the journey passed without

incident. On my return to the Blue Nile I was summoned to Wad Medani to reinforce the staff there because the Governor was worried about the presence of an Egyptian army battalion in the town. The officer commanding was on leave, and the acting O.C. was new to the battalion, with little experience of his officers and men. We had reports of disaffected elements, especially among the junior officers, but fortunately there were no incidents and I was soon instructed to return to Kamlin.

That, however, was not the end of the troubles, for on 19 November Sir Lee Stack, our Governor-General, was assassinated in Cairo and a serious crisis at once ensued. In Kamlin I quickly heard of the events and was of course the only Britisher for many miles, my nearest neighbours being at Khartoum and Rufa'a. On the morning after the news arrived, I arranged a short ceremony in front of the district offices. The police were paraded, the flags lowered to half-mast, the bugler blew the last post, and the police presented arms in salute. The sergeant-major, however, when lowering the Egyptian flag, was not satisfied with leaving it at half-mast; he lowered it completely, rolled it up and when the police marched off he took it away with him and did not return it to me. For a couple of days Kamlin remained only under the Union Jack, until I received a telegram from the Governor ordering me to hoist the Egyptian flag again.

On Wednesday 27 November there was a mutiny in Khartoum of the 11th Sudanese Battalion who planned to join the Egyptian battalion in Khartoum North on the other side of the Blue Nile. Between them they were to secure the only bridge across the river and then march against the British troops whose barracks were just upstream from the bridge on the Khartoum side. The plan failed because men of the Argyll and Sutherland Highlanders intercepted the Sudanese march to the bridge, and the Egyptians gave little support. The Sudanese took refuge in the military hospital, killed three British there, and bravely defended the building which had to be destroyed by shellfire before resistance ceased.

Kamlin was only about sixty miles from Khartoum, and within twenty-four hours, many of the local people were asking what was happening. Was it true that there was fighting in Khartoum? Had the Blue Nile Bridge been destroyed? It was even rumoured that the Egyptian *mamur* at Hassaheissa, Ahmed Atia, had raised a force among the Halawin tribe in that district and was marching against Khartoum. The provincial *muderia* at Wad Medani was also said to be under the control of the Egyptian battalion. I had no news at all and could only report this as reassuringly as possible to my questioners. On the Friday, two days after the events in Khartoum, a southbound train passed through the district from the capital, and I suppose everybody had news – except me. It was not till Saturday that I received a short account of what had happened from Wad Medani, with instructions to carry on normally. Those were anxious days and I felt very isolated, but the people of my district behaved admirably and I had no difficulties with them.

Some weeks later it was decided that all the Egyptian officers seconded to the administration were to be repatriated to Egypt, and I was instructed to send my *mamur*, Hanafi Ali, to catch a train for Khartoum at the station eight miles away. When I passed on these orders to him he wept, poor man, and told me how frightened he was to go to the station because the local people hated him, and the police escort I was giving him – a corporal and two constables – was not nearly large enough to ensure his safety. However, as far as I know, he had no trouble on the way.

Following the Egyptian-inspired incidents, which had in any case passed off quietly enough in Kamlin, life returned to the more routine exercise of administration and justice. It was only a few months after these troubles, in 1925, that I was finally transferred from the district. I left Kamlin with many memories, but above all with the realisation that I had acquired a thorough grounding in the tasks confronting a D.C. On my arrival three years earlier the job ahead had seemed daunting, but by 1925 I had gained both in qualifications, experience and, perhaps above all, in confidence.

# CHAPTER III

# THE WHITE NILE 1925–1930, 1936–1939

Most of my provincial service in the Sudan was centred on the Blue and White Niles. At times it was to seem almost as if I was alternating between one river and the other, but the first move, from Kamlin to the White Nile in 1925, come rather unexpectedly. When I left Kamlin I went home to Britain understanding that on my return I would be transferred to Bahr el Ghazal Province in the Southern Sudan. However, instead of making the long journey there, I was sent to Geteina, a village south of Khartoum on the White Nile; the change of plan may have had some connection with my engagement to be married while in Britain. My news was greeted gloomily in the Civil Secretary's Personnel Office – 'My dear J.W., do you expect me to congratulate you? You have committed the greatest indiscretion' – to which I replied that his reaction on meeting the lady would be reversed. (A year later I was charmed to receive a little note from Personnel: 'Dear J.W., you win.') Marriage could indeed present a genuine problem for the Government, for it was easier to post un-married than married men to remote and unhealthy spots like Bahr el Ghazal. Whatever the reason, I had already booked the journey south and was clearing up in Kamlin when I was informed that I would instead be making a much shorter trip.

Geteina is about the same distance from Khartoum on the White Nile as Kamlin is on the Blue; the country is the same flat, dreary Gezira plain and the people were reputed to be as litigious and as difficult as those of Kamlin. This last similarity was perhaps another reason for my selection, for Geteina required a great deal of thorough investigation in connection with the storage dam which the Egyptian Government proposed to build across the White Nile at Jebel Aulia, thirty miles south of Khartoum. The purpose of this dam was essentially to help regulate the Nile flow in Egypt, but the water stored would inundate towns, villages and agricultural land for some 200 miles upstream. The Sudan Government had therefore set up a commission to examine the implications for the people of the White Nile and esti-mate the costs of finding them alternative livelihood and compensating them for their losses. Much of my time on the White Nile, during both my postings there, was to be concerned with local problems caused by the new dam. In Geteina I was in fact taking over a district which had for some time lacked a District Commissioner, as the previous incumbent had been seconded to the Jebel Aulia Land Settlement Commission. However, it proved essential to have somebody in the district to provide all the necessary information on such vital matters as crop sizes and land holdings, and this was the immediate reason for my posting.

This last problem was particularly urgent, and an enquiry revising land ownership in the area that would be flooded was already under way. The revision entailed the re-opening of the previous land settlement, and the alternation of the register to allow for claims which had either been turned down previously, or had not then been put forward. Unfortunately when the area had first been surveyed, mapped and registered, the people had been unco-operative; in many cases the owners had combined to register their holdings in one man's name, in order to economise on registration fees and the cost of boundary stones. This kind of arrangement worked so long as the registered owner lived and kept his word, and in the great majority of cases the real owner continued to cultivate his land while the registered title holder kept his side of their agreement. Sometimes, however, when the registered party died and his heirs found that legally he owned the whole combined plot, they prevented the other traditional owner from cultivating his portion of the land. A number of such cases arose while I was in Geteina and I tried to get the legal authorities to adopt a new policy that would allow the original register to be adapted to the realities of the situation as easily as possible, for without this the whole payment of compensation would be most unfair. There was much correspondence, culminating in a somewhat acrimonious discussion in Khartoum when my Deputy Governor and I met the Attorney-General, Deputy Civil Secretary and Director of Lands. I must have been rather truculent for as I left the office the Deputy Civil Secretary whispered to me: 'That's right, Robertson – don't let that bloody little Welsh attorney get the better of you.' Our efforts failed to produce satisfactory solutions to all the disputes, but fortunately as the Gezira scheme extended towards the White Nile and became more prosperous, attracting many people to it, some of the rival claims came to lose their urgency.

The Gezira expansion eased the problem of providing a livelihood for the people of the White Nile, but it did not entirely eliminate it, especially for those accustomed to rely on riverain crops. These were the people who passed the summer up on the higher lands tending their animals and perhaps harvesting an exiguous crop on rain-watered ground, and then in the late autumn, when the river dropped, took their families and herds to the riverlands where they erected their tents and planted a special millet known as *sufra* because of its yellow colouring. The soil conserved enough moisture for them to get a reasonable crop in most years; however, the new dam meant that the river would be kept at a high storage level until the spring so that the flats would not be uncovered for long enough to ripen the crops.

My old governor in Blue Nile, Arthur Huddleston, was in charge of the Jebel Aulia Commission, and he recommended that a special area watered from the Blue Nile should be prepared for these White Nile people and that they should be settled there when the dam was built. The cost of what became the Abdel Magid scheme was to be borne from the compensation grant of £E750,000, paid to the Sudan by the Egyptian Government.

The dam took longer to materialise than at first anticipated, and it was another ten years before construction was well under way. I was then brought back again to be involved in the final arrangements to meet the needs of the people of the White Nile. This second period of involvement in the Jebel Aulia scheme was in a somewhat different capacity, though doubtless my earlier experience was a reason for my appointment. In 1926 I had been collecting information, but ten years later as Jebel Aulia Compensation Commissioner, I had to work out a system for assessing losses, paying compensation and arranging the settlement of some of the people on the newly irrigated lands provided for them.

The Government had passed an ordinance which gave the Commissioner the necessary authority and powers, and which also laid down maximum rates of compensation which he was entitled to award for different types of land. It was considered that the very lowest lands, which were longer under the normal annual flood, never produced good crops – as there was insufficient time for a crop to mature, and the land itself was soured by lengthy immersion – though I discovered that, in fact, some of this land produced very good and valuable crops of vegetables such as onions. The very high land was only flooded occasionally when the river was exceptionally high and so was potentially less valuable than the middle levels, which generally flooded each year. Another problem was that some lands had become very dirty, and had not been kept in a cultivable condition by their owners, who had allowed shrubs and grass to cover them. The river grass – known as *diss* – was deep-rooted and stubborn, and needed a great deal of hard physical effort to remove. I was told that since the slaves had been freed by the Government, the landowners had been unable to keep it clean. There was therefore no flat rate for compensation, and a careful scrutiny of the land would be needed before it could be finally assessed.

Although the land had been settled and there was a register of ownership, parts of which had been revised with my help some ten years previously, unnotified sales and deaths of owners in the interim had made the register considerably out of date so that it needed further correction. Also many plots were registered to the heirs of a particular person, and it was necessary to ascertain who these heirs were and the size of their shares under Muslim laws of inheritance.

I went into Khartoum and discussed all these matters with C. H. L. Skeet,* who was then Assistant Financial Secretary, and after consultation with him, it was decided that the best way of tackling this part of the job was to work from a steamer, which would start from the dam and gradually move upriver, as we completed work on the land. It was also agreed that I should require a Sharia *kadi* – Mohamedan law judge – to ascertain the heirs to the various plots and their legal shares; a surveyor, who could identify the boundaries of plots for me, so that I could estimate how much good, bad or indifferent land was included in any one plot; and a Registry official with copies of the existing register. I also thought I should need a corporal and three policemen to summon witnesses and prevent squabbles among the people. All this staff could hardly be accommodated on the steamer and so a barge with cabins for the native officials would also be needed, as well as accommodation for police and servants.

In a surprisingly short time all my requests were approved, and it was not long before we were able to assemble, get settled on board, and start work at Jebel Aulia. The boat was the Amka, an old stern-wheeler, which moved rather slowly. The dam was being built and was an interesting spectacle but my time was well occupied getting my work started, and we had little contact with the dam builders, as we gradually worked southward away from them.

My routine was to go out early in the mornings with the surveyor and ride or walk over an area, marking off my idea of the various grades of land on the maps. Then back to the Amka for late breakfast, and after that, assisted by three or four local sheikhs and elders, I would work on the boat, going through the register of the area I had just seen, and after discussion assess the compensation to be paid for each field. If the registered owner had died, or if the plot was registered to so-and-so's heirs, the *kadi* would then be asked to ascertain who these men were and their legal shares. I had a most helpful and co-

* *C. H. L. Skeet.* Joined Sudan Political Service in 1920 after War Service 1914–18. District work 1921–35. Assistant Financial Secretary 1935–7. Governor Khartoum 1939–42. Governor Equatoria 1942–5. Retired 1945.

operative *kadi*, Sheikh Ahmed El Tai; he came from Hillalia in Rufa'a District and was the son of Sheikh Tai El Sid, whom I had known when I was stationed there in 1923. Finally a clerk compiled a register of all the owners and the cash compensation to which each was entitled according to my assessment. This was a long wearisome business, but once we got into our stride, we got along fairly speedily, though no money was paid out at this time. It was to be held back until the reservoir was filled and the loss of the land actually took place. Then two payments were made with some years' interval between them, so that the compensation was not squandered as soon as it was received: but I had left this work before payment began.

There was no office on the Amka, and I had to use the dining saloon as my workplace. To begin with, the assessing sheikhs and the land-owners were not terribly house-trained, and sometimes spat on the deck. But I managed to stop this by making a local rule, that a spit meant the culprit was asked to leave the ship and so missed the sweet tea and biscuits which the servants dispensed to us once or twice during the sitting.

The riverland varied in width. In some places it was quite narrow, half a mile or so, but elsewhere it might stretch back for five or six miles, with islands of higher ground between the edge and the river. The total area to be dealt with was vast, for the arable land flooded was about 250,000 *feddans* (acres). The compensation for villages was not so difficult, and until we reached Geteina there were no very valuable houses. Thatched huts and dilapidated mud houses were common and were worth little or nothing. I was fortunate in obtaining the assistance and advice of Sayed Ibrahim Ahmed,* then an engineer in the Public Works Department, on the value of native houses, and with the instruction he gave me I was able to work out a formula.

Meanwhile, as this work was continuing on the river, the Government was extending irrigation in the middle of the Gezira inside the White Nile boundary by preparing the alternative livelihood scheme at Abdel Magid – and it was hoped that before the dam was completed and the reservoir filled, a number of the White Nile riverain people would have settled on this scheme, and found a new livelihood for themselves there. The land – 38,000 *feddans* – was taken over from its owners, and the number of tenancies in each annual instalment was divided up among the tribal sections in accordance with the estimated proportion of river-land owned by each section. Tenancies were allotted only to registered owners of river-land. This was no easy task, and as

* *Ibrahim Ahmed.* Engineer in Public Works Department 1936. President of Graduates' Congress 1942. Vice-Principal Khartoum University 1950. Minister of Finance 1956. Subsequently became a banker.

the scheme came gradually into working order, we had to shift people round each year to make the tribal holdings contiguous. An Assistant District Commissioner was appointed to live on the scheme to supervise the administration and deal with the tribal and social problems, and we had an excellent and sympathetic agricultural inspector to supervise the cultivation. In the first year there was no great enthusiasm to obtain the tenancies, and quite a number were allotted to people who had very small holdings of river-land, and who were more or less forced by their sheikhs to take the tenancies. Some were from ex-slave stock, and others were from the poorer and less well-connected families. However, the first year's results were very successful, with the tenants obtaining excellent crops of millet and considerable amounts of cash for their cotton. In consequence, competition for tenancies in the next three instalments was keener, and the new scheme became popular.

The Jebel Aulia dam was the most important single development in my time on the White Nile, but there were also other duties to carry out. On my arrival in 1925 I took charge of Geteina district, but two years later it was decided to amalgamate it with Dueim, its southern neighbour, and I moved there. In 1937 I again found myself dealing with administrative problems on the White Nile following my promotion to Sub-Governor in the new enlarged Gezira Province. With the development of the Abdel Magid scheme, it had been found inconvenient to have an area irrigated from the Gezira canal system under a second and separate administrative authority, and it was considered wiser to unite the two provinces so that the common irrigation and social problems could be dealt with under the single authority of the new province. However, for normal administration, White Nile Province was retained and it was this that I took charge of for two years.

One important new development during these two spells was the progress in native administration which was energetically pressed by Sir John Maffey (later Lord Rugby), who arrived in the Sudan as Governor-General in 1926.* I met him shortly after his arrival, for he visited Geteina while examining the site for the new dam. I have already mentioned that in Kamlin our administration had been very direct, especially in the riverain areas. No native authorities had magisterial powers, and the D.C.s and *mamurs* were directly responsible for everything – maintaining law and order, criminal and civil justice, tax assessment and collection – as well as for all the details of administration. The *nazirs*, sheikhs and *omdas*, although recognised as leaders among their people and often required to help the district officials,

* *Sir John Maffey*. Chief Commissioner N.W. Frontier Province of India to 1926. Governor-General Sudan 1926–34. Later Permanent Under-Secretary Colonial Office and H.M. Ambassador to Ireland.

had no legal authority and were pitifully paid. Sir John Maffey set
the Political Service in the provinces the task of building up local
authorities who could take over much of the work previously carried
out by district officials, and many of my duties while on the White Nile
consisted of trying to inaugurate self-supporting and efficient local
organisations. The main difficulties that I encountered in the early
years in Geteina and Dueim concerned the varied tribal origins of
the people and the jealousy and rivalry which stemmed from this;
in addition, many of the leaders themselves had little education or
intelligence, and the area was very poor. The problems were apparent
even in the town of Geteina itself. Like Kamlin, the town was divided
into two parts, one inhabited by the Ja'alin and the other by Danagla.
Each group had its own *omda*, and relations between the two communities were always poor. The bulk of the people of the district were
of Kawahla stock, but there were also some small towns where Ja'aliyin
and Ga'afera lived. These last, together with some Geteina people,
were the local merchants buying up local products and selling to the
tribesmen such goods as salt, cotton piece-goods, tea and sugar.

The first step in establishing native administration was the creation
of a system of native courts. *Omdas'* courts were given limited powers of
fining people for small civil and criminal offences, and above these the
*nazirs'* courts heard appeals against the *omdas'* decisions. The *nazirs*
were also granted wider jurisdiction in civil matters, excepting cases
involving registered land, and could fine and imprison more extensively
in criminal cases. The District Commissioner had powers of revision
and even of quashing native court decisions; furthermore, initially,
persons sentenced to imprisonment by the native courts had to be sent
to the district prison, where they could, of course, appeal to the D.C.
at his regular prison inspections. Certain types of cases – murder,
manslaughter, slavery and other serious crimes – were not triable
by native courts. No *nazir* could deal with any case on his own; he had
to be supported by a number of elders – *agawid* – whose advice he had
to take into consideration in arriving at his verdict.

Setting up these courts was a task requiring patience and determination. It also involved a good deal of touring in order to sit with the
sheikhs in their courts and inspect their work, as well as reading
the records which all the courts had to keep. Here was another difficulty
to be faced; clerks had to be found and instructed in their duties, and
local candidates with adequate education and acceptable to the sheikh
were not always easy to find. Checks had to be made of the fines imposed,
and I found that the sheikhs and their clerks were often very dilatory
in collecting the money.

Little by little the system developed; the *nazir* required messengers to act as local police and summon accused or take convicted persons to the district prison. The clerks needed safes to keep the fines which had been collected. Gradually, as the responsibilities of the native courts increased, local prisons were required, and some of the old government stations were used for this purpose when the native administrations took over their work. Later came the obvious develop- ment of issuing salaries and paying for local services, which entailed the establishment of accounts offices with experienced accountants to do the work, and finally the transfer of assessment and collection of local and tribal taxes to the new bodies. All this took years to work out, and during the process there were failures and successes and a certain amount of opposition from the town intelligentsia, who looked for a system in which they would dominate the country folk and take the place of the British D.C.s as district rulers.

Once the courts were established, the problem of amalgamating the various tribal units in the area could be tackled, and one of my main difficulties in Dueim was to work out how the non-Kawahla tribes could be induced to unite with the Hassania *nazirate* administration, which we hoped would become the local authority for the whole Northern White Nile area. The different tribes were so intermingled, their lands so mixed together, and the area relatively so small that it seemed untidy and unnecessary to have separate local administrations. When I first arrived on the White Nile, Sheikh Idris Habbani was *nazir* of the Hassania. He was intelligent and good-looking, and had the knack of standing between the authorities and his people – typified by the way in which he promised everything I asked, but in practice scaled down his actions to the lowest acceptable level. During my efforts to collect tax arears he made lavish promises but never carried them out, providing only enough to prevent me from being too dis- satisfied with him and his sheikhs. Sheikh Idris had married the widow of Fadil, son of the Mahdi, who had been killed at Shukaba.* He had a large family and in later years, when religious rivalries had spilled over into politics, some were to become active Mahdists. I got to know him and other notables in the district well, for in the days before motor cars had appeared in any numbers, we toured our districts by horse or camel and generally the *omdas* and sheikhs accompanied us on our journeys in their areas. Sheikh Idris Habbani died in 1927, and tribal opinion among the Hassania favoured the appointment of his eldest son, Abdel Gader, as his successor. Abdel Gader was a mild, ineffective person, with a tendency to piety and seclusion rather than to bustling

* *Fadil el Mahdi.* Interned at Shukaba on the Blue Nile after Battle of Omdurman. Allegedly attempted escape 1899 and captured, tried and executed after a drumhead court-martial with his brother Bushera and El Khalifa Sharif.

action. He had a wet, clammy handshake which seemed to show his weakness. I thought that his nephew Omer was a better man, but it was easy to see that he would have had little chance of success against family and tribal opposition.

The main opposition to unity with the Hassania came from the people of Ed Dueim, Um Gerr, Kawa and one or two *omadias* of non-Kawahla stock, who preferred to be under Ibrahim Hassan, an *omda* in Ed Dueim. His forbears had migrated to the Sudan from Upper Egypt in the 1870s during the Egyptian occupation, and he was a most intelligent man who fully merited the nickname of *Bereigi* – the little bird which couldn't be caught. Eventually I got over the difficulties by persuading Ibrahim Hassan to be *wakil nazir* – deputy – to Sheikh Abdel Gader, to preside over a branch court with similar powers to those of the *nazir*'s court and later on to have a branch office and treasury. He, more than I, put this across at a *meglis* – public gathering – which I called at Id el Ud in the country a few miles from Ed Dueim. In spite of numerous problems, the machinery began to work creakingly and was eventually accepted.

It was interesting, on my return in 1936, to see the developments in the native administration I had established. Among the Hassania, Sheikh Abdel Gader had died and his far more energetic son Idris had replaced him. In Dueim, Sheikh Ibrahim Hassan had died and his son Ali, a weak character who was too fond of the bottle, had to be replaced. Mohamed Umran, a useful successor, was appointed *omda* of Dueim, a post he still held in 1970. Unfortunately, as he never had the position or influence of Ibrahim Hassan, his authority was reduced, and it proved necessary to bring in another man to take charge of the tribal areas outside Dueim. In general the new arrangements seemed to be working fairly well and certainly the level of organisation was better than had previously existed.

As Sub-Governor for the White Nile area I was also responsible for another innovation which had long-term significance. I had felt, as Jebel Aulia Commissioner, that the Abdel Magid alternative livelihood scheme in the far north-east of the sub-province was so far away from the homes and lands of many of those affected by the reservoir that it was unlikely we could easily persuade them to settle there. I had therefore pressed strongly that other schemes nearer the southern part of the district should be investigated, and soil surveys were carried out in several areas near the river. It was realised that such schemes, which would have to be irrigated by pumps, would be economically less satisfactory than lands irrigated from the Gezira canals. The land itself was not so good, and the overhead costs of pumping up the water would be dearer than those of free-flow irrigation. But the grant from the Egyptian Government would not all be required for cash compensation or for the Abdel Magid scheme, and I thought that the balance could fairly be used in this way. It was also obvious that when the reservoir was full, the water level would be constant for six months or so when water would not have to be lifted very far and the costs would not therefore be very heavy.

The Governor of the Province accepted my arguments and supported them strongly with the Central Government so that eventually approval was given for several schemes to be put in hand – one at Fetisa not far south of Geteina, the second on the west bank at Wad Nimr, the third on the east bank just south of Wad El Zaki, and the fourth south of Dueim at Um Gerr. These schemes comprised some 23,000 *feddans* and were so eagerly welcomed by the local populations that the selection of tenants proved quite difficult.

I was the more confident that these pump schemes would be useful additions to the alternative livelihood project, because already on the White Nile south of Ed Dueim a number of private pumping schemes had been started and had proved reasonably successful. Sayed Abdel Rahman El Mahdi, whom I had met first at Kamlin in 1924, had been encouraged by the Government to irrigate the lands he owned on Gezira Aba some miles north of Kosti. Although his support had been useful to the Government during the First World War, it was thought afterwards that if he could be persuaded to devote his energies to agriculture and cotton growing, he might be less inclined to develop his religious and political influence throughout the country, about which the Government felt considerable anxiety. This did not work out as the Government expected, for his influence continued to grow, but in the late 1920s and in the 1930s, Sayed Abdel Raman spent a great deal of time and energy on his land. Helped by the devotion of his followers who worked for a pittance – *belila wa baraka*, porridge and a blessing – he cultivated considerable areas and made good profits. His relations also developed schemes nearby and Sayed Abdel Rahman invested some of his money in their ventures, so that by the late 1930s there were several thousand *feddans* of privately-owned pumping schemes in this area. These of course provided livelihood for the local inhabitants if they were properly run and the tenants were reasonably treated. We were, however, sometimes a little suspicious that the tenants did not always get a fair deal; when water was short, the cotton was irrigated and not the grain crops, and there was sometimes doubt about the equable division of the profits. To rectify these faults we tried to put the organisation of the schemes on to a basis similar to that of the Gezira, with tenancy agreements and occasional checks to see that the owners were playing fair. Often this was far from easy, for the accounts were usually in a mess and in any case the owners did not separate the accounts for their schemes from their ordinary living expenses – so it was almost impossible to see the true cash results of any scheme. Then some of the owners were frequently away, leaving no capable agents to look after matters in their absence, while the engineers in charge of the pumps were often inadequately trained for their responsibility. The expert engineers were in Khartoum and, if required for a broken-down pump engine, usually took a long time to arrive. However, these enterprises staggered along and certainly provided cash for their owners and some livelihood for the tenants and workers.

These owners were regular visitors to Ed Dueim asking for extensions to the area of their schemes. I usually stalled on their proposals, for the water and the land was limited and they had been given licences for their fair share. They would then go to the Governor at Wad Medani to see what they could get from him, but he knew all the answers and was no more forthcoming than I was. I could always warn him by telephone of what was likely to come to him and what I had said. Later on when Sayed Abdel Rahman was deep in politics and I was Civil Secretary, I was often accused by Sayed Ali Mirghani of having built up Sayed Abdul Rahman's power and influence by giving him so much land for cotton; on those occasions I remembered the way I had resisted his attempts to get extensions when I was in charge of the White Nile. He was of course more enterprising than Sayed Ali Mirghani, and it is true that Government agriculturalists and engineers had helped him with advice on the layout of his canalisation, the utilisation of the land and the erection of the pumps and pump stations. But this was the help which the Government was prepared to give to anyone who was enterprising enough to start a scheme of this sort, and was ready to accept advice.

An important innovation which interested me while I was at Ed Dueim was the foundation of a new teacher training college for elementary schoolmasters at Bukht er Ruda, three miles north of the town. The moving spirit was V. G. Griffiths who has since made a great reputation in the field of teacher training, and has recently travelled widely in Commonwealth countries helping with the work of teacher training colleges. He started Bukht er Ruda in a very small way in 1934 and the project grew gradually over the years. The intention at first was to keep the buildings – classrooms and dormitories – similar to those which elementary schoolteachers would find in country areas, and up to 1937 this was adhered to. Of course it turned out to be much more expensive and laborious to maintain mud rooms of a reasonable standard, and gradually Bukht er Ruda buildings became more permanent and sophisticated.

The Institute had some excellent young Sudanese attached to it. Abdel Rahman Ali Taha,* later the first Sudanese Minister of Education, was assistant principal and Sir el Khitim el Khalifa,† afterwards Prime Minister of the Sudan, was also an instructor. Besides training the new teachers, the Institute revised and modernised the elementary school textbooks and thereby was of very great value to education generally, though of course many of these developments took place over a period of years. I understand that Bukht er Ruda is still the main elementary teacher training college in the Sudan.

In my role as a magistrate I frequently judged interesting cases, and I particularly recall three that occurred while I was on the White Nile. Two of these cases were largely investigated by Mohamed Shingeiti,‡ a particularly able Sudanese sub-*mamur* whom I was to know well later as Speaker in the Legislative Assembly. The first which arose while I was in Geteina concerned a murder. The man who had been killed was a small merchant living and working at Shegeig, about twenty miles up from the White Nile on the west bank opposite Wad el Zaki. In September during the rains he left his shop and his family at Shegeig and went down to the river, hoping to cross at Wad el Zaki and catch the post boat to Khartoum, where he intended to buy goods to stock his shop for the next winter. He had a good deal of money with him with which to make his purchases. After he left Shegeig, he was never seen by his relations again. Some two months later, some of his relatives came to Geteina, reported that he was missing and accused certain people in the Wad el Zaki neighbourhood of having killed him. I asked Shingeiti to go to the Wad el Zaki area and make enquiries on both sides of the river to see if anyone knew anything about the missing man.

Shingeiti, in the course of his enquiries, discovered that Mohamed Ahmed had indeed been seen on the west bank, had asked about the ferry and been told it had gone for the evening and would not be back until the next morning. He asked if there was no other way of getting across and was told that a man called Sultan had a raft and might

* *Abdel Rahman Ali Taha.* Educationalist at Bukht er Ruda. Assistant Director of Education. Minister of Education 1948–53. Retired to his home in Blue Nile Province 1954. Died 1970.

† *Sir el Khitim el Khalifa.* Father a merchant at Ed Dueim. Teacher at Bukht er Ruda. Educationalist in southern Sudan. Appointed Prime Minister after end of military rule 1964. Sudan Ambassador in London 1968–70. Minister of Higher Education 1972.

‡ *Mohamed Saleh Shingeiti.* Administrator and later District and Province Judge. Speaker, Legislative Assembly 1948–53.

take him over. He went off on his donkey to find Sultan and was not seen by anyone again. By the time of the inquiry in late December, the river had dropped, so much of the land which had been under water was now dry and Shingeiti and his policemen searched it all carefully. They found in one place some human bones, including a shoulder blade and shin bones. In another place a donkey saddle with a coloured lining stuffed with cotton, and a leather saddle bag with patterns worked on it came to light. These places were on the line of a channel along which the raft would have had to go to make its way through the islands to the main river. Friends of the missing man identified the covering of the saddle and the patterns on the saddle bag as his, and the medical authorities in Khartoum gave their opinion that the bones were those of a man aged about forty, 5 ft. 6 in. tall who had suffered from syphilis (this apparently deduced from the curve of his shin bones), and who had had a wound in his shoulder when he was quite young, as there was a nick in the bone which must have been caused by a sharp weapon such as a spear or a knife. They also considered that the bones were those of a man who had died within the previous six months. Witnesses were produced to prove that the missing man corresponded to these descriptions. Sultan, the accused, agreed in his defence that he had met the deceased, who had asked him to take him across the river, and he had done so, landing him on the east bank near Wad el Zaki. The missing man had left him, gone off to the village to catch the post boat and he had not seen him again. He could offer no explanation of the bones, nor of how the saddle and saddle bags had come to be found in the grass on the west bank. A late witness brought in towards the end of the magisterial inquiry swore that she had seen clothing in the accused's possession covered with blood, and he had been angry when she asked him what it was.

I committed Sultan for trial by a major court, and the case was tried by Judge Creed. The accused was found guilty and sentenced to death, but the sentence was commuted to life imprisonment, as there was 'a slight element of doubt not amounting to reasonable doubt'.

A second case, which caused a considerable scandal in the Sudan at the time, affected me only indirectly. With the help of Shingeiti, now the sub-*mamur* at Jebelein, Tony Arkell,* in the neighbouring Kosti district, unearthed a large slave-running enterprise whereby Negroes from Ethiopia were being sold to Arabs from the Sudan. Sheikh Khogali Hassan, a ruler of Northern Sudan extraction in the

* *A. J. Arkell.* War Service R.F.C. and R.A.F. 1916–19. Sudan Political Service 1920–48. District Officer, Deputy Governor Darfur 1932–7. Commissioner for Archaeology and Anthropology 1938–48. Retired 1948. Lecturer in Egyptology University College London 1948–53. Later ordained, parish priest.

Beni Shangul area of Ethiopia, was transferring the slaves to his wife, Sitt Amna, who lived in the Kurmuk sub-district of the Fung Province. She then disposed of them to Arabs, who took them over the White Nile for onward sale in Kordofan and Darfur. Some hundreds of cases were discovered, and other work in the White Nile area was greatly delayed as *mamurs*, clerks and police were sent to Kosti and Tendelti to assist in the enquiries and prosecutions. Another consequence was that in my district I was instructed to iqnuire into the numbers of domestic slaves who still remained with their masters. Few in fact opted for freedom, but during the next few years, with the rising demand for casual labour on the Gezira scheme, the great majority moved away from their masters to obtain paid employment on their own, though most of them looked on their masters as old friends and were often found paying visits to their homes.

A third outstanding case occurred while I was Sub-Governor; my position did not preclude my being involved. When Hector Watt,* the D.C., was away I was the only first-class magistrate in Dueim, and if the Province Judge could not come across from Wad Medani, I had to try the major court cases. The last big case I tried during my Sudan service was a very complicated and difficult one, which took four days hard going to complete. We started at 7 a.m., and worked through till dark, with two breaks of an hour each for breakfast and lunch, making a twelve-hour sitting every day. It was a major court on which I sat as President and had with me two Sudanese magistrates. There were fifteen accused, all of whom were charged with culpable homicide amounting to murder. There had been some long-drawn-out bickering between two villages some miles from Ed Dueim, mostly about animals from one village grazing on the grain crops of the other, and the local *omda* had failed to settle the dispute. Eventually a lad with his flock of sheep and goats was found trespassing on the fields of the neighbouring village, his animals were rounded up and impounded, and he himself was beaten up and detained in order to hand him on to the *omda*. The lad's companion rushed back to his own village and told the people there that the lad had been killed and the animals seized. It was now late in the day and the villagers assembled, armed themselves with spears, swords and knives and made their way to the neighbouring village where they surrounded a number of huts in the dusk. They raised a shout, and as the other people rushed out from their evening meals to see what was happening, attacked them with spears and swords. Five were killed and a number wounded. Legally everyone who took part in the attack was guilty of murder under the Sudan

* *Hector Watt.* Joined Sudan Political Service 1925. District Officer till 1940. Civil Secretary's Office 1940–3. Died 1943.

Penal Code, but some had been less culpable than others, and the court tried to pick out the ringleaders from the crowd. This was not at all easy, as the evidence conflicted as to who had hit whom: but we eventually picked out seven of the accused, who seemed to us the most guilty. All were sentenced to death; two accused were found not guilty as the evidence against them was insufficient, and we found six to have been among the attackers but to have been less active than the others. These six we sentenced to life imprisonment. In the end five were hanged and eight imprisoned for life; some of these later had their sentences reduced. A fine was also imposed on the village which had been the aggressors, and the *omda* whose negligence had been the cause of all the trouble was dismissed.

I have always thought that I learned as much about the customs, habits and feelings of the Sudanese in trying their cases as magistrate as I did in any other way. One seemed to see the working of their minds, the relationships in a family and in a village, the loyalties and pressures their loyalties implied, and in fact how they lived. I was glad, therefore, that I had had the opportunity of trying scores of cases of all kinds before this work was all handed on to the native courts and town benches of magistrates, or to judges from the Legal Department.

In Dueim an experiment had been made whereby convicts in the province prison were allowed considerable freedom if they could find reliable guarantors to undertake to bring them back if they ran away, and to pay for any damage they might do. I had a few of these men in my garden, and their headman was called Shukrulla. Shukrulla became my small daughter's donkey boy and one could see her riding round Dueim, with him running behind, Carol whipping up the donkey, and calling '*Ta'alla ya Shuki!*' – 'Come on, O Shuki!' Shukrulla was a murderer, whose death sentence had been commuted to life imprisonment; but his murder had been one of those tribal vendetta killings which to the Sudanese implied no personal guilt – by custom he could not have avoided the killing he had to do. He looked after our house when we were away, and was a most honest, decent man. I often had to appear not to hear Carol's tales about Shukrulla, especially when she told us how his wife had come to stay in an empty room in our stables, or how he had stopped in the town to do a little shopping, and other doings which were contrary to the very liberal rules for these guaranteed prisoners. Eventually Shukrulla was instrumental in re-capturing two or three prisoners who had escaped, committed a robbery and run away. As a reward his life-sentence was reduced to one of seven years, and he was released soon afterwards.

Working on the White Nile gave more opportunities for family life than did many other stations in the Sudan. The alteration in my posting which sent me to Geteina instead of Bahr el Ghazal ensured that I would get home leave the following year, and on 21 July 1926 I was married in Huddersfield. In retrospect life in Geteina must have been very dull for my bride as there was little or nothing for her to do, servants did the housework and I was out much of the day. I think she preferred our tours when she could meet the people and see me dealing with cases and petitions. Nor was Geteina a very pleasant spot. During certain months of the year there was a perpetual dust storm, sometimes so thick that the district offices 200 yards from the house were invisible. Our home was no palace – the garden was very poor and I had great difficulty in making the house tolerable for living in. When I arrived I soon decided that I needed a bathroom, a storeroom and, perhaps more important still, a well-constructed earth closet. My initial application to the province headquarters had been turned down, but following a visit by the Jebel Aulia Commissioner and his wife, the necessary additions were made. I was deeply grateful to Arthur and May Huddleston for their help.

It was not long after our marriage that my wife's presence was vital, during one of the worst accidents of my life. In the autumn of 1927 we had an intense invasion of locusts in the White Nile area. My wife and I had returned to Geteina from leave, and I set out to destroy as many locusts as I could, while they were still on the ground in the 'hopper' stage. We had few of the means of doing this which became available later, and we relied on primitive methods. Trenches were dug across the 'hoppers'' line of march, and as they filled up we buried the hoppers. We burned the grass in which they were found, and when they settled in trees and shrubs at midday, we sprayed these with petrol and set them on fire. During one of these exercises, I was badly burned at a place called Goz Abu Kelab about ten miles from Geteina. I was spraying trees and setting them on fire, and my driver – Fadl es sid Fadlu – was by my side carrying a small tin of petrol. By mischance, this caught fire in his hands and he got rid of it by throwing it away; unfortunately, it hit me and set my shirt and shorts on fire. My wife, who was with me, bravely got the fire out by beating it with her hands, making me lie down, and then rolling on top of me. She then somehow got me back in the car to Geteina, put me to bed and got the native dispenser to attend to me. She then arranged for me to get on to a steamer which happened to call, got in touch with the Province H.Q.s at Dueim, and persuaded them to send off the doctor, a man called Voight, in the Province steamer to meet our steamer. I was in considerable pain, and not very conscious of what was happening, but I do remember having to climb from one steamer to another near Wad el Zaki, and then being given an anaesthetic by Dr. Voight, so that he could tidy me up, as my burns were dirty with sand, motor oil and picric acid. At Ed Dueim, we were put in the Governor's house, which was empty, and a longish process started of three daily changings of the dressings. This was extremely painful, and we both became pretty nervous by the end of a few days. The doctor was good at his job but not very careful, and left copies of telegrams about, telling of my critical condition, which was not very reassuring for my wife. The S. G. put me on the danger list and wired my mother to tell her so, which caused some upset at home at a time when one of my sisters was about to be married. However, thanks to my wife's devotion and to my general physical fitness, I began to get better, and was able to go back to Geteina about a month after the accident.

The return to the White Nile in 1936 gave us a further opportunity to expand our family life in the Sudan. By then we had two children who were able to spend the winter months with us. They had come out to Kordofan but at Ed Dueim they were more able to enjoy life. Other members of my family were also able to visit us from Britain. Our house was much grander than that in which we had started married life at Geteina, but nevertheless we were not without difficulties. A bank was being built along the foreshore to protect the town from the rising waters of the reservoir, and the constant noise and dust from the machine was a great nuisance. This work also contributed to the infestation of our house by snakes, and we feared for our children and guests, but fortunately no one was bitten.

My first posting to Dueim as D.C. in 1928 was my first lengthy experience of a province headquarters, and taught me how essential it was for the leading official in a small expatriate community to be sociable and friendly with everyone living in the station. When I first arrived, the Pawsons were in the Governor's house. Guy Pawson* had captained the Oxford University Cricket XI and played for the Gentlemen; his wife Helen was a charming hostess. They had served in the capital and had frequent visitors from there, so that we met leading figures of Khartoum society in their house.

Gardening was a great hobby in Dueim. John Reid,† the Deputy Governor when we arrived, was very keen and arranged irrigation and prisoners to look after the headquarters garden. Similar facilities were

* *A. G. Pawson.* Joined Sudan Political Service 1911. Served in various provinces· Deputy Governor Blue Nile 1923–6. Governor White Nile 1927–31. Governor Upper Nile 1931–4. Secretary International Rubber Study Group after his retirement in 1934 until 1960.

† *John Reid.* Joined Sudan Political Service 1914. District Service in Khartoum and Kordofan Provinces; D.C. Omdurman 1922–3. Deputy Governor White Nile and Blue Nile Provinces 1924–31. Governor White Nile 1931–7. Retired 1938. Served in Second War in O.E.T.A. – Cyrenaica.

available for us privately for a small monthly fee, and we spent much of our spare time making tennis courts and gardening. Reid also grew a plot of cotton, and with the proceeds of its sale made enough cash to build a swimming bath.

Reid later became Governor. He could be cheerful, generous and hospitable, but as his bachelor years wore on he became somewhat self-centred and dictatorial in his governorship. Whatever his faults, his departure from the province to become a personal aide to the Civil Secretary, a post which he held for only a short time, was most memorable. As a governor he was entitled to a certain amount of ceremonial and I arranged a farewell parade and gathering of notables on the river bank before he boarded the province steamer to sail to Khartoum. The police band played, salutes were blown on the bugles, the guard presented arms and as H.E. embarked and climbed to the bridge, we officials came to attention and saluted. Alas, the ship was aground! A score of prisoners or more had to be collected and sent up to their waists into the river pushing the boat before it would move. We again saluted and the cannon fired its tribute. Our saluting cannon was an antiquated weapon, and to increase the sound of the discharge it was customary to fill the barrel with old uniforms and other rags. H.E. departed through a fusillade of smouldering garments fired out over the river.

During these last years for us on the White Nile, important developments for the future of the Sudan were taking place. In 1936 the Anglo–Egyptian Treaty made concessions to the Egyptians concerning the Sudan, which included permitting a battalion of their troops to be stationed in Khartoum. In the same year the Italians overran Ethiopia, and a potential enemy stood on the Sudan border. In 1938 the first mouthpiece of the politically conscious educated class, the Graduates Congress, was established in Omdurman. The latter we particularly noticed, but believed that its foundation was in part the work of John Reid and so presumed that it was along the right lines and blessed by the Government. The great world developments, especially the threat of Hitler, tended to pass us by. We were immersed in our own day-to-day work, which was never-ending and all-absorbing. The tribal and political work, the responsibility in the last resort for all aspects of law and order, the absence of technical officers in the field, meant that the administrative officer still remained the local Jack-of-all-trades. This total involvement in our immediate work left us little time to consider the world at large.

# CHAPTER IV

# WESTERN KORDOFAN 1933–1936

The only area of the Sudan in which I served for any length of time away from the two Niles was Kordofan, the most central province of the country. Western Kordofan was one of the most interesting districts, since it was very large and the diversity of its peoples caused acute tribal problems. In fact it contained representatives of almost all the varied types to be found in the Sudan. In the north there were the nomad camel Arabs, who grazed their herds away to the far north-west with the neighbouring Kababish and Kawahla and returned south for part of the year to Dar Hamar. Then came the great mass of the sedentary village dwellers who cultivated *dukhn* (bullrush millet), melons and groundnuts, and tapped the gum gardens in the sandy rolling country which stretches from El Obeid, the province capital, to Darfur. In the south-east of the district lay the Nuba Mountains, and included in Western Kordofan were several outlying hills, with wild and uncivilised people of Nuba origin who lived on top of the hills, while round them the Baggara Arabs of the Zurug branch of the Messeria tribe cultivated the land and grazed their cattle. Here cotton growing was being encouraged and there was a plan to build a ginnery and small police post at Lagowa. Further south, the Humr section of the Messeria centred round Muglad and Keilak in the rainy season, migrating in the late autumn southwards to the green pastures of the Bahr El Arab, where water and grass could be found in plenty for their cattle during the dry season. The cattle nomads on the river mingled with the tall Nilotic Dinkas, of whom one tribe, the Ngok, was administered by Western Kordofan, and others, the Twij and the Malwal, came north from Tonj and Aweil districts of Bahr el Ghazal Province. In all, Western Kordofan offered the whole Sudan in miniature and was a fascinating posting.

In contrast to most of my previous districts, one of the main problems of Western Kordofan was the scarcity of water, in spite of great efforts to find new supplies. In some areas local ingenuity had led to the adaptation of the tebeldi or baobab trees into water containers. These big, wide trees were hollowed out, and in the rainy season water, collected in a saucer-shaped trench round the tree, was lifted up by bucket and poured into the trunk. The water remained pure for many months, and I have drunk it in April, eight months or so after it had been stored. It was sweet and potable, though admittedly not crystal clear by any means, for it was used by birds and bats as well as by humans. The use of these trees was allotted to the villagers by their sheikhs, and occasioned frequent disputes.

A big hollow tebeldi tree near the D.C.s compound at En Nahud had been used for a different purpose. A predecessor of mine discovered that his cook had taken up a profitable line of trade beyond his normal duties in the kitchen. When on tour with his master he would from time to time acquire a small Nuba or Dinka child whom he brought back with him and hid in this hollow tree until he found a purchaser for him. In the end his illicit trade was brought to light and he paid for it with a long term of imprisonment.

In addition to the trees there were the well fields in a number of places, but the water was a little salty. These well fields got progressively less productive as the year went on, and much depended on the seasonal rainfall, some years being much better than others. The Government had developed a system of deep bore wells, first along the main road from El Obeid to Darfur, and later at other centres as well. The pumps were worked by little donkey engines which gave their name to the installations – el donk – and there was a system of taps for filling up skins and tins, and of troughs for watering animals. In the dry season these well compounds were wonderful scenes of bustle as thousands of animals crowded in to be watered. Little markets sprang up and they became meeting places for local people and nomad Arabs. The system was organised and supervised by the water section of the Public Works Department based on El Obeid, and their engineers were continually on the move maintaining the supply, for a breakdown might mean a real disaster. At Ghibeish, some eighty miles south-west of En Nahud, there were two bores and well yards, and by ill chance both broke down at the same time in the busiest, driest time of the year, when there were thousands of animals and hundreds of people in the neighbourhood entirely dependent on this water. The water engineers made desperate efforts to get the pumps working again, while water was sent in tins by lorry from En Nahud. After two or three days of serious anxiety, the pumps were repaired, and a disaster was averted.

The northern half of the district had the least water of all and was made up of vast expanses of sandy dunes on which grew scrubby bushes and gum trees; in the rains they were green and lush, and the villagers planted dukhn and melons. Apparently the sand dunes absorbed and retained moisture, and it always seemed miraculous that in the dried-up summer months vast numbers of melons were harvested to provide moisture for animals and humans, and masses of melon seed for export to Egypt.

Another local problem was the occurrence of cerebro-spinal meningitis. There was a particularly bad outbreak in the years 1935–6 and several hundred people died in the district. At that time the doctors had not yet discovered a way of treating the disease, at least in epidemic form, and all that was known was that immunity was more likely if the people lived in the open and did not crowd into airless huts. The epidemic we knew would get worse as the weather became hotter, and would rapidly come to an end as soon as the rains fell in May and June. So we forcibly ejected the people from their huts, put the sick into quarantine under supervision, and made those not affected live in grass shelters. We thereby succeeded in lessening the incidence of the disease, but I should guess, though figures are not available, that at least 60 per cent of those who actually contracted the disease died of it. It was remarkable that none of the medical orderlies, police, doctors and administrative officers, who saw many of the sick at close quarters, contracted it; undoubtedly malnutrition was a factor. A year or two later, when sulphonamides were better known, Dr. Joe Bryant of the Sudan Medical Service succeeded in bringing the mortality rate down from 60 or 70 per cent to nearer 12 per cent during an epidemic in Bahr el Ghazal Province.

To administer the district, which was about 44,000 square miles – half the size of the British Isles – with a population of approximately half a million, the District Commissioner had two British assistants, two Sudanese *mamurs* and 110 Sudan police. The District H.Q. was at En Nahud, a town of about 10,000 people, 120 miles west of El Obeid. the capital of Kordofan and the railhead at that time. At Abu Zabad, a small town seventy miles to the south-east of En Nahud, there was an old headquarters where a District Commissioner had once been stationed, but which had by this time been reduced to a police post with one clerk-accountant and a small treasury. Fifty miles south of En Nahud lies El Odaiya, a well centre which boasted a Beau Geste type of district office built only a few years before at considerable expense, but by 1934 handed over as the headquarters of a branch native court and native administration. Then about eighty miles south of El Odaiya is Muglad, the centre of the Humr administration, where there was a small office and a police post. From Muglad it is still another hundred miles south to Abyei near the Bahr El Arab, where Chief Kwal Arob presided over the destinies of the Ngok Dinkas. West of Nahud in the sandhills of Dar Hamar lies Suga'a El Gamal, where the *nazir* of the Hamar tribe had his headquarters and his country residence.

One of the outstanding features of Kordofan was the Sudanese contribution to administration, which was more developed than I had known elsewhere. The *mamur*, Yousef Saad, was a pillar of strength. A Sudanese from Wad Medani, he was probably of slave origin for he was dark and striking-looking. We never had difficulties with junior staff, as Yousef had them well under control, and he somehow persuaded the sheikhs to bring in their taxes in good time. '*Awez filous bus*' – 'I only want money' – was said to be his usual reply to any excuses or apologies. He was good at getting local public works carried out, and we successfully built a second boys' school and a girls' school at En Nahud speedily and cheaply, through his management of prison labour and local craftsmen. He also built the new police post, rest house and ancillary buildings at Lagowa when the ginnery started there.

The Mohamedan Law Court in Nahud was in charge of Sheikh Ibrahim Suwar el Dahab, a member of a well-known family from Burri near Khartoum. Unlike many *kadis* he was very co-operative with the native courts and helped them by advising in Muslim law and training the *ulema* (holy men) for this task. As appeals from the native courts came to the D.C., I was the appeal court for Muslim law cases as well as other cases. I usually consulted Sheikh Ibrahim and always found him ready and helpful when I asked him for his advice in any appeal. He was later given a peripatetic post, which he filled very effectively, as adviser and inspector of the Sharia work of the native courts.

A real character was the Arabic clerk, Wogiallah Karamullah, who was meticulously neat and kept his books in wonderful condition; how careful we had to be not to lose any of his papers or forget to see a decision properly entered in his registers! I well remember the anxiety he felt when one of the Assistant District Commissioners left some papers of cases he had been trying in one of the drawers of his desk, and no one knew what had happened to them.

A junior clerk, Ali Senoussi, was renowned for one especial *bon-mot*. Papers for filing were usually marked 'p.a.' (put away) and one Friday Ali Effendi was found working in the office although it was the weekly holiday. On being asked what he was doing, he answered, 'Sir, I am just peeing away.'

The systematic organisation which I found was the legacy of R. C. Mayall,* who had been the D.C. for several years and had laid the foundations of the local administration. He left in western Kordofan

---

* *R. C. Mayall.* Joined Sudan Political Service in 1920. District Service 1921–33. Civil Secretary's Office (Deputy Civil Secretary) 1934–6. Governor Blue Nile Province 1936–40 when invalided. Sudan Agent in London 1941–51. Public Relations consultant in London to Sudan Government 1951–6. Died 1962.

a routine which was immensely important and which gave me an example I always remembered. On Sunday mornings, whatever happened, there was the Nahud 'town ride', when the senior official present in the station, accompanied by the town *omda*, Sheikh Ahmed Mustafa Abu Rennat, the Sheikhs of Quarters, the *mamur* and one or two policemen, rode around the town inspecting the work of rubbish removers, market sweepers and the slaughterhouse cleaners. We made comments on the general cleanliness of streets and open spaces, and dealt with all applications to build or renovate houses and boundary walls. Nahud had a grey mud, and houses built of mud bricks and plastered over with this looked very attractive, having a pearly grey sheen. I tried to introduce some uniformity, and divided the town into zones, in some of which only mud houses could be built; only outside these zones were straw and grass huts permitted. Our cavalcade riding round the town must have been an amusing sight, especially when it disintegrated and broke up hurriedly which sometimes happened – as, on rounding a corner, we met a few of the stray ostriches which roamed about the town and frightened the horses.

More important was the system of regular inspection of the native courts and treasuries which I found working. During my three years in the district, I always seemed to be trying to catch up on the programme of visiting the main native courts at more or less prescribed intervals. It was easier in the winter months when the three British officials were present, but in the summer during the leave season it was really hard work; the trip to Abu Zabad, Lagowa, Keilak, Muglad, Abyei and back via El Odaiya to En Nahud was about 1,000 miles, and I tried to do this twice each summer in May and June. Then there were the Hamar courts at Suqa'a, Ermil and En Nahud itself and all the junior courts. A typical visit would consist of arriving – at Abu Zabad, for instance – in the evening to receive reports from the clerk and sergeant of police. Early next morning a start would be made checking the books and cash in the treasury. The prison might be next stop to see the inmates and hear complaints and appeals. Then on to the court where after the clerk's books had been scrutinised, petitions from the local people could be dealt with. Usually only enough time was left for a hurried lunch before starting out for the next port of call, perhaps sixty miles away, and starting the same routine again.

Devolution in Western Kordofan had gone a long way beyond what I had known in former districts. Almost all the criminal and civil work was dealt with by the native courts, for the heads of the courts were reasonably competent and well respected by their tribesmen. Appeals were infrequent, and I do not remember having to quash many decisions or transfer cases to the state courts. Most of my legal work was trying homicide cases of which there always seemed to be plenty, and which were outside the jurisdiction of the native courts, but we were helped by occasional visits of the province judge from El Obeid. Then there were incidents of kidnapping, when local Arabs had seized a small Nuba, Dagu or Dinka child and sold her – it was usually a little girl – to the northern nomads. In one of these cases we eventually managed to find the actual kidnappers, an intermediary and the Arab lady who had bought the little girl. They were all sentenced to long terms of imprisonment, but we did not succeed in rescuing the little girl for she, I have no doubt, had been murdered and buried as soon as the hue and cry came close. In this case I learned the unreliability of identification. One of the accused kidnappers admitted his guilt, but the second accused strenuously denied that he had had anything to do with it. However, three little girls who had been with the kidnapped girl picked him out in an identification parade, and were very positive in court that he was the second man. He was convicted. But later, when both had gone to the province prison in El Obeid, the man who had admitted his guilt told the Deputy Governor at a prison inspection that the second accused had been wrongly convicted and that the true accomplice was someone else. I was given his name and address, and when he was brought in to my office in Nahud he admitted that he was the second kidnapper. The man, who had been wrongly convicted, and who of course was then released, had been unable to account for his whereabouts at the time, as he had been engaged on a camel theft the same day as the kidnapping.

Another case concerned the parentage of a little boy of about eight years old called Aboh. He was claimed as their child by a Nuba man and woman, but they admitted that he had been living for some years with a Messeria couple. The Nubas said they had boarded out the little boy with the Messeria during a famine year and now wanted him back. The Arabs said he was their own child. I didn't believe this could be true from his appearance and the thick pigmentation of his skin, and finally I decided that he should go back to the Nubas. A melée ensued when this decision was announced, and there seemed a danger that the poor little boy was going to be torn in two before he was rescued by my assistant, myself and a couple of policemen forcing our way into the crowd and bringing him out. I then decided that we could not safely leave him with either party, so I took him back with me to En Nahud, where he stayed with my cook's family and went to the local school until he unfortunately died of cerebro-spinal-meningitis in the bad epidemic which we had some months later. It was currently said I had taken him away to be my slave!

The district bordered ten other districts, and our people always seemed to be having disputes with their neighbours beyond the district borders. The Rizeigat *nazir* in Southern Darfur persuaded his D.C. to have a Hamar village – allegedly the home of thieves – burned down, and an old feud was thereby resurrected as the Rizeigat had killed the Hamar leader, Sheikh Mohammed es Sheikh, forty years before at Mafura. The Messeria had been attacked by Nubas from Kadugli district, the Western Nuers had built houses north of their border in Ngok Dinka land; the Malwal Dinkas had stolen Humr cattle, and so on. Many of these disputes necessitated tribal meetings and discussions, and during my three years at Nahud I had meetings with almost every one of my neighbours at which the various squabbles and cases between their people and mine were investigated and generally settled. Sometimes the meetings were held in Western Kordofan, or occasionally I went with my sheikhs and their complainants and accused persons to the neighbouring district.

Each year we had a tribal gathering of our own. During one year, with the Humr at Muglad, the Governor-General, Sir Stewart Symes,* arrived with four R.A.F. aircraft. Sleeping and feeding twelve extra people, 150 miles away from our home station, meant a lot of organisation. These gatherings brought together people from all over the district, and after the parades and horse racing were over we got down to administration, while the vet doctored horses, camels and cattle and the medical officer set up a dispensary and attended to human casualties and sickness. These Baggara cattle nomads were highly excitable people and were always having quarrels among themselves, which often took the form of a refusal by one section of a sheikhship or *omadia* to accept the *sheikh* or *omda* nominated by the majority. As excitement rose, shouts of *Ahsan el Sign, Ahsan el Mot!* – better prison, better death! – could be heard, and it seemed that in no way could the squabbling parties ever be reconciled. Usually, however, the recalcitrant party would be placated by some douceur from the majority or their nominee, and the excitement would die away almost as quickly as it had arisen.

In January 1936 we had the Hamar gathering at Nahud when the Governor of Kordofan, Douglas Newbold,† attended, and R. C.

---

* *Sir Stewart Symes.* Served in the Egyptian army and was seconded to the Sudan 1906–16. Served with Sir Reginald Wingate in Cairo 1917–20. Palestine 1920–8. Aden 1928–30. Governor Tanganyika 1931–8. Governor-General of Sudan 1934–40.

† *Sir Douglas Newbold.* Joined Sudan Political Service 1920. District Service 1920–32. Governor Kordofan 1933–8. Deputy Civil Secretary 1938–9. Civil Secretary 1939–45. Died at Khartoum 1945.

Mayall, then Deputy Civil Secretary, came from Khartoum to his old district. Some 10,000 camels paraded at the rehearsal, and the town was packed with people from all over the district and with notables from neighbouring areas. On the morning of the day itself I received a telephone message from one of the water engineers at a station up the Fasher road, saying he had just picked up a wireless message that King George V had died, and then I had the problem of deciding whether or not to continue with the gathering. I kept the message to myself and only told the Governor after the official parades had been duly carried out. I felt sure that this was the right thing to do and showed no lack of respect for the dead King. In all these gatherings the routine was the same; the tribesmen on their camels, horses and sometimes on donkeys or bulls gathered in their tribal sections in a vast circle, and when all were in place the Governor and his official retinue rode on to the ground and made a ceremonial circuit of the parade, greeted by noisy shouts of welcome. Camel whips waved, horses were pulled up on their hind legs and there was great excitement. After the ride round, the Governor dismounted, stood on a platform, and the parade was marshalled into a column, which marched or trotted past the saluting base. Later in the day came the sports, and on subsequent days the crowds began to disperse, except for those with business concerning tribal matters or personal cases to be attended to.

It was fortunate that native administration was going so well in Western Kordofan, for at times travel in the district was extremely difficult. We had motor vehicles, but the sand on the roads was thick, and the route from El Obeid to Fasher in Darfur Province, which passed through the district, was particularly bad. With broad tyres it was usually possible to keep moving, but we carried strips of corrugated iron to lay below the wheels. These were complemented by grass laid on the sand, but brute force was usually needed as well. Some stretches of road became well known as trouble spots, and the tracks spread out for hundreds of yards on both sides of the road as drivers sought firmer ground.

There were also fewer opportunities for trekking by horse or camel than in my previous districts. Distances were so great that it was impossible to spare the time for such leisurely movement, but in one year I sent the animals to Lake Abyad, south of the Nuba mountains, and from there my wife and I trekked southward to the Ragaba Zerga, a tributary of the Bahr el Arab, with the idea of seeing how far the Humr Baggara penetrated the south. We had one or two long waterless stretches which were hard on the horses, mules and bulls in the convoy. Between two of the water holes there was an all-day trek, a waterless

night and then a long morning journey. It was getting very late and
hot on the second morning when I saw a tree ahead and said we would
get a little rest and shade there. But before we reached it one of the
sheikhs with us, the *omda* Riheid Diran, who had been scouting
around, came galloping back in joy with his horse, dripping water
from its haunches downwards, and shouting '*elmi, elmi!*' – 'water,
water!' Our anxieties were over for we had reached the Ragaba with its
abundant pools of water. In this part of the country game is plentiful –
giraffe in scores trotted along on both sides of our moving column,
inquisitively peering over the bushes to see what we were doing, and
herds of hartebeest, tiang and tetel would cross in front of us on their
way up from the Ragaba to their grazing, apparently quite unafraid.
The young Arabs used to come down to chase and kill giraffe, by
running them down on horseback and spearing them, and many an
Arab horse had wounds showing where it had been scratched and torn
by the thorn bush. But I did not find any signs of these hunters' camps
on this trek and I imagined that they had either heard of our proposed
expedition and kept away, as giraffe are protected animals, or we had
gone further south than their usual limits. The game was so tame that
it obviously had not been much hunted. With our cavalcade it was
incumbent on me to shoot something each day for the police, servants
and Arabs to eat, and I found it intensely distasteful to have to kill an
antelope or a buck which was so tame that I could approach within a
few yards of it. I felt as if I were committing a murder every time I
shot one.

This trek ended at Abyei where the cars had come round to meet us,
and here we were in Dinka country. The Ngok Dinka seemed to me
hard to get to know, and it was doubtless foolish to expect to develop
much contact with them in occasional visits of only one or two
days at a time. But I returned several times and have recollections
of some of them. At Muglad I was informed on one occasion that there
had been a bad fight between two sections of the tribe at Abyei, and
on reaching the small dispensary there I found it looking like a casualty
clearing station, with seven or eight dead and about thirty wounded
and badly hurt. Fortunately our medical inspector was at Muglad and
he came to patch up the wounded. Within a few days the Chief and
elders had gathered, and we held an inquiry which ended in a settlement whereby compensation in cattle was paid to cover the losses and
punish the side adjudged to be the agressors, after which things settled
down again.

Chief Kwal Arob of the Ngok Dinka lived in a buffer area between
the Arabs and the great mass of the Dinka to the south. He had the
diplomatic habit of changing his dress to suit his company. When he

came north to Muglad he would don the flowing white robes and turban of an Arab sheikh; going south he wore the topee, shirt, tie and trousers of a southern chief; but in his own country he appeared in the usual Dinka dress – nothing more than a few beads. I often noticed as we passed through the Dinka country a naked figure emerging from a hut, who, seeing the D.C.'s car, would double back and in a few moments emerge again pulling on his shirt.

One year in late June, after the rains had begun, I ventured down to Abyei by car to meet the D.C. of the Western Nuer District in Upper Nile Province, whose people had crossed the Ragaba and built their big cattle *luarks* – thatched huts – on the Kordofan side of the river, thereby trespassing on the Ngok Dinka lands. We decided, somewhat against the grain, to burn these huts and make the Nuer go back to their own tribal lands, thus averting the threatened Dinka attack on the Nuer.

This trek to the Nuer and Dinka was made on a rather uncomfortable borrowed horse, belonging to Sheikh Babu Nimr of the Humr, who came with me, and we got pretty wet as the rains were setting in. One interesting episode was seeing the Nuer and Dinka cutting up a hippopotamus which Sheikh Babu shot for them. It was a gory sight with practically naked men carving off great chunks of meat and lengths of skin, and finally getting inside the enormous beast and discovering all sorts of delicacies there. It was on the way home a little later that Sheikh Babu gave me a few very unpleasant moments. We saw a lioness sitting under a tree not very far from the road and I shot her in the side just by the heart, but she was not killed outright and entered a big patch of thick bush. Sheikh Babu, who had apparently never seen a lion before, chased in after her armed with a light cane. In some trepidation I reloaded my rifle and followed him into the bushes, but fortunately we did not find the wounded lioness, nor did she find us, and it was not till a few days later that the Arabs brought me her tail and claws as proof that she had been killed.

Sheikh Babu Nimr, *Nazir* of the Humr Agaira, was a man of about thirty at this time and very charming and pleasant. He had some education and was intelligent. His father had died young and he had been appointed *nazir* in his place while still hardly more than a boy, so that he had a rather difficult job to win the respect and obedience of his nomadic people. I thought he promised very well, and his court work showed common sense, and fair play. Fifteen years later he represented his area at the Legislative Assembly in Khartoum. In the wet weather he lived at Muglad, but during the dry season he went south and established his camp at a charming shady spot as Ragaba

C

Lau where there was plenty of water. I visited him there several times and enjoyed the pastoral atmosphere; horses and cattle watering in the lake and grazing in the vicinity, as well as the smoke of wood fires. His grandfather, Sheikh Ali Gula, had retired from the nazirate some years before in favour of his son Nimr, Babu's father, who had only lived for two or three years after his appointment. Ali Gula was still alive and exercised a good deal of influence in the tribe. He was a great raconteur and had many tales of the past; he told of the days when Gordon was Governor-General and had passed through the Humr area on his journeys to Darfur to put down the traffic in slaves. He had been one of those selected to meet King George V at Port Sudan in 1912, on His Majesty's return from the Indian Durbar, and when I came back from leave Sheikh Ali always asked me if I had seen the King, and wanted to know how he was. He would then go over again the wonderful occasion at Port Sudan and his conversation with the King.

The other sections of the Humr, the Fellaita, had a separate *nazir* in my time, Sheikh El Hag Abgar, who was a charming old gentleman. He was a Mahdist and had been wounded at the Battle of Omdurman, when he fought in the Khalifa's army; he was proud to display the mark of a bullet wound in his leg and always did so if the conversation made it at all appropriate. He had several sons, who helped him in administering his tribe, and they all usually lived to the east of the district at Lake Keilak.

The Humr, Agaira and Fellaita are parts of the nomadic Messeria tribe, though in my time we regarded the Messeria Zuruq as separate. They lived north of Lake Keilak along the foothills of the Nuba Hills. Their *nazir* had been Sheikh Mohammed Defa'ala but he had been dismissed shortly before I went to Western Kordofan, and Sheikh Hemeida Khamis had been appointed in his place. He was not a strong man, and had difficulties with the sons of Mohamed Defa'alla and of another ex-*nazir* Mohamed El Fagir Wadel Gaburi; for although both these elderly worthies had been exiled to El Obeid some distance away, they were still near enough to cause trouble to Sheikh Hemeida. After I left Western Kordofan, the three sections of the Messeria joined up into one united local administration under the supreme sheikhship of Sheikh Babu Nimr, and so the tribe was reunited after many years of separation. I always thought that this successful reunion was chiefly due to the diplomatic gifts of Sheikh Babu, but there were also economic advantages, for union gave the Messeria Zuruq the liberty of wider grazing than their previous, rather straightened tribal boundaries had allowed them.

The Baggara are fearless horsemen. I have already mentioned the way in which they rode down giraffe in thick bush and on uneven, cracked soil. I had first-hand experience of their ability in the game of polo. I played at Muglad with Sheikh Babu and his young men. I used to borrow horses from the police or the Arabs, and was fortunate in never getting a bad injury. The rules of the game were not well-known to all the players: crossing was common, sticks were used for more than hitting the ball, and players never appeared to mind their ponies being tripped up, or an opponent's stick whistling past their heads. It was fun, and I always hoped that by joining in these fierce games I gained some reputation with the Humr.

Kordofan in 1933-6 was a go-ahead province. Douglas Newbold, our Governor, was imaginative and sympathetic, full of ideas for the advancement and benefit of the people, and he inspired the same ideals in those working with him. He was energetic and travelled widely in the province, though to us in Western Kordofan it seemed he devoted too much of his time to Nuba development. But he came on two or three treks with me in my district, and I found him a most interesting and charming companion. One year we went to the north-west and our car broke down near Foga so that we had to walk some miles to our camp at Um Bel. During the walk I first noticed how lame Newbold was and remembered this lameness, which was due to an arthritic hip joint, when he died tragically in Khartoum in 1945. Another year we toured south from Abu Zabad, through the Messeria country and the scattered hills to Lagowa, spending a day at Tuleishi. This particular hill was one of our problems, for the unsophisticated people were like children. They seemed overjoyed to see visitors and crowded round in large numbers, laughing and singing, and appearing to be as good as gold. But they were quite unreliable, and were always getting into mischief by stealing Messeria cattle and fighting with the young Arabs. There were feuds in the hill too, and the chiefs had little control over their people. A year or two after I left Kordofan they had to be brought down from their hill-top villages to more accessible sites, where they could be more easily kept in order.

I went several times to Tuleishi and found that the sultan was on bad terms with two of the villages on the hill. Once in late June he accused people in these villages of keeping the rain away, and I didn't know what to do about it. However, I sent one of my police to bring four of these gentlemen to see me. They assured me that they had done nothing to keep away the rain, and I asked them to go to the holy rock at the top of the hill and swear that they had not and would not keep away the rain. They agreed to do this, and before I reached the rest house at the foot of the hill an hour or two later the heavens opened and a magnificent night of rain ensued.

In his efforts to improve economic conditions throughout the province, Newbold used to hold an annual meeting at Dalami in the Nuba mountains of D.C.s from that area and from Western Kordofan. There were usually some experts on various subjects from Khartoum – agriculturalists, veterinary inspectors, doctors and educationalists – and we discussed economic and social development. These meetings greatly stimulated us in the task of helping our districts to make progress. Of course the main difficulty was financial, but there was also the problem of getting new ideas across to the mass of the people, a process requiring great patience. My recollection of the result of these efforts in my district is not very clear, but I think we made some advances. Gum and melon-seed auctions were inaugurated in the Nahud market, and ensured that the cultivators and gum tappers obtained a fair price, and were not done down by having to sell in private to small traders. Market prices were cabled through daily from Khartoum and posted in the auction room. Educational advance was more obvious to see, with a second boys' elementary school at En Nahud and expansion of the sub-grade elementary schools in various places throughout the district.

After one of these Dalami meetings I went back to En Nahud and invited the *omda* and some of his elders to come and see me. I suggested that we might start a girls' school – there was one at El Obeid, another at Bara; surely we should not lag behind. The *omda* and elders asked for a few days to consider this proposal, and about ten days later came back saying they agreed that En Nahud should have a girls' school, but no girl should go to school after she was seven, and no man should be allowed to enter the school unless he was over seventy. Anyhow we went ahead, and when I went back to En Nahud on a visit in 1943 there were two girls' schools with some 200 pupils in them, and I was requested to do my best to get the town a girls' secondary school.

Eventually in 1936 I was told that I was to go back to the White Nile in the autumn as Jebel Aulia Compensation Commissioner. So once again we had to pack up, and endure the usual farewell parties. There was a big tea party at the native club, at which the *kadi*, my friend Sheikh Ibrahim Suwar el Dahab, made the farewell speech. He eulogised my work in the district, and started to enumerate the various things I had done, such as touring, checking administration books and other jobs. Then he said: 'Look at the public works that have been completed'; he paused, trying to remember them and finally exclaimed: 'Did he not make a concrete floor in the storeroom of the girls' school?'

We felt sad to be leaving a place we had grown to like very much, and people for whom we had developed affection and admiration.

They lived hard and difficult lives, for water was scarce and food often none too plentiful. But they were brave, tough, patient and friendly; above all I felt they had great freedom, and if they experienced hardship they were not wage slaves, nor did they have to worry about time or spend their days in the monotonous routine of factory or workshop. Their mode of life was despised by the educated classes and town-dwellers, but who can deny that it has some advantages? We were both in tears as we drove out of En Nahud.

# CHAPTER V

# THE BLUE NILE 1930–1933, 1939–1941

## *Roseires* 1930–1933

The second time I found myself posted to the Blue Nile came in 1930, when I was transferred from Dueim to Roseires District. The journey was not in itself very long by Sudan standards, but it was the first time I had to transfer my goods and chattels any distance. For a young single man such a move was quite easy, but a married couple after four years in the same district accumulated a good deal of luggage. The route to our new station entailed a voyage upstream in a stern-wheeler from Ed Dueim to Kosti, followed by a train journey to Sennar, across the bottom of the Gezira between the two Niles, and then nearly another 200 miles up the Blue Nile by boat and road. Luggage thus had to be transhipped twice. We went ahead ourselves with one or two servants and light trek kit, leaving the rest of the servants to look after our heavier belongings, and it was something of a relief when all eventually arrived safely.

In 1930 Roseires District was part of the old Fung province, named after the kingdom which dominated the area from its capital at Sennar between the sixteenth and nineteenth centuries. The Province head-quarters was at Singa between Sennar and Roseires, and there we broke our journey to meet the Governor, Charles Thomson, and his wife, and his Deputy, Guthrie Monteith. Another resident of Singa at that time was an army officer, Orde Wingate, who commanded the Eastern Arab Company stationed there, and who in 1940 was to return to take charge of the invasion of the Gojjam region of Ethiopia. Already in 1930 he was reputed to be a tough character who rigorously trained his company in the most difficult terrain available.

The Southern Fung District, which I took over from C. G. Davies,* covered a large area along the Ethiopian frontier. To the south it bordered on Upper Nile Province, while to the west it stretched about two-thirds of the way to the White Nile. The Sudan–Ethiopian frontier runs through hill country cut by innumerable small *khors* and a few

---

* *C. G. Davies.* Joined Sudan Political in 1920. District Service 1921 to 1936 (at Roseires 1925–30) Assistant Financial Secretary 1937–40. Governor Upper Nile Province 1941–5. Sudan Agency in London 1946–55 (Agent 1951–5).

large valleys. Mostly the boundary leaves the larger hills on the Ethiopian side, and many of the Sudanese hills are not part of any range but rise in isolation from the plains, often just pinnacles of rock with trees growing from cracks in the stone. Near the border the Ingessana hills are more substantial, and are pleasantly green for much of the year. The country is wooded with stretches of very high grass in the clearer spaces. Through the middle of the district flows the Blue Nile, in many places through rapids; very different from the navigable stream which I had known at Kamlin. Steamers could ascend the river only as far as Roseires, about 100 miles from the border, for the cataract at Damazin prevented further progress.

In addition to the district headquarters in Roseires, there were two sub-district centres, one at Wisko in the Ingessana hills under a sub-*mamur*, and the other at Kurmuk, where an Assistant District Commissioner was in charge. Kurmuk and Geissan were two small market towns on the frontier itself, and in the dry weather there was considerable motor traffic between these places and Roseires, in connection with local trade across the border. The Ethiopians used to sell their coffee, a popular drink in the Sudan, and to buy such things as salt and cotton piece goods from the Sudanese and Greek traders. Communication throughout the district was poor, for the roads were rough and became impassable in the rainy months. Roseires was connected to Singa by telegraph, but there was at first no telegraphic communication southwards.

The people were varied, being composed of several tribes. The Ingessana were a compact, homogeneous tribe of energetic, hardworking cultivators. Few spoke Arabic and over the centuries they had successfully resisted the attacks of Arab invaders. The Berta were the largest tribe, and were made up of two well-defined sections, those who had never been enslaved, and those who had been released from slavery and settled in villages along the river at some distance from the Ethiopian frontier. The free Berta villages in the hills were much more progressive and self-reliant, usually with good crops and well-made huts. The ex-slaves, usually runaways from the Beni Shangul region in Ethiopia, were much less self-reliant, and were often to be found badly off and looking for assistance from the Government when their crops failed. The Berta language was the most widely spoken in the district and had been adopted all along the river right up to Fazogli, the home of the chief, Mek Hussein. There were also pockets of the Gumuz tribe on the east bank opposite Fazogli and in various other places. They had their own language and some customs which differentiated them from their neighbours.

The people were shy and easily frightened, compared with the

Arab peoples further north, and I found them very diffident in coming to see me when I first toured their villages. However, it turned out that this was merely a precaution while they assessed my character, for after a few months they apparently realised that I was reasonable enough, after which they crowded round the camps dancing and singing most of the night. Late one evening at Falabut, torch-lit processions could be seen wending their ways down from the hill villages to our camp, where they gathered round our beds, singing and dancing and brandishing their torches for several hours while my wife and I nervously wondered whether our mosquito nets would catch fire above us.

I thought that my main duty was to travel as much as I could, and try to win the confidence of these shy people; consequently, schemes of devolution – establishment of native courts and native administration – did not make much progress during my time in the district, though in one or two places the chiefs did begin to exert more authority than they had previously. It was too soon to expect them to keep proper records, for there were no clerks of adequate calibre. Though many of the people were nominally Muslims, they did not talk Arabic fluently and the variety of languages in the district made it difficult to learn any of them. I tried to pick up Ingessana and reached the stage where I could make a little small talk, and try a simple case – and I actually passed an exam in it just before I left the district when I was tested by the Governor, Charles Thomson, and Hassan Sid Ahmed, the sub-*mamur* at Wisko. The examination consisted of Thomson asking me to pass on to the interpreter in Ingessana instructions about action to be taken, and the interpreter then reported to the Board what I had told him; the procedure was then reversed from Ingessana into English. This I successfully accomplished, but it was less easy to have lengthy conversations with the locals when I met them. I missed the evening talks with the sheikhs round a fire outside my tent, which were so common in the North, and found it much more difficult to get any idea of what the ordinary people were thinking and what were their troubles.

It was obvious, however, that they were most superstitious, believing deeply in black magic and witchcraft, and frequently cases came up for trial which gave me some idea of the terrible danger of these things. I had to try four young men at Kurmuk for murder, and under the law there seemed no doubt of their guilt. Their elderly father was sitting at the door of his hut in the early morning eating his breakfast, when a young man passed by and greeted him. The young man went off to his fields and thought no more of what had been just a normal encounter until the four accused came upon him some time later, tied him to a tree, and told him they would beat him until he removed the spell which he had put upon the old man as he had passed him in the morning. Since the old man had been seized with severe gastric pains and was at the point of death, they believed that the young man must have put the evil eye on him. They proceeded to belabour him with sticks until he died, protesting all the time that he was entirely innocent. With their beliefs, the four accused had done what they thought right, and of course the sentence of death, which by law had to be passed, was commuted in due course by the Chief Justice.

Another interesting case concerned a man dying in Roseires Hospital. Dr. Pratt,* the medical inspector, came over to my office and told me that as far as he could see there was nothing wrong with him, but the sick man was convinced that he had been bewitched, and that unless the spell were removed he would die. The doctor had discovered that the patient believed a certain woman had put the spell on him. I sent a policeman to bring the woman to see me, and when she came to the office I taxed her with having bewitched the sick man. She did not deny it; so I told her that if he died, she would be tried for murder, and probably hanged on a tree just outside my office. At this the 'witch' agreed to come with me to the hospital and remove the spell. We stood round the patient's bed, and she asked for a bowl of water in which she washed her hands. She then made some passes over the man's head, and crooned some words which I didn't understand. After this she put her lips on his and sucked hard, then turned and spat a little piece of root, about half an inch long, into the bowl. She showed this to the patient and said that it was the root that was killing him. I presume she had been hiding it in her cheek. I let her go with a warning that if the sick man did not get better she would be arrested and tried, but he immediately began to improve and in a week or ten days was discharged from hospital and went home perfectly fit.

Some of the crocodiles, of which there were a great number in the river, were believed to have magical powers, and I once witnessed an accident which was attributed to this. At a village called Malua, some miles upstream from Roseires, there was a very large crocodile which the villagers said was taking their goats, and it had also tried to snatch a little girl who was drawing water. I was asked to kill the crocodile for them. I went with a policeman called Mismeith, and we lay down on a little knoll above the pool where the crocodile lay. Eventually it came up to the surface, and getting a good target of its head and neck, we both fired together. There was a swirl of water as the crocodile writhed about, lashing its tail, and I was pretty confident that we had hit it. But I saw Mismeith holding his wrist in some pain and moaning.

* Dr. E. P. Pratt. Joined Sudan Medical Service 1927. Senior Medical Officer, Roseires 1930–3. Director S.M.S. 1948–51.

The doctor could find nothing wrong with his wrist, but it continued to give him so much pain that he couldn't use it , and in the end he had to be invalided out of the police force. He believed that he had shot a 'witch' crocodile.

An interesting aspect of the district was its ethnological and anthropological history. Dr. A. N. Tucker circulated a questionnaire about linguistic affinities in the region, and following this I was stimulated to write a couple of articles for *Sudan Notes and Records*. The Mountains of the Fung had been famed since the Middle Ages for their gold-bearing rivers. During the Egyptian invasion of the Sudan in 1821, their army had penetrated as far as Fazogli, where they built a fort at Famaka above the Blue Nile gorge. I was fascinated to read accounts of this invasion in Caillaud's book *Voyage à Merowe au Fleuve Blanc*. Gold was still found in the sandy bottoms of many small water courses and was patiently washed out by the natives. Taxes were frequently handed over in gold dust, and on occasions I collected little bags of the precious metal from the village sheikhs to save them trekking into Roseires. There were dangers in this, as the price of gold fluctuated with world markets: and sometimes the dust I received fetched more than was due, though more often it turned out to be too little. Nowhere was gold found in any large quantities, nor were there any large nuggets, so presumably the original reef had disintegrated, or it was situated in some particularly remote place in Ethiopia. At any rate, it has not yet been discovered.

One of the main problems of the district was caused by the situation along the Ethiopian border, which had really been sited incorrectly and was too far to the west ethnologically. The area known as Beni Shangul had been occupied in the early nineteenth century by Northern Sudanese, who had fled before the Egyptian invaders and had carved out little empires for themselves in the hills. They had enslaved the local inhabitants – mainly Berta – and intermarried with them, the mixed progeny being known as *watawit* – bats – neither animal nor bird! They still retained numbers of slaves, whom they treated badly, as far as I could discover. As a result many used to run away from Beni Shangul and cross the frontier hoping to settle down in the freedom which the Sudan Government offered them. These escapes were usually followed by somewhat peremptory demands that I should return the runaways, who were always accused of having committed murder, adultery, theft or other serious crimes. Sometimes I met and discussed the cases with the Ethiopian potentates, Dejazmatch Ahmed Tor el Gori at Geissan, or Mek Hamdan abu Shok from Gubba, or the Chief of Dul, near Kurmuk, and I normally agreed to hear witnesses who could give evidence about the alleged crimes. Sometimes witnesses were sent, but it was usually obvious that they had been told what to say, and a little cross-questioning proved the contrived nature of their stories. One day I was in the Kurmuk office when a Witwati sheikh from Dul came in telling me that a murderer from his village was in the market at Kurmuk and asking me to have him arrested. His name was Guma'a and he had allegedly murdered a man called Kheirulla. I summoned Guma'a and asked him about Kheirulla, only to be told that Kheirulla was also in the market. When I sent for him, the sheikh from Dul had to admit shamefacedly that he had been mistaken and it was not Kheirulla that Guma'a had murdered but someone else. Guma'a went free.

The most serious frontier trouble in my time arose from an incident which occurred some fifteen miles from Kurmuk at a place called Shima, in June 1931. The Shima raid later featured in Foreign Office telegrams and in questions in the House of Commons. Between thirty and forty men, women and children, who lived just on the border in Ethiopia, considered that they were oppressed by their Watawit masters and migrated *en bloc* across the frontier into the Sudan to Shima, settling down there a few miles from the border at a place called Ora. Before news of their arrival reached Kurmuk and they could be brought in for their own safety and for enquiries, a body of armed Watawit crossed the frontier and took them back forcibly to Ethiopia. I happened to be in Kurmuk, as I had trekked up in June to spend a few days there to tidy up in the office and deal with outstanding matters before the rains set in; immediately the raid was reported I went to Ora with about a dozen police to find out what had happened. I was sorely tempted to go into Ethiopia and rescue the Shima people, but in the end decided that it would probably be impolitic to do this, and that I should follow more diplomatic methods. My report went to Singa, on to Khartoum and finally to the Foreign Office in London, and some nine months later a conference was convened at Kurmuk to which three Ethiopian delegates and Sheikh Khogali Hassan, the Witwati ruler of Beni Shangul, were sent by the Emperor. The Sudan Government was represented by the Province Governor, myself and my assistant at Kurmuk. The British Consul, Erskine, from Gore in Ethiopia, was also there. Discussions were protracted, due partly to language difficulties and to the Ethiopian attempts to raise bogus counter-charges against the Sudan, but chiefly because the delegates had apparently no authority to come to any decisions themselves, and had to refer almost everything to the Emperor at Addis Ababa. This could be done only by sending runners three days into Ethiopia to a telephone whereby messages could be transmitted by relay to the capital.

The result was much delay and frustration, with nothing concrete emerging from the conference and no agreement reached; but frontier control on the other side improved as a result, and we had fewer incidents thereafter. In any case the people of Shima had almost all succeeded in getting away from their oppressive masters again and were safely settled in the Sudan by the time the conference ended.

It was when I was at Kurmuk in June 1931 that I received telegrams sent on by messenger telling me that I had been awarded the M.B.E. I was worried at being unable to acknowledge the congratulations of the Governor-General and the Civil Secretary until I returned to Roseires, by which time it seemed silly to bother as so much time had passed. I never knew why this award was given me, except that Guy Pawson, my previous Governor in the White Nile, told me my work in the Dueim and Geteina districts had been outstanding. One or two of my friends pointed out that in the same list the postmistress at Lossiemouth had been honoured with the same decoration for looking after Ramsay Macdonald's mail!

The District also received migrants from within the Sudan. Each year the nomad Arabs from the Northern Fung district, the Rufa'a el Hoi, Rufa'a el Sherg and the Kenana, came south with their herds as the country dried up. They worked their way slowly down the west bank as far as the Yabus river where there was water and grazing in the driest years, and on the east bank to the Dinder game reserve where they poached and did much damage by fire. We district officers tried to regulate their progress, so that they did not come south too soon, before the local sedentary population had harvested their crops: for trespass and damage to the crops led to fighting and bloodshed between the Arabs and the Negro tribes.

The R.A.F. used to come to Roseires and were welcome visitors. We had a landing ground at the Damazine Rapids, a few miles south of the town, and in the high river float planes could land just below the town. I had several trips round the district in these rather primitive aircraft – Fairey Foxes – in which one sat in the open behind the pilot, strapped in to avoid the danger of being bounced out. On one lovely trip, I went with Squadron-Leader Searle, who was shortly afterwards killed in Equatoria, to see the Dinder game reserve, and I shall always remember flying over a large herd of giraffe, who sensed danger but didn't know where it was, and rapidly formed into a square with females and young in the middle and the young males as guards around the perimeter. On another trip four aircraft flew up to Geissan where the leader touched down but would not allow the rest of us to land because the air-strip, which I had made, was too short and bumpy. So he took off again and we flew round Jebel Kashankaro towards Kurmuk, where the strip was marked. Our leader didn't see Kurmuk, and we flew on and on into Ethiopia until I told my pilot – by standing up in the cockpit and shouting in his ear – that we had passed Kurmuk. He said that he couldn't break formation, but I eventually persuaded him to do so, and we went back to land safely. My pilot, Flight-Lieutenant Banks, was then ticked off by the O.C. until I broke in and said that I, as D.C., had ordered him to take me back. The Wing-Commander went off southwards to Malakal in Upper Nile Province after lunch, and I returned with Banks to Roseires, tree-hopping down Khor Offut looking unsuccessfully for game.

We had a pleasant house at Roseires, with three excellent rooms and good verandahs. It was sited on a little hill with a flat field below where we could hit a polo ball about. The station was surrounded by big tebeldi trees, and some neem trees had already been planted; to these I added some hundreds more, which I was delighted to find had grown well and made fine shady avenues when I came back in subsequent years. There was a little garden where we grew our vegetables with fair success. The club was a friendly centre where we sometimes met in the evenings to chat to our clerks and other Sudanese officials, and it was possible to organise an occasional game of tennis. During the cooler winter months we had visitors fron the north, coming for a few days to see the mountains and the game. Judge Holford, with whom I had become more closely acquainted after our first meeting in Rufa'a, came regularly at Christmas for a few days' leave which he spent fishing; we had the Minister from the British Embassy at Cairo and his wife on one occasion, Lord and Lady Stratheden on another, and then there were the usual routine visits by officials. But in the wet, rainy months it was a lonely place, and once the roads became impassable, mails only arrived once a month by steamer. As the steamer stayed only a few hours before going north again, there was always a great rush to get the urgent and important letters answered, and then we had four weeks in which to cope with the rest of the official mail and twenty-four copies of *The Times* to read. I could never decide whether to work chronologically and patiently through them or read the last first to get the latest news. Radio had not yet made its appearance, but we were not without information, as in every station in the Sudan which had a telegraph office we received a daily Reuter news telegram, still headed 'A.U.N.' – Army up the Nile – the relic of an arrangement said to have been made by Lord Kitchener with Reuters at the time of his expedition to reconquer the Sudan in 1897–8. This arrangement was still in force when I left the Sudan in 1953.

We organised the leave of the administrative staff so that no one was too long on his own. The annual leave which we had in the Sudan has often been criticised as extravagant, but in lonely stations like those in the Southern Fung it was most necessary as one often became depressed mentally in the rains if one was all alone, and perhaps had occasional attacks of malaria. I found also that if I never saw another European for weeks on end, it was difficult to keep my sense of proportion and I became in danger of developing exaggerated ideas of my own importance.

In the three years that I served in this district, I trekked up to Kurmuk each year in June with horses and mules after my two colleagues had gone on leave. I went along the Blue Nile to Abu Shenina and then struck up the Khor Tomat by Bikori to Geissan, where I spent a couple of days at the police post checking the general state of affairs. I then trekked round by Jebel Kashankaro to Keili, where Mek Nail lived, and was able to see how his affairs were progressing. Then into Kurmuk for five or six days, to tidy up the office, hear any cases that had arisen, check the accounts and the safe, and see that all was in order. In 1932 I had a bad attack of malaria at Kurmuk and felt pretty ill, as besides the fever I had an outbreak of herpes. There was no doctor and the medical orderly at the dispensary was not at all skilled. I was worried about the ride of about 120 miles back to Roseires, and thought I would never be able to manage it. I sent off a policeman with a letter to Province H.Q. telling the Governor I was unwell and didn't know when I would get back. Two days later I was terribly disappointed when the policeman returned in very bad shape, having lost his mule, his rifle and most of his kit in a flooded *khor* which had washed him away. My letters had also disappeared in the torrent. Fortunately, once the fever had gone, I felt better, and could get back to Roseires through Wisko without too much difficulty, having ridden about 300 miles in all on the round trip. However, I made proposals for a wireless telegraphic link between Kurmuk and Khartoum for the future and this was installed during the next dry weather. After that there was no excuse for arbitrary rules about the time, and it was possible to take down a notice, on the official notice board at Kurmuk, which had always amused me. It read: 'The sun will rise at 6 a.m. and will set at 6 p.m. by order R. B. Knox, Major, District Commissioner.' I never met this man, my predecessor but one, who had been in Roseires district for many years and was known to everyone. From all the tales about him it was clear he had been a martinet. He was said to have shot the *mamur's* pony because it grazed on the polo ground, and then cut it up. He once replied to the Governor's request for information about a complaint which had arisen from one of his decisions by saying: 'These Sudanese natives must learn to do as they are told!' He had enhanced his reputation locally by letting it be believed that Mrs. Knox was the sister of the King of England. How apocryphal these tales were I never knew; in any case, the locals had great respect for him and seemed to believe that any dictatorial attributes he possessed were suitable in a *hakim* – ruler. Other officers of similar type were also much esteemed, and I am sure this was because the people recognised their single-minded desire to do the best they could for their district, and their entire lack of self-seeking.

Major Knox had built a rest house at the Damazin Rapids about six miles upstream from Roseires, and it was a favourite resort of the three or four Europeans in Roseires on a Friday or on a public holiday. The Nile ran through a narrow gorge formed of volcanic rocks, and we used to fish there for Nile perch which were plentiful up and down the river, and spend the day lazily. When I last went to Roseires in 1962 I found that the new dam was being built across the Damazin Rapids, a new town had been built on the west bank, with a railway, a bank and other civilised amenities, and the site of our rest house had been obliterated under piles of soil. *Eheu fugaces*! But I was happy on that occasion to breakfast at old Roseires in my former home, as guest of the Sudanese District Commissioner, and to meet a number of friends of thirty years before.

Another interest at Roseires, which I had not found in the Northern Blue Nile, was the wonderful variety of game, which one could hardly fail to meet on tour. Elephants once walked round our camp at Saoleil in the early morning, and my wife and I lay undisturbed in our beds thinking they were cattle going to water. On another occasion a buffalo charged out of a clump of bushes straight at a body of local people and myself as I was trying to settle their cultivation dispute. We slithered down a steep bank and saw him proudly snorting at us from the top. A week later a kindly villager brought his head into my office, and told me that this was the buffalo which had insulted me: he had shot it with his bow and arrow. There were herds of roan antelope, countless gazelle, a few kudu, numerous giraffe, dikdik, and even a pack of wild hunting dogs which I saw chasing a roan antelope. I got a few heads, but was not very keen on shooting these beautiful animals. Monkeys and baboons were plentiful, and the latter could sometimes be rather nasty, as when Guthrie Monteith, my wife and I were climbing Jebel Menzeh. The baboons that inhabited the rock disliked intruders and seemed to be trying to surround us, snarling and barking at Guthrie's dog. Lions and leopards were less numerous, but I still remember feeling rather nervous at Khor Doleib, on hearing heavy breathing at the foot of my bed. When, greatly daring, I looked up, I found it was a baggage camel which had wanted my company, and not one of the lions we had heard roaring a little earlier.

Shortly after I left Roseires on transfer to Kordofan, the Fung Province was amalgated into the Blue Nile Province, and I heard on the bush telegraph that the new Governor, having visited Roseires, asked what Robertson had done there as it all seemed so backward. I asked that the reply should be: 'He climbed the hills, got to know the people, and fished.'

## Wad Medani 1939–1941

It was a further six years before I again returned to work in the Blue Nile area, by which time my responsibilities had increased considerably, and some of the circumstances in which I was to serve were both unforeseen and unwanted. The experience I had gained of Roseires district was to prove most useful when the Italian declaration of war on Great Britain, on 10 June 1940, turned a long-recognised threat into an established fact – the invasion of a province which by a combination of promotion and chance had become my responsibility.

I was on leave, staying with my family in Northumberland, when the imminence of the Second World War interrupted my holiday. In late August 1939, together with other officials of the Sudan Government, I received orders to report to Glasgow for a swift return to duty. On 3 September, while in Glasgow, I heard Mr. Chamberlain's formal announcement of a state of war between Britain and Germany.

The *Montcalm*, an old Canadian Pacific liner on which we were sailing, formed part of the first convoy to leave Britain during the war, and we were naturally excited and somewhat apprehensive, especially when we saw ships returning with the survivors from the *Athenia* sunk off the north coast of Ireland, However, our departure looked brave as a dozen fine ships steamed out in glorious weather and passed Bute, Arran, Ailsa Craig, to be met by an escort of destroyers. We had a blackout and repeated lifeboat drill during the journey, but fortunately experienced no more than one or two alarms, when destroyers rushed about dropping depth charges.

The Sudan passengers on board numbered about 350, including a number of quite senior officials and our bishop, Bishop Gwynne.* We afterwards heard that it had been said in Khartoum that the loss of the *Montcalm* would have brought great sorrow there but also great promotion! Most of us had no abnormal kit with us, but 'Stuffy' Arm-

* *Bishop Gwynne.* Missionary and Bishop in Egypt and the Sudan 1900–45, when a new Diocese of the Sudan was formed. Continued in Cairo for a short time.

strong, Governor of Upper Nile Province, was reputed to have in his haversack iron rations and everything he might require if forced to abandon ship, even down to the currency of several of the countries on the shores of which he might possibly be washed up. My only discomfort on the journey was being in a cabin close to the boilers in a ship designed for the North Atlantic route. In a Mediterranean summer it was impoosible even to put my hand on the wall.

The convoy broke up in the eastern Mediterranean, we disembarked at Port Said, and after a period of delay a special train took us on to Cairo. Then we found some difficulty, but by going immediately to the booking office I was lucky enough to get a sleeper on the night train going south, an acquisition which led to some argument with one or two of my seniors who had not been so fortunate or far-sighted.

From then on the journey was routine and I arrived in Wad Medani to take up my duties as Deputy-Governor of the huge new Gezira province, incorporating what had once been White Nile, Blue Nile and Fung. Although the phoney war was in progress, province life continued very much as normal. One of the first pieces of advice I received was on the importance of establishing good relations with the senior members of the cotton syndicate who managed the Gezira scheme from their headquarters at Barakat just south of Medani. Unfortunately, soon after meeting them, I 'crossed' the General Manager while playing polo, an accident which cost him two broken ribs, but he was very nice about it.

In December 1939 R. C. Mayall, the Governor had a bad attack of malaria while on tour, and the resulting weakness coupled with the tension of the war situation resulted in his return to Britain on sick leave in April 1940 – never to return to the Sudan, as it turned out. I was left to carry on as Acting-Governor and was to continue so until the end of July 1941.

The younger British staff were very restless, and, many wished to resign and go home to join the forces. The British Government's policy was that the Sudan's small army should not be expanded, for fear of antagonising the Italians who were in Ethiopia; instead, British manpower in the country should be retained and used militarily if necessary. The rationale was unfortunately not explained, and caused considerable resentment among younger officials of the Government and the syndicate. However, we were allowed to start forming a 'home guard' – the Sudan Auxiliary Defence Force – the members of which were given some training in infantry drill and rifle practice. District officers joined and were given distinguishing marks which enabled them to command their police, who had been incorporated into the S.D.F.

In spite of these developments the Government forces in the province fell far short of the numbers deployed by the Italians on the other side of the frontier. The bulk of the Italian forces were facing the neighbouring Kassala Province on our north-eastern border, but we estimated their strength facing the Gezira at 3,800 men, mainly colonial troops with Italian officers and some N.C.O.s. Their armaments included machine-guns, pack artillery and aeroplanes. There were no troops, Sudan Defence Force or any other, in the province at the time, and the bulk of the men we had were local police under the leadership of S.D.F. officers. Roseires District had about 120 policemen in all. Most of the N.C.O.s had seen service in various parts of the province, but many of the men had been locally recruited and as such were thought to be more sensitive to enemy propaganda. The major concentrations of these men were at Roseires, where there were about fifty, and at Kurmuk on the border, where there were usually about forty men, and the district office was fortified with barbed wire and slit trenches. The police were armed with ·303 rifles but had no machine guns or other weapons.

When Mussolini finally declared war it was not immediately clear whether the Sudan would be involved, for Egypt, one of the two co-domini, was not a belligerent. I had, however, made a number of precautionary arrangements and by the time the Governor-General's Council had decided the Sudan was at war – 1 a.m. on the day following Mussolini's declaration – we had already mounted guards at vulnerable points and arrested for internment all the Italian subjects in the province. Most of these were Greeks from the Dodecanese, which at that time was under Italian rule, but one or two were truer Italians who had shown Fascist sympathies and who we feared might prove dangerous.

The first major event after the declaration was the resignation in August of our Governor-General, Sir Stewart Symes. His departure had apparently been considered two years previously, but the imminence of war prevented his intended successor, Sir Bernard Bourdillon, then Governor of Nigeria, from taking over. However, when the war came it was felt that a senior military officer was needed to lead the country, and while Symes went to South Africa, General Sir Hubert Huddleston took over the governor-generalship.

Symes had been criticised in the Sudan because he appeared not to support the country's war effort strongly enough. This is of course untrue, but at one time he had held the view that the war was a matter for Europeans and that the Africans should not be dragged into it. He also had a habit of debunking what he thought was stupid or unnecessary, sometimes including practices which many felt had a useful psychological effect. For instance, once when I was reporting to him in Khartoum, he asked me: 'How are the Gezira goosesteppers getting on?' – a rather sneering reference to the Sudan Auxiliary Defence Force, numbers of which were motoring twenty or thirty miles after their day's work for military training. When I mentioned the enthusiasm that one eighty-year-old sheikh had shown personally to fight the Italians, he presumed that I had told the octogenarian volunteer not to be such a bloody fool. Stories like these got around and caused comment and uneasiness, but they were consistent with his character and meant nothing more perhaps than a desire to shock. I was once most upset when he gave me an almighty rocket for confirming the sentence of execution on two Italian agents – both Watawit from Beni Shangul – who had been caught distributing Italian propaganda leaflets. Technically I can see that he was correct, but the Government could hardly expect us to carry out the strict procedure of a major court under the penal code, when the police were involved in operations against the enemy, and the District Commissioner was collecting information and helping to wage the war, as well as distributing arms and ammunition to those Ethiopians already beginning to revolt against Italian rule. I had earlier asked for the Legal Department to introduce a simplified code of procedure for areas where there was fighting, but nothing had been done.

In the first month after Mussolini declared war there was little military activity, though it became clear that the Italians were sending troops from Asosa to Dul, opposite Kurmuk, and were obviously preparing to attack. There were one or two air raids on Kurmuk which did no damage but caused some panic among the more uneducated local people. Non-essential staff left, but in order not to cause unnecessary alarm the *merkaz* civil staff were not evacuated, nor were the merchants advised to leave. The orders given to the D.C. were to hang on to Kurmuk as long as he could, not to retreat before threats or small forces, but if he saw the approach of an overwhelming force, he should send away what he could of the government stores, and retreat.

By 6 July the news from Kurmuk appeared so menacing that orders were sent to the D.C. to send away his civil staff with the office registers and treasury under a small escort. A few hours after the message had been sent the post office reported that there was no reply from Kurmuk, and it was realised that the attack must have taken place, though it was several days before there was news of the garrison's fate.

Kurmuk faces Dul, which lies about ten miles away across a valley. The market and native town of Kurmuk are so placed as to blanket the district office buildings from the Dul road. Late at night on the 6th, the enemy, about 600 or 700 strong with some guns, left Dul and spent the night in the *khor* near Kurmuk, where they were seen and fired on by one of our scouting parties. Two Italian aeroplanes then appeared about 5.30 a.m. and bombed the district offices for about an hour. This kept our men in their slit trenches, while the enemy troops worked their way round and behind the town under good cover and began to shell the defended area with their artillery. By about 6.30 they got within short range of the defenders, and a spirited engagement took place, with the enemy trying to surround the garrison. Though our force had suffered almost no casualties and inflicted a considerable number on the enemy, the D.C. decided that he must retreat or he would be cut off. The retreat was orderly, and the force re-formed about four miles to the west, having lost one man killed and one wounded. Fortunately the discipline and fire control of the enemy was bad, with machine-gun fire passing over the heads of our retreating men at almost point-blank range. Most of the mules were saved, but their saddlery was lost and the men had no food or stores and only the clothes they stood up in. The civil staff and the police families had all got safely away, but they were in a similar plight. The D.C. then decided to retire as far as Wisko, where he could be sure of getting food, water and shelter, but before moving he sent back a police patrol to see what the enemy was doing.

They found Kurmuk in a state of chaos. The Italians had withdrawn their troops, fearing a counter-attack, but the market, which had been fully stocked with supplies for the rainy season, was being sacked by bands of Italian native troops, and Watawit from both sides of the border. Several merchants were killed trying to defend their shops, and great quantities of goods were being transferred to Dul. The warrant officer in charge of the patrol found the district office area unoccupied, and he methodically set fire to the thatched roofs of the buildings, the grainstore and two motor-cars. He met the cashier's Berta servant who by some chance, contrary to financial regulations, had the keys of the treasury, and he then collected the cash amounting to about £E.1,100. They also found several mules, and one or two police who had been cut off before returning safely to the main body.

When I visited Kurmuk in March 1941, shortly after its recapture from the Italians, the district office was still unroofed, and there were just a few sheets of corrugated iron taken from shops in the market, laid across the half-burnt rafters. Three officials' houses had been demolished, and the stones used to build a rampart round the headquarters. The market was standing, but about a quarter of the shops had no roofs, and the whole place was dirty and deserted. A small graveyard had been made in front of the fort and I counted forty Christian graves, one of an Italian officer, the rest of Ethiopian Christians. Other graves without crosses and without names were said to be those of Muslim troops.

Meanwhile at Wad Medani we had heard nothing, and it seemed best to send instructions to the small Geissan border post to withdraw immediately. A few days later they retired on Bikori, about 40 miles down the Tumat, and the merchants of Geissan, fearing a repetition of the Kurmuk looting, sent word to the Italian *Tenente* at Belfodio. He then occupied Geissan without incident. The Italian radio at Bari hailed this as a great victory and reported that a British division who were occupying the surrounding hills had been driven out. Thus by 15 July we had had to withdraw from the frontier and were very anxious lest the Italians would follow up their success.

The next phase involved preparing new forces and awaiting the enemy's next move. Back at Roseires, strenuous efforts were being made to prepare for an àttack, while throughout the province men were enlisting and training. By mid-August over 100 additional trained police had been drafted to the Fung, and about 180 more were in training to reinforce them. An irregular force known as Banda Fung was also enlisted, and by the end of October the police and Banda strength in Roseires had been raised to about 350. These men were gradually organised into platoons and equipped as mounted infantry. In late July, C. G. Davies, Assistant Financial Secretary, was sent to Roseires with some Lewis guns, and a number of police were trained to use them. Some small forward posts were also established. They were intended to prevent enemy infiltration, collect news and reassure the local population. Constant patrolling was carried out with the object of misleading the enemy with regard to our numbers. To keep this up we scoured the province for mules while the stores and Ordnance Department performed miracles in producing saddlery out of nothing.

However, during the three months of July, August and September the prospects were so disheartening that the officers and men at Roseires and the forward areas must have been frequently depressed and very uneasy about the future. They were alone, close to a much stronger enemy, living uncomfortably in bad temporary shelters, often wet and tired, surrounded by a population which was thoroughly unhelpful and undermined by enemy propaganda – all the more effective due to our early withdrawals. It is greatly to the credit of the police that they did not panic, and in only one case did they show any signs of uneasiness. Many of the local people retreated from their frontier homes and sought the greater security of Roseires, while thousands of others took to the hills as they had so often had to do in the slave-raiding days of the past.

During all this time there was much military work to be done in areas farther from the front. Plans had to be made as to where we should try to hold the enemy should he advance in great force, for our forward positions were scattered and communications difficult. We were afraid of outflanking movements by the enemy especially as a captured Italian map marked the rough track from Jebel Gule to Singa as a first-class highway. The final dispositions decided on were that the roads south of Roseires should all be blocked, a company of the Frontier Battalion moved to Roseires as soon as possible, with orders to defend it at all costs on both sides of the river, while any forces should be concentrated at Singa. We pushed on with the defences at Roseires and Singa and blew up the roadway through the pass at Wisko. Precautions were taken against harm coming to the steamers by camouflaging them and mooring them under trees, instead of at their usual stations. Locally everyone was cheered by the news that troops might be expected soon, and that offensive operations might then be possible. All that actually arrived was the single company of the Frontier Battalion, only recently enlisted, which reached Roseires in mid-September.

We were consolidating quite well by the end of September, when we were once more thrown into a state of great anxiety. It was later reported that the Italian commander of the forces facing us, a Colonel Rolle, had approached the Duke of Aosta, the Governor of Ethiopia, and suggested an overland expedition to the Blue Nile to distract our attention from the Eritrean front in Kassala Province, where our reinforcements were causing concern to the enemy. His plan was approved and he began to advance at the head of between 1,500 and 2,000 men. Our small posts, in danger of being over-run or cut off, had to retreat, although a number staged spirited engagements when opportunity occurred. The Italians advanced 80 miles from the frontier, the furthest penetration into the Sudan during the war, and were only 25 miles from Roseires. However, having reached Khor Uffat on the Nile, the advance halted, apparently to rest and re-group, and we pushed forward our troops as well as making use for the first time of aeroplanes sent from Khartoum to reconnoitre their position.

Colonel Rolle was a tough and experienced African campaigner, having fought in Libya as well as the Ethiopian conquest, but he appeared to have made the mistaken calculation that his force could live off the country. The main crops were not yet ripe and the villagers had taken their food stocks when they fled. The advance had been hard, for the Uffat valley was overgrown and in places almost impassable. The troops suffered a great deal from thirst, and there were no local people to show them the spots in the sandy valley beds where water holes could be successfully dug. When they eventually arrived at the river, the men were completely exhausted. Rolle also discovered that he appeared to be facing stronger forces than he had anticipated, and he therefore decided to retire. He hurried back along the road to Geizan, leaving numbers of stragglers who were cut off and killed by the local inhabitants, or taken prisoner by our patrols following up the retreat. Our troops could not follow quickly because they were still rather raw, and the road-blocks we had set up to impede enemy mechanised columns now constituted an obstacle to our own men. In all, the Italians lost about 400 men, mainly from illness and exhaustion. Many rifles were captured by us, but a large number fell into the hands of the Ingessana and the Berta. Several of the rifles were marked 'Somaliland Police' and had been captured by the Italians in the British Somaliland campaign. I was particularly pleased by the success of our irregular forces in harassing the Italians throughout the incursion.

By early November 1940 the situation had reverted to Italian domination of the frontier and we were preparing to advance. Our hopes were high, for throughout the summer we had been successfully encouraging the Ethiopians to revolt. British officers had gone into the country issuing rifles, stores and money, most of which had been transported by armed camel trains on long and arduous journeys. At the same time, we increased direct pressure on the Italian frontier positions. In January I went up to Roseires with Douglas Newbold, then Civil Secretary, and found the place a hive of activity, full of men of the King's African Rifles, Sudanese troops, Ethiopian contingents, batteries of guns and British officers trying desperately to organise the whole affair. Camels were pouring in from the Gezira and Kordofan to reinforce the motor transport. The road forward had been cleared and graded, and convoys left for the front almost daily. As our troops advanced the Italians made little endeavour to oppose them and on 4 February 1941 they finally evacuated Kurmuk. The war in the Fung was over, leaving mainly the memory of those anxious days six months previously when there seemed a real danger that the Blue Nile lay at their mercy. I still recall the fright I had on waking one night, as I slept on my roof in Wad Medani, to see a line of cars approaching with lights blazing. I was relieved when I heard singing and realised that it was not the Italians but a Sudanese wedding party.

Most of my work as Acting Governor consisted of taking whatever action seemed necessary to support our front in the province, while maintaining the administration as normally as possible. I had refused to be given any military rank as I believed I would be more independent as a civilian and could argue with the military if I disagreed with proposals. On one occasion in September 1940 the area military commander, Hugh Boustead, wanted me to withdraw all police guarding the frontier right back to Sennar in case the Italian advance left them totally cut off. I resisted this, feeling that their departure would further undermine local morale, and after putting my views on paper went to Khartoum to see the G.O.C., who supported my view.

The Sudanese were wholly behind the Government's war effort and showed this in many ways. Once permission was given to expand our forces, there was no difficulty in recruiting for new formations and for the irregular bodies which were raised. As British officials of the Sudan Government and men from the Plantation Syndicate were released for the new formations, the Sudanese leaders took over more responsibilities from them. I went round the province giving pep-talks to assemblies of sheikhs, and found the greatest keenness to help. The Italians were heartily disliked by the Sudanese because of reports which had come to the Sudan about their behaviour to the Senoussi Arabs in Cyrenaica, when they had conquered that country, and we benefited from this.

The foreign troops also excited Sudanese interest, especially the Indian divisions passing through Wad Medani *en route* for Gedaref and Khashm El Girba on the Eritrean front. The local Sudanese were vociferous in their welcome, and gathered round the station, clapping their hands, cheering and singing. A trainload of Sikhs caused tremendous excitement when they detrained and were allowed to go to an open piece of ground to say their prayers and comb their hair, and a battalion of the Highland Light Infantry were also given a fine reception, especially when the pipers played on the station platform. My wife, who had come out just before the Germans invaded the Low Countries and France, organised the other women into a reception committee and provided tea and soft drinks at the station for all these troop trains, a service which was much appreciated.

My wife was also in charge of ciphers and codes, and we had some fun over them. One code which we used had five letter groups, and in a telegram I was sending to the Governor Upper Nile about some police movements there was a gap of four letters in the last group. She filled this in with letters, which when decoded read L.O.V.E. I was told afterwards that the recipient had complained to Khartoum that I was not taking the war seriously enough. We also received long coded telegrams about the trains coming through giving details of British, Indian, Sudanese and other personnel, and lists of the military stores on the train. These telegrams took hours to decode and I couldn't see why time should be wasted in decoding information about rolls of toilet paper and other such articles. However, when I suggested this to Khartoum I was told that an intelligent enemy could deduce the size of the force opposed to him from the amount of such articles being supplied. At railhead for Roseires – Suki station on the line to Gedaref – there was one British officer who had to spend so much of his time decoding these telegrams that there were quite serious delays in getting urgently required materials sent off to Roseires.

There were difficulties with the Sudan Plantations Syndicate. In September 1940 I had to break the news to the Manager that the Railway Department was going to remove railway lines from his ginning factories to expand facilities at Gedaref and Khashm El Girba where our troops were being concentrated in the autumn, and this of course might mean delays in getting away the future cotton crop. Later in November, then Wingate's expedition was preparing to go into Western Ethiopia, I had to commandeer camels from the Gezira, and this again was a blow to the Syndicate's management, as camels were essential for the cartage of cotton from the fields to the light railways, which carried it to the ginneries. However, after heated arguments both over the telephone and face to face, military necessity was accepted and loyal co-operation achieved.

The devolution of authority to *samads* – headmen – to take the place of the British inspectors who had gone to the war and to supervise the tenants' work on the irrigated area caused some anxiety. Policy had been that these *samads* should be elected by village councils, and be responsible to them in a democratic way; but with the need for haste it was inevitable that such methods were often omitted, and appointments made direct by the Block or Group Inspector, so that the result was much more autocratic than was theoretically desirable.

After the Battle of Keren and the fall of Asmara a few days later, I was informed that we were being sent several thousand prisoners of war, and soon trainloads began to arrive. Before I left Wad Medani in July 1941 the numbers had grown to nearly 10,000, of whom about 1,500 were Italians and the rest native troops. We also received some eighty elderly guards, retired and re-enlisted policemen and soldiers. The camp consisted mostly of straw huts and was surrounded by barbed-wire apron fences. I was anxious about security to start with as the guards were not very reliable, but after a few escapes in the first week had ended in the escapees being captured, beaten up and returned by local villagers, the prisoners stopped trying to get away. Except for the difficulties of feeding and finding work for them, they caused very little trouble thereafter. One morning, when riding round, I found a Vickers machine-gun loaded with a belt of ammunition standing in the open not far from the P.O.W. camp, with no one apparently in charge of it — and I saw not far away in the camp several white Italians standing talking together. I went on slowly and then galloped to the nearest telephone to speak to the Commandant of Police. He took immediate action and had the gun removed. It turned out that police were being trained in the use of the gun, and when their lesson was over they had been marched off and the gun had been forgotten.

I used to talk to some of the Italians who knew English and discuss the war with them. They told me that they had surrendered at Keren because there was no point in being killed here in Africa. The war would be won in Europe, and when it was over the Germans and Italians would be able to take all they wanted from the British. They were members of an Alpine battalion and were tall, good-looking men whose apathy and lack of initiative seemed very odd. Inside the province we began to consider the return to normal conditions. The local population round Kurmuk and Geissan had suffered to a certain extent, for the Italians had driven off large numbers of livestock, and when I was there in March 1941 there were certainly few cattle, sheep or goats to be seen. Neither were there many people about, and the villages were either tumbledown or had been burnt when the inhabitants had fled to the hills. But by the end of May, when I again visited the frontier *omadias*, there was a great change. Many houses had been rebuilt, and the usual sprinkling of children, goats and cattle were everywhere to be seen. It was remarkable how soon things became normal again. The grain situation was the most worrying, for in 1940 confidence had been rudely shattered and the harvest had not been gathered in. But in those areas a state of semi-famine is unfortunately no unusual thing, and the people know a good deal about the use of wild plants, roots and leaves for food. We did our best by helping merchants to take in grain, and by supplying big dumps of it in places which merchants could not be expected to serve. The Sudan War Relief Fund Committee made a generous contribution, and this was distributed to those who had lost animals or houses by enemy action. These people also had one great asset in recovery from misfortune not possessed by people in other places. If they liked to work hard they were able to wash gold out of the *khors*, and with the current high prices they were able to buy the grain which had been brought to the markets.

In the spring of 1941 I was told that I was to take some leave and then go to Khartoum to the Civil Secretary's office as Assistant Civil

Secretary. I was disappointed at having to revert to my proper rank as Deputy Governor, after acting as Governor of a big province for sixteen months, with apparent success. But there was nothing to do but accept the decision, and in the meantime enjoy wartime leave in East Africa.

So ended nearly nineteen years in the province, which I had enjoyed to the full. It was a wonderful life and somehow amazingly rewarding, chiefly because one was so closely in touch with the Sudanese and learned to appreciate their patient courage, cheerfulness and friendliness. I went into the Secretariat most unwillingly, partly because it was a new unknown world, but also because I felt that I could never again be in such close touch with the ordinary people, and would have to make decisions on other people's proposals and on other people's estimates of what was best to be done.

# PART TWO

# SUDAN CIVIL SECRETARY

# CHAPTER VI

# THE POST-WAR SUDAN

## *First Steps in the Secretariat*

It was with very mixed feelings that I first went into the Secretariat in September 1941. Although I had been a long time in the Sudan there was much to learn about the central organisation in Khartoum, which had grown in size and complexity since 1922. It was obvious that our way of life would be changed too, for while the capital afforded far less opportunity than the provinces for informal contact with the Sudanese, it also involved a much fuller official social calendar.

The organisation of the Sudan Government differed from that of Britain's colonial territories. Instead of a Chief Secretary, who was responsible to the Governor for the administration as a whole and to whom everything of importance was referred, the Sudan had three Secretaries, Civil, Finance and Legal. In the eyes of their juniors they sometimes seemed like a lesser Holy Trinity, co-equal in power in their various spheres – though by no means always of one mind; and each of them was individually responsible to the Governor-General for the matters in their respective portfolios. The Civil Secretary was the 'funnel' for various departments – Health, Education, Agriculture and Forests, Surveys, Local Government and Native Administration, Police and Prisons, Aviation, Information and, later, the Labour Department. The Financial Secretary had of course Audits, Customs and Excise, and the Gezira scheme, with the whole question of irrigation. He was also responsible for Sudan Railways. The Legal Secretary resembled the Lord Chancellor; he looked after legislation, the staffing of the legal services such as the state and *sharia* courts, as well as being responsible for the Lands Department and the Land Registry. It can be seen from this brief survey that these responsibilities were bound to overlap. The Civil Secretary had responsibility for the political and social aspects of the Gezira scheme and, as the Governor-General's foreign secretary, could not afford to be ignorant of what the Financial Secretary and the Director of Irrigation were saying to Egypt about Nile waters. The Civil Secretary also received all the political repercussions if there was agitation about matters which fell under the portfolios of the other Secretaries, such as labour troubles in the Sudan Railways.

There were two reasons why this system worked reasonably smoothly in my time. First, when I became Civil Secretary in 1945, I was junior to Jock Miller,* the Financial Secretary, and Tom Creed,† the Legal Secretary, but they were both longstanding personal friends and were extremely co-operative and helpful. When they left the Sudan in 1947 I was well entrenched as Civil Secretary, and had worked closely with their successors, Louis Chick‡ and Charles Cumings,§ both of whom I knew well; but even so, if we had not been good friends and able to co-operate, the system could have been very difficult. Secondly, the Governor-General could always step in to ensure that his secretaries worked in unison. During my time in the Secretariat, the Governor-General held a meeting every Sunday morning with the three Secretaries and the *Kaid* (the Commander of Armed Forces), during which important matters could be raised; after discussion the Governor-General would give his opinion and then a decision could be made. Later on in Nigeria, when I was Governor-General there, I was to see the Chief Secretary system working and I was inclined to think that too much work was thrown on to one man, which sometimes prevented the Government acting quickly and decisively, and so led often to delays.

However, in 1942 the rival merits of these two systems lay ahead of me, and I had two and a half years in which to learn the workings of central government before becoming Civil Secretary myself. Douglas Newbold, my Governor when I was D.C. in Western Kordofan, had been Civil Secretary since the autumn of 1939 and as such he had supported me wholeheartedly when I had been in charge of the Gezira Province. He was a very charming and delightful person and did an immense amount of work for the Sudan during his service. He never spared himself and during these war years never let up or took a proper holiday. He was very well read, interested in history and literature, and had in his early years done some exploration in the northern parts of Kordofan and the Sahara. He had a quick, inquiring mind with immense curio-

* *Sir Edington Miller.* Sudan Political Service 1920–49. District Administrator 1920–7. Financial Department 1928–49. Financial Secretary 1944–9. British Council 1949–50. Iraq Government Development Board 1950–4. Died 1957.

† *Sir Thomas Creed.* Sudan Political Service 1922–48. District Administrator 1922–6. Legal Department 1926–48. Iraq Government 1931–5. Chief Justice Sudan 1935–41. Legal Secretary 1941–9. Principal Queen Mary College, London University 1952–67. Died 1969.

‡ *Sir Louis Chick.* Joined Sudan Finance Department 1930. Deputy Financial Secretary 1944. Financial Secretary 1949–53. Commissioner to Nigeria 1953 and Malaya 1954. Chairman White Fish Authority 1954–63. Died 1972.

§ *Sir Charles Cumings.* Sudan Political Service 1927–30. Transferred to Legal Department 1930. Advocate General 1943. Chief Justice 1945. Legal Secretary 1947–53. Retired to Rhodesia.

sity about everything and a quizzical, cheerful personality. He inspired affection in all with whom he talked and had a wonderful gift of showing his interest in the difficulties and anxieties of young officers in their loneliness and separations during the war. His wide outlook, ranging far beyond the day-to-day problems of the Sudan, put our work in a broader perspective and reconciled what we were trying to do with the world-wide scene. Newbold was somehow able to put himself across to the Sudanese, so that although a number of the things he did disturbed them tremendously, they never thought for a moment that he had made these decisions because he was out of sympathy with them.

The most important of these incidents was the row with the Graduates' Congress in April 1942, soon after I first went to Khartoum. I had nothing to do with political matters at that time, but it was common knowledge that Newbold had sent back to the Congress a memorandum which they had submitted on behalf of the Sudanese people, on the grounds that Congress had no right to claim to speak for the people as a whole, or make such highly political demands. This action, about the background of which I know little even now, always seemed to me most unfortunate, as it was inevitably considered an insult by Congress members, who included almost all the country's intelligentsia. Subsequent reconciliation proved very difficult. In fact this decision always seemed to me to have been the beginning of the divisions among the intelligentsia, which continued until the Sudan became independent – the one part trusting the Sudan Government and the British to lead them to self-government and independence, and the other part looking to Egypt for assistance against the British. The brusque refusal to receive the memorandum seemed to me most unlike Newbold and indeed very unlike the Governor-General, Huddleston. It would surely have been much better to acknowledge it, draw attention to the Sudan Government's preoccupation with the war and its effects, and make one or two polite remarks upon the Government's inability to accept the Congress as the mouthpiece of the Sudanese as a whole, though its contents would be studied carefully. However, in wartime when everyone was tired, overworked and under-staffed, it was possibly not so easy to be wise and patient when presented with a foolish and impolitic list of demands.

Newbold, in 1942 and 1943, came to the conclusion that it was politically essential to speed up the promotion of Sudanese into higher posts in the administrative service, and consulted most of the governors of provinces and the senior British officials. He was disappointed to win no response from most of them: John Humphry* at Kassala,

* *J. M. Humphry.* Sudan Political Service 1920–46. District Service 1921–38. Assistant Civil Secretary 1938–40. Governor Kassala Province 1941–6. Died 1964.

D

who had fairly recently been in the Civil Secretary's office, and I were the only ones who wholeheartedly agreed with him. There was, of course, a serious problem in that the most senior Sudanese administrative officers were of the old solid type – honest, decent, unimaginative officials who had had little more than elementary education and could not perhaps stand up to the young intelligentsia, or win their respect.

Furthermore, the governors feared for the efficiency of their provinces, and were not convinced that Sudanese administrative officers would allow the heads of the local administrations, which had been set up with great hopes and much travail, to carry on their work without interference. This was a problem which I later had to face myself both in the Sudan, when I was Civil Secretary, and afterwards when I first arrived in Nigeria as Governor-General and found that Africanisation there was terribly behindhand. Newbold at the centre could estimate political necessities much better than the provincial governors, yet he had to carry them along with him, so compromise was necessary. Fewer promotions were made at once than Newbold believed desirable; only a few of the bright young men were pushed on and still fewer of the older characters were given a rise in grade. For the next ten years or so we continued to give a few consolation prizes to the experienced officers while concentrating on the younger and better educated men. The pace was set by Pridie,* the Director of Medical Services, whose young doctors, on passing out of the Khartoum School of Medicine and being appointed to government service, were rapidly pushed on into senior posts, thereby creating a precedent which was impossible for other departments to ignore.

There was also the problem of the younger expatriate civil servants who had come into the service before these political factors had assumed this new importance. How would they react to the rapid promotion of Sudanese who were less well educated, and perhaps less reliable, and who might also threaten their careers? This was a problem which I first began to think about in 1942–3 but which continued with me during the rest of my service.

In all the anxieties of the war, with its gloom, defeats and unremitting work, it was often difficult to remember that there would be a future to cope with if we survived, but in the moments when we thought of this, we realised new policies had to be devised. The Atlantic Charter, and the encouraging remarks Stafford Cripps made on his stop at Khartoum Airport *en route* for India were notable events which stirred

* *Sir Eric Pridie.* Sudan Medical Service 1924–45. Director Sudan Medical Service 1953–45. Health Councillor British Embassy in Cairo 1945–9. Chief Medical Officer Colonial Office 1949–58.

the Sudanese to consider the future. Strangely enough, although the Sudan was governed for the benefit of its peoples as we saw it, and although consultation with the Sudanese individually had always been a characteristic of administration in the district and at the centre in Khartoum, nothing had been done before the war to create any sort of central assembly, legislative council or parliament. The Sudan was still governed autocratically by the Governor-General assisted by a Council, the members of which were all British officials appointed by him. In most of Britain's overseas territories, even in Africa, some sort of legislative council including representatives of the indigenous peoples had been created years before this – even though the people of these territories were no more advanced than the Sudanese. It seems odd, looking back on it now, that nothing had been done in the 1920s or 1930s to associate the Sudanese more closely with central government, although on local matters town councils and tribal councils existed as consultative bodies throughout the country.

In 1942 Newbold began to work on a proposal to set up a consultative body which would be mainly composed of Sudanese, and he studied what had been done in other similar countries. He found, as I did a few years later, that we in the Sudan were very much on our own, and that we had no one to provide us with advice on how to set up national bodies representative of the people, nor did we know the difficulties and the advantages of varying forms of constitution. The Foreign Office, to whom we looked as our sponsor in Britain, was uninterested and uninformed in these matters, and as a condominium under Egypt as well as Britain, the Sudan could not turn to the Colonial Office for help. Both Newbold at this stage, and I myself later, had to obtain our advice and information through personal contacts in Britain.

Newbold set up a small committee of senior British officials to advise him, and he and this committee hammered out a scheme which eventually came to life in 1944 as the Advisory Council for the Northern Sudan. This was a purely advisory body, consisting of twenty-eight members, who were appointed from the Northern provinces only. It was criticised by the Congress and the intelligentsia generally as having no executive power, for not covering the whole of the Sudan, and for being largely composed of nominated members. In fact three members were elected by each of the six Northern Province Councils, two by the Chamber of Commerce, and only eight were nominated by the Governor-General to represent the educated and professional classes. The three Secretaries were vice-presidents and attended all the meetings. The Governor-General was President but only opened and closed each session. Newbold presided over the first two meetings and I had to take his place at the next six meetings, after his death. The Advisory Council discussed several important matters, and its resolutions about education, the Gezira scheme and the definition of 'Sudanese' were carefully considered and largely accepted by the Government. Newbold was nervous about the Advisory Council before it opened in May 1944, and I believe that he felt it a great strain to preside over it.

When I first went into Khartoum I was only an observer of most of these new developments, but I gradually became more involved between the autumn of 1941 and Newbold's tragic death in April 1945. In my early days I found the transition from provincial life difficult. It was a complete change to settle down in an office with little opportunity of getting away, and with the prospect of being far less on my own and of having much less direct responsibility than previously. Furthermore, having never been in the secretariat before and knowing neither how the machine worked nor the answers to current problems, I found that for three or four weeks I had very little to do. I was by-passed by both my seniors and my juniors as they could get decisions or action much more quickly by ignoring somebody who would need to have the background of any subject explained to him. After about four weeks I began to have enough to do, and during the next eleven years, until I retired in April 1953, the difficulty was to find the time and the energy to do all that I had to do. But the first few weeks were desperately dull.

The British clerks in the office eventually rallied round and gave me some training in my duties, and I owed much to these excellent officials. They were always cheerful and co-operative, they worked hard and took a great pride in the reputation of the office. As Sudanisation progressed and they retired, it was noticeable that the Sudanese who took their places could not produce the same standard of work. More routine drafting had to be done by the senior officials and instructions for subordinates had to be much more carefully and precisely worded.

From the autumn of 1941 as Assistant Civil Secretary (Departmental) I acted as the Civil Secretary's representative and executive in most matters which came to his office from the various departments. Representing the Civil Secretary, I sat as Chairman of the Central Board of Public Health, as Chairman of the Public Works Board and of the Roads Board. I was required to supervise the Civil Secretary's office Personnel section, which had responsibility for the appointment, posting and promotions of the clerical service as a whole as well as for the recruitment and promotion of Sudanese junior administrative officers. I also found that I had to help in considering the transfers and promotions of the Political Service personnel and producing recommendations for the Civil Secretary to decide upon. During the war there were numerous other tasks. I had to plan and put into action with the Post and Telegraph engineers a system of wireless warning stations all across the Northern Sudan, so that German aircraft operating from bases in North Africa could not reach our Sudan airfields and petrol dumps without some warning – although, as far as I know, they never tried to attack us. A rather unhappy assignment was the conscription of the young Greek manpower of the Sudan, which the British Government had apparently agreed with the King of Greece. Our young Hellenes were rather weedy youths, most of whom worked behind counters in the Greek stores and did not look like fighting men. However, some 220 were called up and in the end, following some training and the donning of uniforms, they paraded at the station, were reviewed by me and a somewhat fascist-looking Greek colonel called Caloumenos, after which they entrained for Egypt. What they did for their country I do not know; I always remember being told that while I should shout *Zeeto Hellas* to them, I must not shout *Zeeto Basileu* as most of them, while patriotic enough Hellenes, were republicans and not royalists. The Colonel, for my pains, presented me with a beautiful volume of Thucydides' History in the original Greek.

One of my main duties as Assistant Civil Secretary was to work with the various authorities to facilitate the passage of aircraft from West Africa and South Africa to the Middle East on the reinforcement routes. This meant co-ordination with the provinces, the R.A.F., the Public Works Department and the Posts and Telegraphs and, on occasions when aircraft were overdue, arranging for searches. During the war some 14,000 aircraft passed through the Sudan on their way to Egypt, and to supply sufficient petrol for refuelling these numbers at Geneina and El Fasher, which were far from rail-head, was no small task, especially when the roads were so bad.

In 1942, before the victory at Alamein and the defeat of the German and Italian armies, we had to consider what might happen if Cairo and Egypt were lost, and considerable efforts were devoted to a scheme named AFLOC, whereby a reinforcement route was reconnoitered from Matadi at the mouth of the Congo, up that river and then across by land to Juba in the Southern Sudan, whence supplies could be delivered either northwards by the Nile to Khartoum or southwards to Uganda and Kenya. Fortunately the victory at Alamein came before too much time or money had been spent on these various projects.

Another consequence of defeat in North Africa for which we had to prepare was the possibility of a large influx of people. We prepared plans to house the headquarters of a British army in Khartoum, and we also expected to accommodate some hundreds of girls – A.T.S., Wrens and other services. In the end the girls got no further up the river than Aswan, where an official of ours had been sent – with facetious comments from his friends – to look after them. The only group actually to arrive were refugees from Cyrenaica and Palestine, who had collaborated with the British and had to be moved in case they were captured.

The Sudan Agent's office in Cairo was tremendously busy in June and July that year, as all sorts of people wanted to get away from Egypt to avoid Rommel and Mussolini. Ted MacIntosh,* who knew Egypt well, was sent down to help our Sudan Agent to cope. Apparently fortunes could have been made by accepting bribes during the first scare in June and July if any of our officials had wished to succumb to temptation.

When Ted MacIntosh went as Governor to Khartoum Province in 1943 I was appointed Deputy Civil Secretary, and thus was fortunate to have more than two years' service as Newbold's deputy, and to work in close contact with him. In both 1943 and 1944 he took a short local leave and left me in charge of the office for several weeks, when I had to take his place on the Governor-General's Council, the Establishments Committee and the Council of Secretaries. During those years our friendship deepened, and usually we fitted in well together, although sometimes Douglas could procrastinate over office work. We all have our failings, and no doubt those who worked with me found me at times impossible to deal with. With Douglas I sometimes felt irritated when papers, which I had submitted to him with careful minutes asking for his decision – yes or no – on some matter or other, sat on his table for days while he wrote scores of his wonderful letters, in his beautiful clear hand, to D.C.s and other friends, or prepared a lecture on a Crusader for the Clergy House Supper Club after Sunday evening service. Once or twice I went in to his office when he wasn't there and removed files which I had sent for his decision days before, and minuted under my own minute 'C.S. being absent, decision is (a) above' – but he was a fine colleague and had the real guts of the matter in him. He loved the people we were working for and inspired us all to follow his example. I was lucky to have these years working in close

* *E. H. MacIntosh.* Sudan Political Service 1921–45. District Administrator 1922–37. Assistant Civil Secretary 1937–8. Sudan Agent in Cairo 1938–41. Deputy Civil Secretary 1941–2. Governor Khartoum Province 1942–5. Re-employed as Labour Officer 1945–8.

contact with him and to acquire from him something of his spirit of service to Africa.

It was not only the nature of my work which made life in Khartoum appear very different from my earlier experiences. The social life was very active, especially during the war when dozens of people of all nationalities were passing through the capital. The Khartoum riverside houses with their gardens, palms, bougainvillea, oleanders and other flowering shrubs set in lawns, possibly with a tennis court, were delightful. We were fortunate enough to have a small one just east of the Catholic church: my wife ran what was more or less a guest house or a nursing home, for it was always full of visitors. We took our share of serving the Anglican Cathedral canteen for troops and got some amusement there, especially when a tough battalion of the Argyll and Sutherland Highlanders come down from Gondar in Ethiopia, and seemed to think that Khartoum should be treated much as they had treated Gondar. I was told by one chap that he'd have 'sausages, fried eggs and bacon – and see they're hot!' Lady Huddleston was told 'Come on now, mither,' and one friend of ours was asked 'Ye'll no be a Greek, will ye?'

Leave was obviously difficult during the war, but a combination of inspections and local leaves permitted some escapes from the seemingly endless meetings in Khartoum. Internally I visited a number of the provinces and was able in 1944 to make a prolonged tour of the Southern Sudan, a region already causing us concern, which later became acute. One incident which I remember vividly occurred on my way back from Egypt in 1943. When we reached Shellal on 18 July the Nile was so low that the ship could not sail, and there was no firm information to tell us when the flood, which was already late, would arrive and allow the ship to move. At Shellal the ships for the Sudan moored in a backwater: when the river was low there was no current and it seemed to me that if some four or five hundred people lived on the steamers and barges, the river would be quickly fouled and the water supply defiled. I therefore arranged to send the 1st Class passengers to Luxor by rail and the 2nd Class passengers to Aswan, and for their board and lodging in the hotels to be paid by the Government. I obtained tents for the 240 3rd Class passengers to camp ashore under arrangements which I made with the Governor of Aswan. The 3rd Class passengers complained that they had no money to buy food, so I promised them free passages on the steamer to Wadi Halfa, which allowed them to use the money they had been saving for their fares for food. We could not leave Shellal until 2 August and it was 8 August before we got back to Khartoum. On my return I was naturally concerned at the possible reaction of the Financial Secretary, for I had spent quite a large sum of money without authority. However, on my going to make my apologies, he thanked me for my efforts, saying he thought it fortunate that I had been there to take charge – so all was well.

## Civil Secretary

Towards the end of 1944 I even managed to get home leave, although there was much to do while I was in London, discussing our post-war plans. It was delightful to be with all my family again, for I had not seen the children for five years. However, on my return to Khartoum I found that Newbold was not fit. He had had a bad hip for a number of years, and it was giving him much pain, especially after he bumped it one day against the corner of a desk. By 11 March he was ordered to bed and then into hospital, where he died on Friday, 23 March. His death was due to septicaemia and complete weariness and exhaustion.

This was a terrible loss to the Sudan, as the Sudanese certainly realised: his obviously genuine devotion to them was well known, and an unassuming friendly manner had won him a host of friends. There were immense crowds at his funeral the next morning, and for weeks letters of sympathy poured into the office from all over the country.

But work had to go on. There was no indication at first who would succeed Newbold as Civil Secretary. I was his deputy, but this ranked as an ordinary provincial governor's post which had no special seniority or entitlement, and I was junior to several of those in the provinces. I supposed Bredin* at Wad Medani to be the most likely, and Campbell† at El Obeid was also senior to me and had had Secretarial experience. The appointment rested with the Governor-General, who was not obliged to get approval from the Co-domini. Huddleston did not take long to make up his mind. He consulted the senior people in Khartoum, and on the 28th, only five days after Newbold had died, I received a note from him in his own immense scrawling hand saying that he proposed to appoint me, and the appointment would be officially notified on Monday, 2 April, after some of the governors had been informed privately. So I found myself appointed to the top post in the Political Service, which I was to hold for the next eight years. I was naturally very pleased, but also a little concerned about the scale of

* G. R. F. *Bredin*. Sudan Political Service 1921–48. District and Provincial Service 1922–39. Deputy Civil Secretary 1939–41. Governor Blue Nile Province 1941–8. Member of Governor-General's Council 1945–8. Fellow and Bursar Pembroke College, Oxford 1951–69.

† *Ewen Campbell*. Sudan Political Service 1921–47. District Service 1922–35. Assistant Civil Secretary 1935–6. Deputy Civil Secretary 1936–8. Governor Kordofan Province 1938–47.

the task on which I was embarking, and especially diffident about succeeding such a distinguished and well-loved man as Newbold, whose personal qualities I could never expect to emulate.

The roles of the Civil Secretary were varied, and one into which I found myself thrust almost immediately was dealing with foreign affairs. In July 1945 I was sent to represent the Governor-General in the British Middle East Defence Committee. I attended under Lord Killearn's* wing, as he was still High Commissioner for the Sudan – or looked upon himself as such – and so I was privileged to drive with him in his big Rolls-Royce through the streets of Cairo from the Embassy to the British Middle East Minister's office with the Union Jack flying and outriders in front. This was the style of his predecessors, but one which was shortly to die out. The meeting had to prepare recommendations for H.M.G. about the future of the occupied territories, and the Sudan was really only concerned with one of them – Eritrea, which had a frontier with our Kassala Province and was inhabited partly by people tribally akin to our Hadendowa and Beni Amer. The Sudan Government had, and constitutionally could have, no territorial ambitions, and I said so; we were particularly reluctant to take over the high plateau land of Eritrea, whose inhabitants were Christians and were much more like the Ethiopians than the Sudanese. We would not object so much to taking over the Beni Amer tribesmen of the lower hill country, the cousins and relatives of our own Beni Amer, but we would only do this to assist the Allied powers to make a good arrangement for the future, for such a settlement would be economically expensive and would bring in little or no revenue to the Sudan, which had no money to spare. We did think that to have all the Beni Amer tribe under one administration and not divided in two by an international boundary would lead to better control and maintenance of law and order, and prevent frequent international trouble arising from petty tribal bickering. General Paget, the C.-in-C., was emphatic that 'never again should British troops have to storm the heights of Keren' – though why they should was hard to see; and the Admiral and Air Marshal wanted air bases on the high plateau to be denied to any possible enemy, for 'we must never forget the Straits of Bab El Mandeb'. These two phrases were repeated periodically throughout the discussion rather like the strophe and antistrophe of a Greek tragedy. Nothing of course came of all this, for in 1952 the United Nations handed over the whole of Eritrea to the Emperor of Ethiopia, who has had trouble there from time to time ever since.

Although I could not foresee all the future complications facing the Sudan, it was clear in 1945 that I was taking over as Civil Secretary

* *Lord Killearn.* British High Commissioner in Egypt and Ambassador 1934–46.

at a difficult time, for we had to catch up with affairs which the war had forced us to neglect, while at the same time we were confronted by the new expectant post-war world. On the whole, as the war in Europe and the Far East drew to a close, it was evident that the Sudan had been relatively little affected. The Italians had invaded the east of the country in 1940 and 1941, but their defeat had been followed by four years of internal peace. There had been economic difficulties, but not severe ones, and most of the country had ticked over comfortably on a care and maintenance basis. But inevitably there had been a certain amount of neglect. With the shortage of skilled manpower and the impossibility of obtaining recruits for the civil services it had been impossible to initiate many new developments, and the end of hostilities had brought a general urge for new activities, especially economic development. There were, however, a number of problems. Much of the transport in the country had become run down and needed replacement, but there was little money with which to buy it, and in any case the industrial centres of the world were not themselves in a position to supply it quickly. Ordinary people could not understand why, with the war coming to an end, shortages of all kinds remained and rationing had to be continued.

On the political side the Advisory Council was in existence and it now became my job to chair its biannual meetings. In my view there were useful discussions on a number of subjects, such as the Gezira and education, and the views expressed were taken very seriously by the Government. It meant a good deal of extra work for me, preparing papers for members and being cognisant of all relevant information concerning the various subjects, and I am sure it educated all its members in the conduct of a political assembly. However, there had always been considerable criticism of the Assembly, and to these attacks were added the expectations of the post-war world, encouraged by the statements of Allied leaders. The Sudanese nationalists could be expected to redouble the call for their wartime demands and thereby create tension between the intelligentsia of the towns and the conservative rural populations, whose leaders feared a loss of influence and position if too much power was handed to the small educated class. The beginning of such a situation were reflected in the development of political parties at the time I became Civil Secretary. A small group of pro-Egyptians known as the Ashigga – the brothers – was seeking the support of Sayed Ali Mirghani and the widespread Khatmia sect, while anti-Egyptians were rallying around Sayed Abdel Rahman, forming the Umma (nation) party.

There was also another and immediately more serious problem in which I found myself directly involved after only a few months in

office and which intermittently recurred throughout my years as Civil
Secretary. The Egyptians had long been discontented by the limited
role they had been allowed to play in the Sudan, claiming that from
the beginning the Condominium Agreement had been used by the
British to dominate the country. The reason for this exclusion was of
course the Egyptians' refusal to accept the Agreement from its inception, and their several attempts over the years to upset it, ending with
the mutiny at Khartoum in 1924. Furthermore, the corruption and
incapacity of the Egyptian ruling classes was well known and led the
Sudan Government to reject strongly any idea of allowing the Egyptians
a share in senior positions. However, the worldwide post-war movement against imperialism and colonialism was having an effect among
our northern neighbours and it became apparent that the Egyptians
would soon be seeking sweeping amendments to the Sudan's constitutional arrangements. I wrote at the time that nothing would content
them except the complete evacuation of British troops from Egypt
and the incorporation of the Sudan in Egypt.

As expected, in the closing weeks of 1945 the Egyptian Government
submitted a formal note to the British Government asking for negotiations to be started with a view to revising the 1936 Anglo-Egyptian
Treaty. This Treaty, negotiated when Mussolini's expansionist policies
seemed to be threatening both British and Egyptian interests in the
Middle East from Libya to Ethiopia, gave the British valuable facilities
in Egypt in the event of a war with Italy; and it was certainly largely
due to the alliance with Egypt under the terms of this Treaty that
Britain was able to defeat the Italian and German threats in the Middle
East in the 1939–45 war. Now that the situation had radically altered
with the defeat of the Axis Powers, it was not unreasonable that Egypt
should seek to revise the Treaty, although it was originally intended to
last twenty years; moreover, since the Treaty had also reaffirmed the
Condominium with only minor concessions to Egypt, the Sudan was
bound to be included in the negotiations.

At the beginning of 1946, British ministers were faced with immense
problems all over the world as they tried to tidy up the legacies of war
and prepare new policies; consequently there was some delay in reply-
ing to the Egyptians, whose attitude hardened. Violent anti-British
disorders occurred in Cairo and Alexandria, and the stern measures
taken to counter them by Nokrashi Pasha's Government led to its
downfall. By the time the two delegations eventually met in Cairo
in the latter part of April, Sidky Pasha had taken over as Prime
Minister.

I was invited to Cairo to meet Embassy officials and discuss the
whole question of the Treaty negotiations with them. During my visit

I met the new Ambassador, Sir Ronald Campbell, and members of his staff, and called on Sidky Pasha, the Egyptian Prime Minister. I spent an hour and a half with him, and we had a long talk about the Sudan. I started in my hesitant French, as I understood that he spoke no English, but I had stammered no more than a sentence or two when he suggested that we switch into Arabic. He asked me many questions about the country and its administration, and made copious notes, the result of which was clear a month or two later, when the Governor-General received a long despatch from the Egyptian Government asking for explanations of much that I had told the Pasha. He was a pleasant, cheerful little man, but like so many others, could not understand that although I was a British citizen, I had nothing to do with the British Government but was a Sudan civil servant. This inability to appreciate that a British subject could be a loyal servant of another government was very common among Egyptians, Americans, not a few British, including some ministers and civil servants and, to a lesser degree, Sudanese. The Sudanese who knew us well realised that we were ready to disagree with or oppose the British Government, if we thought they were acting contrary to Sudanese interests, and in the next few years it was not uncommon for us to do so.

Embassy officials believed that the best way for the Sudan Government to counter Egyptian pressures was to hasten Sudanisation, both of the civil service and of the organs of government, and it was suggested by Dr. Pridie that a whole province should be Sudanised forthwith. I explained the difficulties involved in such a rapid timetable and outlined the plans on which we were working. But their arguments had some effect on me, and it was only a few days after this on 17 April that the Governor-General, in his address to the meeting of the Advisory Council, announced on my advice that he was going to set up an Administration Conference to propose ways of associating the Sudanese more closely in both Central and Local Government, and to appoint a Sudanisation Committee, as a sub-committee of the Advisory Council. These bodies were convened almost immediately, and their appointment had considerable effect at the time in persuading the Sudanese that the Government was sincere in its intention of preparing the Sudanese for self-government. Nevertheless I approached this meeting of the Advisory Council with anxiety, and was glad when it was over after reasonably amicable discussions, and without any Sudanese members resigning.

The lack of Sudanese participation during the 1936 negotiations had been one of the reasons for the creation of the Graduates' Congress, thus when the 1946 talks began, a number of the educated Sudanese were determined to try to press their views on the Co-domini. An all-party delegation went to Cairo early in the talks and caused us a certain embarrassment. The British Embassy agreed to treat the Sudanese politely but modestly, for they had no official status, although they obtained interviews with a number of prominent Egyptians. However, their impact was lessened by internal dissension, and after a few weeks the supporters of Sayed Abdel Rahman returned to Khartoum.

The spring and summer of 1946 were marked by unrest and student demonstrations, though none of these did much harm. I was telephoned occasionally by anonymous voices asking 'When are you going to give us our freedom?' to which I would make facetious replies such as 'Oh! are you in prison?', and on occasions I received letters saying 'We have rifles and revolvers and you are number one on our list.' But there were no attacks or incidents. I handed these letters to the police, and on subsequent nights was awakened by the tramp of heavy footsteps on the gravel round the house. When I asked whose they were and what they wanted, I was told 'We are the Secret Police.' I complained to the police authorities, and the next night when I came in a little late I found two men who looked like beggars sitting at my gate; when I asked who they were and what they wanted, they leapt to their feet and saluted – again the 'Secret Police'.

Meanwhile in Cairo the negotiations continued, but in the early weeks the emphasis was all upon the Egyptian demand for evacuation of the British troops from Egypt, and the British delegates refused to consider the Sudan until this question was settled. Lord Stansgate, who led the British delegation, went back to London in June for consultations, but returned fairly soon, and it appeared that there was some chance of an agreement being reached on the military clauses. In July I went to Egypt again and met the British delegation at Montaza Palace in Alexandria. I found Lord Stansgate in his dressing-gown with a bad cold. It was very hot and the delegation was wilting. Lord Stansgate appeared far from sympathetic towards my views about the Sudan, but I hoped he was only irritable because of his cold.

I then went home on leave, and was enjoying a holiday in Scotland when the news came that the Treaty negotiations had broken down, and that Sidky Pasha had resigned. I went to London to see the Governor-General, Huddleston, and to discuss our position with him and the Foreign Office officials. The Governor-General thought that we both should remain within touch, and that I should not return to the Sudan at the beginning of October as I had intended. King Farouk persuaded Sidky Pasha to continue in office and he came to London in person to see Mr. Bevin. On 7 October Huddleston and I received the news of the still secret Bevin-Sidky Protocol. In private talks with

Ernest Bevin, Sidky had persuaded him to reconsider the Sudan question, and together they had worked out a form of words, which both
could accept, although it turned out later that each put a different
interpretation on them. I noted in my diary, 'It was on this day that
we first heard that Mr. Bevin intended to do what he knew to be wrong:
to sell the Sudan to Egypt to buy his Treaty. It was a very great
shock.' The clause of the proposed new treaty which caused us such
concern read:

> The policy which the High Contracting parties undertake to
> follow in the Sudan, within the framework of the unity of the Sudan
> and Egypt under the common crown of Egypt, will have for its
> essential objective to assure the wellbeing of the Sudanese, the
> development of their interests and their active preparations for
> self-government and consequently the exercise of the right to choose
> the future status of the Sudan. Until the High Contracting parties
> can in full common agreement realise this latter objective after
> consultation with the Sudanese, the Agreement of 1899 will con-
> tinue and article 11 of the Treaty of 1936.

We foresaw many difficulties for the Sudan in this proposal. It
acknowledged the unity of the Sudan and Egypt, which most Sudanese
did not accept; it stated what we, in the Sudan, had never recognized –
that King Farouk was King of the Sudan in a way different from King
George VI: and it was not clear whether the Sudanese had the right
of self-determination and independence if they wished, or if their
status was always to be under the common crown. We thought the
Egyptians would claim this, and we also thought it would be difficult
to maintain the existing administration of the Sudan if the Egyptians
tried to exercise the sovereignty which this Protocol seemed to give
them. General Huddleston saw Bevin and other British ministers and
pointed out the likelihood of disturbances and bloodshed in the Sudan
once the Sidky-Bevin Agreement was made known. However, great
pressure was put on the Governor-General and he eventually said
that he thought there might just be a chance, if he had time to put it
across properly, that the Sudanese pro-independents might accept the
Protocol. According to the British interpretation, the Egyptians were
for the first time conceding the right of self-government and eventual
self-determination to the Sudan. This would be a great advance and a
real charter of future independence if they, the Sudanese, wished that
eventual goal.

Huddleston and I went back to the Sudan, arriving late in the
evening of 29 October. On my return I was very unhappy. My British
colleagues were polite and sympathetic, but I felt that they thought we
had sold the pass and let them down; and the Sudanese, who usually

came to meet me on my return from leave, were silent and unwelcoming. However, the reason was not so difficult to discover. Sidky Pasha had returned to Cairo a few hours earlier and on landing had announced to the crowds awaiting him that he had brought back *seyada* – sovereignty – over the Sudan. In Arabic *seyada* can mean the authority of a master over a slave and this was what the Governor-General and I were thought to have agreed to.

The next day a very large demonstration was organised by the Umma party and the followers of Sayed Abdel Rahman El Mahdi. The demonstration came to the Secretariat and crowded the lawns between my office and the river. It was orderly, although it must have been composed of about 10,000 people, and the leaders – many of them old friends of mine – were not hostile. They handed over a protest against the reported concessions to Egypt and declared their refusal to co-operate with the Sudan Government if it tried to carry on in such circumstances. The next day the pro-Egyptian Ashigga party organised a counter-demonstration, but it was not nearly so big.

During the next week the situation in the Sudan was difficult. The Mahdists had brought large numbers of rather wild tribal supporters into the Khartoum area, and we were anxious lest law and order should be affected. There was an almost fanatical feeling abroad, which seemed to affect elderly and staid leaders of opinion in our conversations with them. We thought this change in the situation – and the likelihood of serious and prolonged disturbances if such a Treaty was concluded – should be made quite clear to the British Government, especially as it seemed certain that considerable force would be needed to enforce the proposals. Creed, the Legal Secretary, Miller, the Financial Secretary, and I composed a memorandum to the Governor-General explaining the position as we saw it, describing our fears, and saying that we did not think that we could possibly remain in the Sudan to force a Treaty on these terms upon the Sudanese. In this I think we were voicing the opinions of the entire British staff of the Sudan Government, on whom the orderly running of the country chiefly depended. The Governor-General decided to return to London to leave H.M.G. in no doubt about the situation, and had interviews with the Prime Minister, Mr. Attlee, and other British ministers. He determined to remain in London until he obtained a definite answer to his recommendations.

The local situation calmed down a little when Huddleston returned to London, and we received a reinforcement in Khartoum of a second battalion of British troops. Sayed Abdel Rahman El Mahdi promised me that he would keep his tribal followers in hand and would not allow them to start any disturbances. But we were still faced with the need to convey to the Sudanese the symbolic nature of the Egyptian crown, to which so many of them were fanatically opposed. At this point Sayed Abdel Rahman went to London himself and was able to put his point of view to Mr. Attlee.

During Huddleston's stay in London it began to be clear that Sidky Pasha put a different interpretation on the Protocol from that of the British ministers. He said in Cairo that the Protocol did not allow the Sudanese the right of secession from Egypt, whereas the British held that after a preliminary period they would be entitled to an independent choice of their future status, including the right to secede from the Egyptian crown if they wished. The Governor-General, therefore, asked Mr. Attlee to give him written instructions to stand fast on the British interpretation, and these were eventually given him, whereupon he set out on his return journey to Khartoum. When he reached Cairo, however, he received a telegram asking him not to make use of the letter containing these instructions. He wired back saying he could not return to the Sudan until he received an answer to the hypothetical question, which he was bound to be asked when he returned to Khartoum, 'Have the Sudanese the right to secede from the Egyptian crown or not, when the time for them to make their choice arrives?' He said that unless he received an answer in the affirmative he could not return to the Sudan.

I wrote on 3 December: 'There has been a marked lessening of tension in the Sudan since the beginning of November, due, I think, very largely to the personal influence of the Governor-General and British officials on the people, and partly, of course, to the realisation that there was to be a choice of complete independence in the future, and that we were not handing over the Sudan, body and soul, to the Egyptians.' I went on:

> Reports coming in from all Provinces and conversations with many Sudanese go to show that there is a great fund of goodwill felt towards the British officials of the Sudan Government. Moderates and reasonable Sudanese everywhere realise that any lessening of the authority of the British in the Sudan will at the present moment mean chaos and anarchy with the likelihood of bloodshed and return to conditions of the Mahdia. In the country districts anti-Egyptian feeling is strong, and tribal leaders everywhere throughout the country fear the prospect of any change in the present administration very strongly. They dislike the prospect of being handed over to Egypt. Followers of Sayed Ali Mirghani are as convinced of this as anyone else: they hate Sayed Abdel Rahman, but certainly do not want Egyptian domination. His Excellency's visit to London and the obvious dislike of most British

officials in the Sudan for the Protocol have been appreciated. The feelings of mistrust which were felt so strongly at the beginning of November have modified, and it is generally realised that the Sudan Government is in no way responsible for the present state of affairs. There still remains suspicion and distrust of the British Government, however, and attempts to whittle down Mr. Attlee's interpretation of the Protocol will be disastrous.

Having received the assurance for which he had asked, Huddleston returned to Khartoum on 6 December and we, his Secretaries, met him and discussed an announcement which he proposed to make the next day. This quoted the British Prime Minister's letter and, while it had a reassuring effect in the Sudan, it caused great offence in Egypt. Sidky Pasha resigned on the 9th and Nokrashi Pasha formed a Government and took office the next day. Opinion had hardened both in Egypt and Great Britain about the Sudan, and the basic views of both Governments seemed more opposed than ever. The Egyptians clearly wished to dominate the Sudan and incorporate it in the Egyptian state, whereas the British wanted to develop self-governing institutions in the Sudan, and assist in the economic and cultural development of the Sudanese, until they were able to decide for themselves what their future should be. The attempt to negotiate a revised treaty, therefore, broke down in January 1947, and Nokrashi Pasha announced that he would refer the dispute to the United Nations. Mr. Bevin, reporting in the House of Commons, spoke highly of the Governor-General's efforts to protect Sudanese rights and we in Khartoum were especially delighted at the passage which regretted Egyptian press attacks on him. This for a month or two ended the major crisis in our overall constitutional position, which had occupied most of my time for nearly a year, and I was able to get back again to more constructive and rewarding work.

Following the Governor-General's statement and before the final breakdown of talks, we made efforts locally to explain the situation. One opportunity to do so came when the postponed Advisory Council met in January 1947. At a private meeting of members Huddleston spoke at some length about symbolic sovereignty, and so perplexed and confused were Sayed Abdel Rahman and a number of other members that I had to call a further meeting the following evening to try to clarify matters. General Huddleston also made visits to the provinces, and his active role was influential in easing the tension in the country at large.

Although the general situation was quieter, Egyptian problems could never be forgotten, and a variety of incidents arose in which I was involved. One example was the case of the Grand Kadi. Since

the Sudan Government had been established in 1899, the Chief Judge
of the Mohamedan Law Courts, with their cadre of Sudanese Sharia
judges, had always been an Egyptian. On one or two occasions it
was suggested that a Sudanese should be appointed, but it was never
done, and Sheikh Hassan Mamoun, another Egyptian, was appointed
in 1941. His term of secondment from the Egyptian Service was now
due to end, and the Legal Secretary, Sir Thomas Creed, considered
that the Mufti, a Sudanese called Sheikh Ahmed El Tahir, was sufficiently qualified to be appointed, and furthermore, under the terms of
the 1936 Treaty, a non-Sudanese should only be appointed to posts
for which no qualified Sudanese was available. The Sudanese watched
with interest to see what the Governor-General would do: the Egyptians
asked the British Government to prevent the Governor-General appointing a Sudanese, and there was a lengthy exchange of telegrams
between Khartoum, the Foreign Office and the Cairo Embassy.
Eventually some months later, Sheikh Ahmed El Tahir was appointed
after quite a long period of 'acting', and proved a very adequate successor to Sheikh Hassan Mamoun.

The lull which followed the breakdown of negotiations also provided
an opportunity for the Governor-General to retire. General Huddleston
had been seriously ill in 1945, and at one time it was thought he might
die. Fortunately he had recovered and in early 1946 had made a
number of tours which he regarded as farewell visits, but when negotiations began he felt it his duty to remain until the country's future was
settled one way or another. Early in 1947 the time was considered
suitable for his departure and he left the Sudan on 5 April.

His contribution to the Sudan had been immense. On his arrival in
1914 as an officer in the Egyptian army, Darfur was virtually independent under Sultan Ali Dinar, and Huddleston was responsible for its
conquest in 1916, from which time it became a province of the Sudan.
By 1924 he had returned to the Egyptian army and was Acting Sidar
in Khartoum at the time of the mutiny when, as well as displaying
great personal courage, he managed a difficult situation admirably.
When the Egyptian army left the Sudan, he was the main architect of
the Sudan Defence Force, which was then formed. Now in 1947 he was
completing nearly seven years as Governor-General at a time when his
personal qualities had been of the greatest value to the country. In the
dark period of the war he was the rock in a weary land on whom
everyone, British and Sudanese, relied: he was courageous, wise and
full of common sense. I found him a wonderful man to work with for
he was decisive and clear; one always knew what he thought, and
there was never any occasion when I left his office in doubt as to what he

wished me to do or to say. He was shrewd, quick-witted and well read, with an excellent memory for the apposite quotation and analogy. I admired him tremendously and was most sorry when he left. He had done much for the Sudan, but perhaps his greatest service for the Sudanese was his steadfast struggle against great odds to prevent the British Government giving away the right of the Sudanese eventually to choose their own future. He cut through the maze of words and the ambiguity of the proposed Protocol, and forced the two negotiating powers to define clearly the interpretations each of them put on it. It took great determination and moral courage to do this, and it is mainly to him that the Sudanese owe their independence as a sovereign state.

I summed up the general situation at this time as follows:

'It has surprised me that we have not had more serious troubles after eighteen months of uncertainty about the future, and after a great deal of intense propaganda playing on a comparatively ignorant and un-sophisticated population. The strength of character, patience and common sense of the Sudanese have stood them, and us, in good stead and in spite of all that has been said and done the great bulk of the population is little affected.'

For me it could hardly have been a more difficult start to my service as Civil Secretary, and showed the complexity of the task, involving constant discussion with many different people, held in places as far apart as Omdurman and the Foreign Office in London. There had been few moments for relaxation, but on those that did occur I was able to enjoy one of the perquisites of the office. In the summer of 1945 we moved to a larger riverside house. It was very roomy and had a lovely garden which we very much enjoyed, though on feast days the religious exercises in the neigbouring Coptic Church could be quite noisy. The main problem was the number of snakes. I encountered one on the stairs, and another was discovered under a discarded blanket on the floor by my bed. My wife sought the help of the Public Health authorities who promptly sent a man along, but instead of fumigating the house he proceeded to play on his pipes. No snakes appeared, whereupon my wife again rang Public Health. The official expressed no surprise at the failure and replied that the musician was only a substitute for the expert – he was on leave.

# CHAPTER VII

# CIVIL SECRETARY 1947–1948

Sir Hubert Huddleston was followed as Governor-General by Sir Robert Howe, a career diplomat, who had been the first British Ambassador in Ethiopia after the war, from 1942 to 1945, and had then served in the Foreign Office where he was concerned with Middle Eastern affairs. Some of us were a little anxious when his appointment was announced, in case he was coming to alter the Sudan Government's policy and bring it more into line with what some of us suspected the Foreign Office wanted – the appeasement of Egypt. Huddleston, however, was very definite in his view that whoever sat in the Governor-General's chair in the Palace where Gordon had once lived, and where he had been killed, would soon become pro-Sudan, and he proved to be right. We could not have had a more devoted supporter of the Sudan's right to self-determination than Sir Robert became during the next few years.

On 6 May the new Governor-General and Lady Howe arrived at Wadi Halfa on the border with Egypt, where I met them. We almost immediately entrained for Khartoum and started on the twenty-four-hour journey which was to take us first across the empty wastes of the desert and then from Abu Hamed upstream along the green banks of the Nile to the capital. We had much to discuss and I found them very much interested in the Sudan, so that the time passed quickly until we arrived, meticulously on schedule, at 8 a.m. the following day. The Financial Secretary and acting Governor-General, Sir Edington Miller, greeted Sir Robert, who inspected Sudanese, British and Egyptian guards of honour and was introduced to a number of notables. H.E. and Lady Howe then drove in state to the Palace through streets lined with troops and great crowds of welcoming people. There were no untoward incidents, but that night something went wrong with the air conditioning plant in the Palace and there was a loud bang. 'That's the first!' Lady Howe was reported to have exclaimed, thinking it was a bomb.

Setting to work almost at once, Sir Robert presided over a meeting of the Governor-General's Council and opened a session of the Advisory Council. The latter was particularly important, as we debated the proposals of the Sudan Administrative Conference for the establishment of a Legislative Assembly and an Executive Council in place of the existing Advisory Council and the Governor-General's Council. There was a large measure of support for the proposals and an appreciation of the difficulties. I tried to make it clear that in the half-way stage between an autocratic and a fully representative government, there were bound to be anomalies and illogicalities. Until the Condominium Agreement was altered, the Governor-General with his constitutional responsibility to the Co-domini could not hand over his ultimate powers for the good government of the country. He had to be given powers to overrule these proposed bodies should any action of theirs appear to him contrary to the Condominium Agreement.

One outstanding difficulty concerning the proposed Assembly was deciding whether or not the Southerners should be represented in it. The Administrative Conference had recommended their participation, but doubts about the wisdom of such a policy still existed in some quarters. I planned the next stage in the implementation of the conference report to be a meeting in June with Southern representatives to be held at Juba, the provincial capital of Equatoria. Meanwhile the Legal Secretary was in England discussing the question of the constitutional transfer of power to colonial peoples. I hoped that when he and I had completed our tasks all three secretaries would then be in a position to review the whole matter of the Legislative Assembly prior to final decisions at the Governor-General's Council in July.

The Southern Sudan was perhaps the most difficult problem of all those with which I had to deal while I was Civil Secretary. Failure to solve it speedily led in 1955 to civil war, which continued sporadically in the Southern districts until January 1972. Much has already been written about the South and I do not wish to go over all the ground again. But I must give a very brief account of the background.

The Turco-Egyptian invaders of the Sudan after 1820 penetrated to the far South, and by their firepower were able to overcome the Shilluk, Nuer and Dinka who had resisted past invaders from the North without difficulty. The result was that during the rest of the nineteenth century, except for a few short intervals at the time of Sir Samuel Baker and General Gordon, the Southern Provinces were in a continuous state of unrest against the Government of Khartoum. The defeat of the Egyptians in the 1880s and their withdrawal before the Mahdi did not improve matters, and when the Condominium Government began to move southwards at the turn of the century it found great fear and suspicion among the Southern peoples. It took twenty to thirty years before civil administration could be properly established over all the Southern provinces. As a result, educational and social development was far slower in starting than in the North, with the

South remaining very much on a care and maintenance basis – administration consisting chiefly of keeping law and order and trying to win the confidence of backward, frightened and suspicious people. Finance too was limited; it had to come from the North, and the development of social services and economic progress there had necessarily to have first call on the slender resources of government. Especially was this so since the South seemed unlikely in the foreseeable future to pay dividends on investments made to develop it.

It was mostly to save money that Sir Stewart Symes amalgamated the Mongalla and Bahr el Ghazal Provinces into one Equatorial Province in 1937. The new Governor of Equatoria, Martin Parr,* was then asked to administer this vast area from Juba. To give an idea of the size of this province, it was further from Nagichot, the most easterly of the district headquarters, to Raga in the extreme west, than it is from London to Moscow. Moreover, communications were poor and administrative districts were too large to be fully controlled.

These problems of the South lay behind the special policies which were adopted for the area. In working to win the confidence of the Southern people, the Government had earlier instituted a Closed District Ordinance which made it necessary for Northern merchants and traders to have special permits to trade in the Southern provinces. This was intended to restrict the number of Northern traders, and to prevent Northern pedlars – *gelaba* – travelling about in the Southern districts. Although ordinary Northern citizens were not legally excluded, administrative authorities certainly did not encourage them to visit the South. The aim was to create a barrier against exploitation of the simple, uneducated inhabitants of the South by astute and untrustworthy people, and thus prevent the continuation of the hatred between North and South. It was hoped that behind such a barrier the Southern peoples would develop until they were able to stand on their own feet and meet the Northerners on equal terms. The trouble was, however, that right up to the time of the Second World War very little seemed to be happening behind the barrier. Educational and medical services were for many years in the hands of missionary societies, and although devoted men and women laboured unceasingly with inadequate means to provide the services required, they could not hope to make any real impression on the vast field requiring attention. Only in the 1920s did Government begin to assist the missions by subsidising

* *M. W. Parr*. Sudan Political Service 1920–42. District Service 1920–4. Civil Secretary's Office 1925–7. Private Secretary to Governor-General 1928–33. Governor Upper Nile Province 1934–6. Equatoria 1936–42. National Association of Boys' Clubs 1944. L.C.C. Education Committee 1946. Alderman L.C.C. 1954.

and supervising their educational and medical work and by establishing its own medical services. Progress remained slow.

By the mid-1940s the Northern Sudanese and the Egyptians had begun to blame the Sudan Government openly for the situation in the South. Opposition focused not only on the Closed Districts Ordinance, but also on such aspects of policy as the exclusion of the South from the Advisory Council and the refusal to allow the Council even to discuss matters concerning the South. Further criticism was directed at the teaching and official use of English and local vernacular languages in preference to Arabic; the sending of students for higher education to Uganda rather than to the Gordon Memorial College, Khartoum; and above all the absence of Muslim missions in an area where Christian proselytising was encouraged. In addition, remarks made casually and unofficially about possible amalgamation of the Southern Sudan and Uganda were seized upon and given much more authority than such *ballons d'essai* deserved.

My predecessor, Douglas Newbold, when working on the proposals for the Advisory Council in 1943, had begun to sense this problem coming to a head. He allowed me to make a long tour of the South in 1944, and in the same year spent eight weeks or so in the Southern Sudan and Uganda himself. I do not know how his mind was working, but after his death I realised that this was a problem which had to be tackled positively, and I was sure that he would have aimed at a more open door.

The problem became particularly urgent as a result of the deliberations of the Administrative Conference. Two committees had been appointed by the Conference to report with recommendations on local and central government, and the committee dealing with national affairs favoured the establishment of a Legislative Assembly with considerable powers, composed of representatives from the whole Sudan – including the South. This recommendation was accepted by the Conference as a whole, and the Government was therefore faced with the need to make a decision on this difficult problem. Was the South to be brought fully into the Sudan and to be administered like any other area, or was it to remain separate and administered differently?

There seemed to me to be three possible solutions. First, we could carry on as we had been doing with the ultimate aim of detaching the South from the North or at least of leaving such a possibility open. Secondly, we might establish the South as a separate administration federated to the Northern Sudan, with its own lieutenant-governor and a separate advisory council responsible for its local government. The final option was to treat the South as an ordinary part of the Sudan, open it up to development, repeal the closed district legislation and admit its representatives to the Legislative Assembly as recommended by the Conference.

As for the first possibility, I did not see how the Southern Sudan could be linked with Uganda, and we had never had any indication that Uganda would willingly take on such a poor and undeveloped area. Any possible rearrangement of borders ran into complex tribal problems. Although the Acholi and Madi tribes were divided by the existing boundary between Uganda and the Sudan, the Zande were shared not with Uganda but with the Congo, while the Bahr el Ghazal Province bounded with neither but with French Equatorial Africa. To the East, the Toposa were neighbours of the Turkana of Kenya towards Lake Rudolph. So it looked as if any transfer of territory would mean slicing the area up like a cake, into at least four portions. Then again, where would the Northern boundary be set? There seemed to be no natural boundary. The line of the Bahr el Arab running from west to east into the main White Nile as far as the Sobat, and then from the Sobat to the Ethiopian border, looks possible on the map. But it would not be a good boundary for the rivers do not divide; they rather bring the different tribes together in the dry season, and they also provide the established routes of communication in a difficult swampy country. Finally, the railway which was said to be coming from Soroti in Uganda to Juba had still not been built, nearly thirty years after its proposal. In all, I could not see the Southern Sudan being cut up, and its parts being distributed to the territories south of it.

The second suggestion, that the South should be administered separately in a federation with the Northern Sudan, would have been difficult. It would have been expensive to establish a lieutenant-governor with staff and full headquarters. The Northern Sudan would have had to finance it, and many Northerners would have been critical of paying for an organisation over which they would have little control and which would work only for its own conception of the Southerners' interests. In addition, few Southerners were capable of staffing such an administration, and Northern staff might not in some cases be suitable to work in the South. Even those who seemed suitable for transfer there might be unwilling, especially as so many in the North were hostile to the whole scheme of a separate administration. There was an element in the South which favoured such an idea, believing that the North had gained a political advantage through experience in the Advisory Council. It felt that the South, excluded from the Council, should have an opportunity of learning a little about government through having an Advisory Council of its own before joining up with the North. I thought, however, that this solution would cause a tremendous outcry in the North and in Egypt, and would add substance to the suspicions already held that the Sudan Government was trying to separate the North from South for some deep and subtle reason. One of the allegations was that the South was rich and full of minerals, and the British were sitting on them. In addition, some Southern educated staff thought that the British intended to separate the South from the North, because in this way they could continue to pay low salaries to the Southerners and not bring them up to the Northern level.

The third policy – that of bringing the South into the unified Legislative Assembly, and abandoning the protective ordinances – had the disadvantage that the Southerners were in the main politically uneducated and unsophisticated in comparison with the Northerners. I hoped that with experience over a number of years, and with the development of education and economic schemes in the South, they would become more self-reliant, but meanwhile there should be some safeguards in the legislation to prevent a Northern Government from ill-using them.

While these were my general ideas, I thought that before advising the Governor-General in Council about this matter I ought to satisfy myself about the capacity of the Southerners to sit in a Legislative Assembly and play a constructive part in its discussions and deliberations. With the three senior British officials in the South, I arranged to hold a conference at Juba in June 1947 to discuss the whole question of the South's participation in the proposed national assembly. There were no provincial advisory councils in the South at this time and so no way of electing representatives to come to my Juba conference. Instead, those asked to attend were leading tribesmen and officials considered by the Governors to be sufficiently educated and intelligent to discuss the matters before the conference. I looked upon the conference solely as a means of finding out the capabilities of the Southerners, and it was therefore quite inaccurate for some people to say later that at the Juba conference the Southern representatives agreed to come in with the North. No decisions could be made by the conference, since members had received no mandate from their peoples.

The only decision resulting from the conference was taken by myself. I decided that I could, after what I had seen of the Southerners who attended, endorse the recommendation of the Administrative conference, and ask the Governor-General-in-Council to accept its proposal that the new Legislative Assembly should be representative of the whole Sudan. I found at the Juba conference that a number of the Southerners there were quite as able as many Northerners to take part in discussions of this kind, and that they were no less intelligent and capable, though very few of them at this stage had had the education of the best type of Northerner. I was, however, rather disturbed by the sudden change of mind which occurred during the conference. On the first day the general view seemed to be that it would be best to begin with a separate advisory council for the South, and then possibly after some years to join the North and come into the full Legislative Assembly. The next day this view had altered very considerably. A few of the Chiefs still remained of the same mind, but all the Southern educated members were now in favour of going in at once. I guessed at the time that my friend Mohamed Shingeiti, one of the Northern Representatives I took with me, had been busy during the night persuading the Southern officials that Northern rates of pay would surely come to the South, if they agreed to come in with the North. This apparently persuaded Clement Mboro* and others that it would be better for them if the country were administered as one area, and after the conference we had further discussions about the Southern rates of pay, which were in consequence improved.

On 19 July the Governor-General's Council met for a final discussion on the Legislative Assembly and I submitted the following note on the South.

One of the main problems of the report is its recommendation that the Southern Sudan should send representatives to the Legislative Assembly, and for better or for worse become wedded to the Northern Sudan, which on its part will have to endow the South with much of its worldly wealth. It will be remembered that in December last I issued a circular on Southern policy in which I asked for views about the future, giving it as my own view that historically, geographically and economically the South was inextricably connected with the North.

The majority of replies have confirmed this view, but all have stressed the necessity of safeguarding the cultural and social integrity of the South against domination and mismanagement by a Government composed mainly of Northern Sudanese. Without protection the Southerners will not be able to develop along indigenous lines, will be overwhelmed and swamped by the North, and deteriorate into a servile community hewing wood and drawing water for a superior Northern aristocracy.

In order to gauge Southern views I held a meeting in the South recently, where a widely representative body of Southerners endorsed the view that they should not be separated from the Northern Sudan, but emphasised their backwardness and their fears of Northern infiltration and domination.

In my opinion, the South must be administered as an integral part of the Sudan: it must be encouraged to set up organs of local

---

* *Clement Mboro.* Clerical Officer Southern Sudan. Promoted to District Commissioner and later to Deputy Governor in Darfur. Minister of the Interior 1964.

government speedily, with Provincial Councils which initially should appoint representatives to the Legislative Assembly. The Legislative Assembly and Executive Council should legislate for the whole country, but power should be reserved to the Governor-General (in cases where legislation or administrative order appears to him to have possible unfortunate results in the South), to order that action should be suspended until the Southern Province Councils have considered it. A further safeguard could be that one of the Southern governors should be appointed 'adviser' to the Executive Council to explain Southern views and point out the implications of proposed policy to the Council where necessary.

I do not fear that if powers of legislation are given to the Legislative Assembly there will be dangers for the South: the necessary safeguard for Southern development along healthy lines lies in the maintenance in the Southern Sudan of a British–controlled administration, with British Governors and D.C.s., and carefully chosen Sudanese assistants. If such an administration can be maintained, I have no fear that the entry of Southern Sudanese into the Legislative Assembly will have other than the excellent effects of unifying the country and widening the outlook of the Southerners.

Strong views are felt however in some quarters against 'handing over the South to the North', and action of the kind envisaged above is compared to handing over the Northern Sudan to Egypt. There are many parallels: there are some differences. The Northern Sudan finances the South: if the Northern Sudanese are to be asked to spend nearly £E.900,000 a year on the South they are surely entitled to have some say in its administration. It seems extremely doubtful if the Southern Sudan could ever stand on its own as an independent unit: the Sudan as a whole could. The infiltration of Moslem missions, etc., is feared. I do not see how we can keep out Moslem influence without immense political difficulty, even if it were morally right for us to try to do so.

There are noticeable tendencies among semi-educated Southerners to blame the Sudan Government for the backwardness of the South. I am convinced that should Southern representation in the Legislative Assembly be delayed, or should the Legislative Assembly not be permitted to deal with the Southern Sudan, agitation, which would be inevitable in the North, would be echoed in the South: we should lose the trust of many Southerners and be accused of wishing, to their detriment, to maintain a sort of human 'Whipsnade' in the Southern Provinces. I believe it is to the ultimate welfare of the South to be opened up and to have a chance of ultimate cohesion with the North, and of playing a part in the development and advance of the country as a whole.

The Governor-General's Council approved in principle the decision to include the whole country in the Legislative Assembly, but noted that 'safeguards be introduced into the legislation setting up the new constitution which will ensure the healthy and steady development of the Southern people.'

I was handicapped in dealing with the South by never having served there – a point frequently stressed by protagonists of the old policies, who said one could know nothing of its problems without direct experience. I tried therefore to make up for my deficiency by assiduous visiting. I saw every Southern district during my years as Civil Secretary, except Yirrol, which somehow I never managed to reach. In three of my Deputy Civil Secretaries, Hancock,* Nightingale† and Beaton,‡ I had men with long Southern experience, and I believe that there was no lack of consultation with those serving there.

Looking back on the subsequent troubled history of the South, and with the hindsight of more than twenty years, I still think that the decision of 1947 was right. The Southern Sudan had to be opened up and brought into touch with reality. The people there could not be segregated any longer into a kind of human zoo. The tragedy was that political independence impinged on an unsophisticated people before they were adequately prepared, or even fully understood what was taking place, and the early removal of the British District Officers in accordance with the Sudanisation clauses of the Anglo-Egyptian Agreement of 1953 left them without one of the safeguards which I had thought necessary. Few people in 1947 could have foreseen the sudden change in the world situation which led to the rapid colonial emancipation of the 1950s and 1960s. I certainly never guessed in 1947 that the Sudan would be independent less than a decade later.

The corollary of the political and constitutional decision was the need for parallel economic development. Dr. Tothill,§ who came to the Sudan in 1939 from Uganda where he had been Director of Agriculture, was the author of a plan to develop the Southern Sudan. This consisted of agricultural projects, combined with the establishment of a trading company. The main project was to grow cotton in the Zande area near the Congolese border, and produce both cloth and soap

* *G. M. Hancock.* Sudan Political Service 1924–50. District service 1925–42. Assistant Civil Secretary 1942–5. Deputy Civil Secretary 1945–6. Governor Kassala Province 1946–50.

† *E. H. Nightingale.* Sudan Political Service 1926–54. Education Department 1927–30. District service 1920–50. Director Local Government 1950–2. Deputy Civil Secretary 1952–3. Governor Equatoria Province 1952–4.

‡ *A. C. Beaton.* Sudan Political Service Education Dept. 1927–30. Provincial service 1930–50. Director Local Govt. 1950–2. Deputy Civil Secretary 1952–3. Permanent Under Secretary Ministry of the Interior 1954.

§ *Dr. J. D. Tothill.* Colonial Civil Service 1926–39. Sudan 1939–44. Principal Gordon Memorial College 1944–7.

from the crop in local factories. This enterprise required a reorganisation of traditional Zande agricultural methods, and 'Tiger' Wyld* (D.C. Yambio), one of the best district administrators I have known, did a fine piece of work settling the great mass of the Zande into new, more compact cultivation areas. In the flat river lands around Wau, experiments with rice growing were proposed, and near Mongalla a pilot sugar scheme was visualised. Meanwhile it was thought that if a supply of trade goods were made easily available to Southern peasants, they would be stimulated by their appeal to work harder in order to make enough money to buy them. My part in all this was to support the plan at the Board of Economics and Trade, at the Governor-General's Council and in discussions with Jock Miller, the Financial Secretary. I thought that the F.S. was too sticky about money for these projects, but at the same time some of the schemes proposed had not been adequately worked out, and the Departments concerned should have produced more detailed plans before expecting large financial grants. However, soon after the proposals had been put up, the Attlee Government in the U.K. made a grant of £2 million to the Sudan Government, as a contribution in gratitude for the way in which the Sudan had kept prices down and saved H.M.G. millions of pounds on the price of meat and other articles made available to the British troops in Egypt and the Sudan during the war. This British gift allowed us to find funds to meet the capital cost of the Equatoria development. It took some time to get the projects started and I was anxious lest too much emphasis be put on the Zande scheme and there would not be enough diffusion over the whole region. But by 1953, when I left the Sudan, great progress had been made, and it was only after the mutiny of August 1955 that there was gradual slowing down, soon leading to the end of our hopes for speedy educational and economic advance.

However, the South was by no means the only problem in 1947, for the Egyptians had decided to take their dispute with Britain to the United Nations Security Council at Lake Success. The Sudan Government decided that the Legal Secretary, Sir Thomas Creed, and two or three other officials should be sent so as to be available if the British or Egyptian delegations required information or assistance in the course of the discussions. I had wished to send two Sudanese as members, but it was impossible to find any uncommitted Sudanese of the necessary quality, and in any case both the Umma and Ashigga parties sent representatives. Our delegation was of some use, I think, in helping the British representatives, but the Egyptians did not recognise

* *Major J. W. G. Wyld.* District Service in Southern Sudan 1925–51. Organised Zande Scheme in Equatoria, grouping scattered cultivation into manageable areas.

them or call them in for advice at all. We also prepared a pamphlet entitled *The Sudan*: a *Record of Progress 1898–1947*, which was widely distributed in the Sudan, the United Kingdom, Egypt and New York.

The hearing at the United Nations, which took place in August 1947, has been fully discussed elsewhere, and I need only say that on the whole the discussion was fairly favourable for us. The Egyptian complaint against the Sudan Government was effectively dismissed since it was felt that not enough was known of the viewpoint of the Sudanese, and it was implied that they should have the right of self-determination once they became self-governing. The decision was welcomed by the supporters of an independent Sudan, but pro-Egyptian groups were less enthusiastic. For a short time it also meant a lessening of Egyptian propaganda, which had been pretty intense since the breakdown of treaty negotiations the previous year; but we knew this was only a respite, as Nokrashi Pasha, the Egyptian Prime Minister, had told the Sudanese at Lake Success that activities would soon be intensified.

Once this worrying interlude was over it was possible to get down to the task of drafting the ordinances creating the Legislative Assembly and Executive Council. About half my U.K. leave in the autumn of 1947 was spent in London, where, in addition to routine matters, I helped our legal draftsman, Mavrogordato,* with a first version. On my return to Khartoum – a much friendlier one than the cold welcome from my previous leave at the time of the Sidki–Bevin Protocol in 1946 – I continued to supervise the ordinances until the time of their consideration by the Advisory Council in March of 1948.

In addition to incorporating the Southern Sudan and making the Legislative Assembly more representative than the existing body, we intended that the Government should appoint some of the Sudanese members of the new Assembly as ministers and under-secretaries in principal departments where they would be given appropriate responsibilities. It was also intended that the ministers and some under-secretaries should fill six seats on the Executive Council when it replaced the Governor-General's Council. British and Egyptian representatives finally met in Cairo to discuss the draft ordinance in May 1948, and a series of meetings took place over the next few weeks. The Egyptians tried to get participation in the actual administration of the Sudan by having some Egyptian officials appointed as heads of department and by making an agreement that any difference of opinion between the Governor-General and the Legislative Assembly should be referred to

† *J. G. Mavrogordato.* Legal Department 1946–61. Advocate-General 1946. Legal adviser to Governor-General 1953. Senior legal counsel Ministry of Justice 1958–61. Legal draftsman to Sudan Government.

the Co-domini. Their aim, in general, was to restrict the Governor-General's powers as much as possible. We had agreed at the Foreign Office that in order to get acceptance of the ordinance from the Egyptian Government we should include the proposals that the Governor-General should appoint two Egyptians to sit on the Executive Council; that a joint Council composed of British, Egyptian and Sudanese members should be set up to supervise the progress of the Sudanese towards self-government; and that a joint British and Egyptian commission should supervise the forthcoming elections. However, these concessions were not enough, and a number of further amendments were suggested. A few were purely verbal and, though distasteful to our legal draftsman, innocuous; others, to meet Egyptian susceptibilities, were more substantial but not unacceptable. We agreed that if any irrigation matters came to the Council, the representative of the Egyptian Irrigation Department in the Sudan should be co-opted as a member for that item. I spent many hours on the telephone talking about those proposed amendments with our Sudan Agent in Cairo, E. C. Haselden,* and giving him our views about them after talking them over with my colleagues and the Governor-General. An agreed text was reached by 28 May, but it then appeared that Khashaba Pasha, the Minister leading the Egyptian negotiating team, had not kept his Government informed about what he was doing and still had to persuade them to approve the agreement that he had accepted. We had now two drafts of our ordinance, one with concessions which we had given the Egyptians, the other nearer to the original draft in case they even now refused to accept the first.

Locally, in Khartoum, we had had the usual difficulties with Sayed Abdel Rahman el Mahdi and the Umma party, who raised their normal cry that we were betraying them in making concessions to the Egyptians. The Governor-General saw Sayed Abdel Rahman and at least partly persuaded him that Egyptian approval of an advance to self-government was worth some concession, which might help to lessen both Egyptian propaganda in the Sudan, and their subsidies to the Ashigga party and others. However, in early June the Egyptian Government finally decided to reject the agreement reached by the British Ambassador and Khashaba Pasha, on the grounds that they were not being given an equal share in the administration of the Sudan, and that they preferred nothing at all to half a loaf. After we had been told that the British Government now had no objections to our proceeding, the original ordinance was passed by the Governor-General's Council on 15 June and promulgated in a special Gazette

* *E. C. Haselden.* Sudan Political Service 1925-53. District Service 1926-45. Sudan Agent in Cairo 1945-53.

a few days later. Council also passed an ordinance to define Sudanese nationality, the qualifications for voting and membership of the Assembly. At last the long battle, which had begun two years before, was ended and we had now to get down to making the new constitution work. I hoped that it might be possible to hold the elections for the Assembly in November so that it might open in the following month. But there was much to do: we required a new building to house the Assembly; we had to work out electoral rules; an electoral roll had to be made for each constituency, and arrangements made for printing notice papers, minutes, order books, bills, reports and amendments, and there were many other tasks. Standing Orders for the Assembly had to be drafted, and consideration given to the appointment of ministers and under-secretaries, although, as these appointments were to be made after consultations with the Leader of the Assembly, such plans could only be tentative.

While these preparations were under way, duty called me to Cairo and London. In Cairo I had an interview with the Egyptian Prime Minister, Nokrashi Pasha, who sat fingering a *sibha* (rosary) while he discussed the affairs of the Sudan in good English. Although polite and courteous, he was critical of our administration and the failure to give Egyptians a fair share in the Government. I then made the usual business visits to the British Embassy and the Sudan Agency before flying to London for similar tasks. At the Foreign Office the Governor-General and I went over the various facets of our political differences with the Egyptians, and discussed the possible impact of communism in African territories. My own feeling at this time and for some years afterwards was that the Sudanese were not really interested in communism, but that because the Russians supported anyone who worked against the established colonial regimes, some anti-colonial Sudanese pretended to subscribe to these doctrines for the sake of the assistance they received. Moreover, much of the heady literature smuggled in by the Communists made exciting and forbidden reading. I also spent some time at the Colonial Office in discussions with Mr. Creech-Jones and some of his officials about progress to self-government in their territories. I met the Chief Secretaries of Nigeria and Kenya, with whom I talked about our common problems, and I was struck by the similarities.

I returned to the Sudan in October to find the political temperature rising as the elections for the new Assembly drew near. Disturbing demonstrations took place in Khartoum, Atbara and Port Sudan, although none constituted a major threat to the authorities. I found the election results disappointing, since they reflected the split in the nationalist movement between the pro-British and pro-Egyptian factions. We were faced with the position that the Khatmia – the followers of Sayed Ali Mirghani – had more or less boycotted the elections and, though they constituted a considerable and influential part of the Sudanese people, were represented in the Assembly by only one or two tribal leaders. The Assembly was therefore not truly representative of the Sudanese people. I saw two dangers in this: first, that to the world at large the Assembly would be less credible as the voice of the Sudan; and secondly, that Sayed Abdel Rahman and the Umma party might try to use their majority in the Assembly to pass measures which the Sudanese as a whole would not accept. I found Sayed Abdel Rahman already implying that anyone who failed to agree with him was an enemy of the Sudan Government.

But all this was for the future, and our immediate job was to get the Executive Council and the Assembly into being. We had to see that suitable men were nominated to the Assembly by the Governor-General, and we had to manage this in a way that would be acceptable to Sudanese opinion. I spent a good deal of time talking, and consulting possible nominees. As soon as the Assembly had met and chosen Abdulla Bey Khalil* as its official leader, he and I had to consult about the Sudanese appointments to the Government. To broaden the base of support I hoped to include Mirghani Hamza† as Minister of Works. He was a leading Khatmi and supporter of Sayed Ali Mirghani as well as having been an outstanding figure in the Advisory Council. My conversations with him had suggested that he might be willing to serve, but it transpired that Abdulla Bey's prediction of a refusal was correct. I also made an approach, through an intermediary, to the leader of the pro-Egyptian Ashigga party, Ismail Effendi el Azhari, to see if he would accept nomination to the Assembly and appointment as a minister, but he too declined the invitation. In the end we had three Sudanese ministers, all identified with the Umma party – Abdulla Bey took Agriculture, Dr. Ali Bedri, Health, and Abdel Rahman Ali Taha, Education. With an additional three undersecretaries, the Sudanese occupied half of the seats on the Executive Council. As well as the three secretaries and the *Kaid* (Commander-in-Chief, Sudan Defence Force) two further British members were appointed by the Governor-General. One of these, R. J. Hillard, was head of Sudan Railways and the other, Arthur Gaitskell, head of the

---

* *Abdulla Bey Khalil*. Sudanese officer in Egyptian army; saw action Gallipoli 1915. Continued service in Sudan Defence Force 1926, and retired as brigadier. Later Secretary, Umma party, and Minister of Agriculture. Prime Minister 1956–8.

† *Mirghani Hamza*. Official in Public Works Dept; became Asst. Director. Member Advisory Council 1944. Leader of Khatmia group 1955. Deputy Prime Minister 1956.

E

Sudan Plantations Syndicate and elder brother of the late Hugh Gaitskell, resigned after a few months to be replaced by Sheikh Mohammed Ahmed Abu Sin,* thus giving the Sudanese an overall majority.

The Governor-General formally opened the Legislative Assembly in 23 December 1948. His speech from the throne had, in accordance with British practice, been prepared by the secretaries and ministers and approved by the Executive Council the previous day. The ceremony passed off successfully and without incident, although there was not nearly enough room in the gallery for all who wished to attend. So ended the long process of getting a parliamentary body started in the Sudan, after two and a half years of work and argument. The opening ceremony could have been held a year earlier if we had not had to wait while the Egyptian and British Governments negotiated, and in the end disagreed. The same delay was to be repeated at the next stage which lay some years ahead.

I consoled myself at the time by writing as follows:

> The growth of nationalism and emergence of a rather tiresome political class is not a sign of failure – the emergence of the great dominions of India, Pakistan and Ceylon, whose Prime Ministers have recently played an equal part in the Prime Ministers' Conference, is not a loss, but a magnificent step forward, and the fruition of the devoted work of many administrators, educationalists, judges and other Britons from the days of Warren Hastings onwards. Macaulay, the Lawrences and others in the early nineteenth century looked forward to the goal – we should surely not lament when it has been achieved.

I continued by writing that in Africa we were working towards the creation of African states with African governments, in which British control and guidance would gradually be lessened until it disappeared. I concluded:

> This will be a far more difficult operation than direct administration of backward peoples, but surely it is worth doing, and on the way in which we do it, and deal with the growing forces of nationalism, depends the future of these people committed to our care.

* *Sheikh Mohammed Ahmed Abu Sin.* Head Sheikh of the Blue Nile Shukria tribe. Member of Legislative Assembly and of Executive Council 1948-53. Minister in Abdulla Khalil's ministry 1956-8.

# CHAPTER VIII

# A TIME OF CONSTRUCTION 1949–1950

Once the Co-domini had finally halted their negotiations and the Legislative Assembly had been established, it was possible to give more attention to social and economic affairs. Internationally most of 1949 and 1950 was a quieter time for the Sudan, but locally I found a mounting urgency to tackle many post-war problems, and my job became if anything more demanding.

The new institutions of government, the Executive Council and the Legislative Assembly, were of course among my major responsibilities, and involved more work than their forerunners. The Council took a little time to settle down and work together, but I soon noticed an improvement in its general efficacy, and meetings became more frequent. Apart from the formal meetings presided over by the Governor-General when official business was done, I presided over unofficial meetings every Sunday – before the three secretaries went to see the Governor-General – and at these we discussed the coming week's business for the Assembly, decided the line we would take in dealing with the matters which were on the Order Paper, and settled who would speak for the Council in the various debates. This weekly gathering became a habit, and after some months there was little or nothing which we did not discuss. A team spirit began to appear and we British members began to get a better knowledge than ever before of how government policy and actions would be interpreted by the people at large. Our Sudanese colleagues had no inhibitions in giving their views, which were usually sensible and moderate, though of course in the early days there were no very controversial matters for decision. It was obvious, however, that Council meetings were going to take longer than those of the old Governor-General's Council simply because the business arising required more explanation than was necessary when all the members were senior Government officials who, from their long service and experience, knew the background of most matters coming up for decision. I felt that much of our duty in Council and Assembly was to educate and train, and show our colleagues how to consider all the pros and cons of any proposal before reaching a decision.

Abdulla Bey, as Leader of the House and Senior Minister, proved a tower of strength, for he was sensible and not easily upset. It was his duty to speak for the Executive Council in the Assembly, and though he was Secretary of the Umma party he soon began to look at things in a wider and more impartial way, as befitted his new position. I got to know him well during these three or four years, and had a great admiration for his courage and imperturbability. The Minister of Education, Abdel Rahman Ali Taha, was himself an educationalist, and knew his subject. He was more dynamic than Abdulla Bey, but more emotional and easily excited. He was a nationalist and very strongly anti-Egyptian, and it was often he who raised allegations of Egyptian propaganda and interference with students and schoolboys. Dr. Ali Bedri, the Minister of Health, and himself a graduate of the Khartoum Medical School, was the son of old Sheikh Babikr Bedri (see p. 20), who was a prisoner-of-war in Egypt after the attempted Mahdist invasion of that country in 1889, and he was a strong opponent of the unity of the Nile Valley. They both seemed to me to be much more in charge of their departments than Abdulla Bey, who was Minister of Agriculture as well as Leader of the House. This may have been in some part due to the personalities of the British directors of departments; it was a difficult transition for them, after being in charge of the policy of their departments, to hand over the ultimate responsibility to Sudanese who had perhaps been their juniors or who had little or no knowledge of departmental work. The integration of departments into the ministries responsible for them was a problem, as I also found later on in Nigeria, where both in the Federal Government and in the Regions we had difficulties of personality and of definition of functions. In one or two cases in Nigeria, departmental heads had to be removed before proper integration took place, and in the Sudan it took some time before the directors learned that they were now permanent under-secretaries (to use the British term) and were no longer in complete charge of their departments' policies.

Since I had been personally involved in designing as well as establishing the Assembly I felt bound to attend a great number of its sittings at least until it had settled down into a working routine. This limited the time I could give to the work in my office, and necessitated long hours in the early mornings and evenings for my normal departmental, administrative and political work.

The Assembly was finally composed of ten members directly elected by ballot in the towns, forty-two elected by electoral colleges in rural areas, twelve elected by the newly constituted Southern Province Councils, and ten nominated by the Governor-General. In addition there were eleven members of the Executive Council (including six British members) appointed on an *ex officio* basis. as well as Abdulla

Khalil, a nominated member of the Assembly, who had been elected its leader and was thus automatically the twelfth member of the Council.

We followed the Westminster model and before the Assembly opened the Speaker, Shingeiti, who had been my sub-*mumur* at Geteina in 1925, spent some time in London at the House of Commons, and the clerk, M. F. Keen,* was attached for three months to the Clerks' Office at Westminster. We had a translator, again an old acquaintance of mine, Mohamed Amir Beshir †('Furawi', the man from Darfur – to give him his nickname – the son of my sub-*mamur* at Kamlin in 1924). His duty was to translate Arabic speeches on the spot into English in précis form for the benefit of those Southern members who couldn't speak Arabic. I used to tease him occasionally by making the odd speech in Arabic, and asking him to translate into English, but he usually responded by saying I could do my own translation, as the ministers did.

The members speedily began to appreciate the fun and the value of question time, and we had a mass of questions on all subjects, usually about local needs and requirements, and it became quite an onerous duty for the departments to prepare the answers. I insisted that draft answers on questions which I had to answer should be submitted to me as early as possible so that I could vet them, and this, together with preparing speeches for the Assembly, took up a good deal of time.

I see from my diary that on 27 December we dealt with finance Bills, on the 28th we debated the incursion of students and schoolboys into politics, and on the 29th motions were put forward about the police and clemency to so-called political offenders. I wrote at the time:

> We have had a number of rambling debates: we have been handicapped by the delay in getting the Standing Orders translated and printed in Arabic. These orders, based on parliamentary practice in the 'Mother of Parliaments', are not easy to follow, and our infantile arguments about points of order and what is a 'motion' and what a 'question' have not been helped by the ignorance of the Speaker and the members of the proper way of conducting business. The language difficulty is considerable and translations not easy. Furthermore, translation slows down debate and makes proceedings

* *M. F. A. Keen*. Sudan Political Service 1926–54. District Service 1927–47. Clerk of Legislative Assembly 1948–53. Clerk of House of Representatives 1954.

† *Mohamed Amer Beshir*. Translator to Legislative Assembly 1947–53. Son of Amer Beshir – sub-*mamur* at Kamlin (see page 17). Later newspaper editor and journalist.

stilted and unnatural. Another snag has been the lack of legislation to lay before the Assembly. There seem to be very few ordinances coming along at the moment and the Assembly obviously needs something heavy to get down to. We have had too many motions about local matters. The Council has not yet got together as a team and this will take a little time.

On 12 March 1949 the Financial Secretary introduced the Budget in the Assembly, and it was finally passed on the 31st. I wrote about this at the time:

> The House was in committee for quite a large part of the time and went through all the headings fairly closely. Much information was imparted to members, and a good deal of hot air was talked, but on the whole I think the Assembly have got down to their work and are beginning to know better what they are trying to do. They still wish to interfere too much in purely executive matters: they find the procedure hard to follow and our Chairmen of Committees, apart from the Speaker himself, are pretty poor. 'The Terrible Twins', Ahmed Yousef Hashim* and Mohamed Ahmed Mahgoub,† suffered one or two heavy defeats in the Committee stage of the Budget. The Assembly has shown that it is not to be rushed into foolish nationalistic motions.

The 'Terrible Twins' were nominated members, the former a newspaper editor, and the latter a retired judge. They constituted themselves as an opposition and enjoyed needling the Government spokesmen. I took it as a proof of our impartiality that they had been recommended by me to the Governor-General for nomination as members of the Assembly, and they performed a very useful function by their opposition, though at times it seemed annoying.

The Assembly was adjourned on 7 April and did not meet again until October. We had expected that it would not meet continuously, as there was seldom enough work for it to do for more than three or four weeks at a time, and there were clauses in the Constitution enabling the Executive Council to pass Orders in Council to deal with urgent matters during a recess. These had to be confirmed later by the Assembly when it met again, and this system seemed to work reasonably well and to be accepted. Until the Governor-General returned from the U.K. in November, I was 'Acting' and so could not attend the Assembly myself during its first few weeks that autumn, and my work there was

---

* *Ahmed Yousef Hashim.* Newspaper editor and critic of the Condominium Government. Member of Legislative Assembly 1948–53.

† *Mohamed Ahmed Mahgoub.* Retired district judge. Led opposition in Legislative Assembly 1948–53. Foreign Minister 1957–8, 1964. Prime Minister 1965–6, 1967–9.

effectively done by Abdel Salam el Khalifa,* my Under-Secretary. He was a son of the Khalifa whose armies Kitchener defeated at the Atbara and Omdurman in 1898, and a charming, friendly, intelligent person.

By October 1949 I was beginning to consider how best to amend the Executive Council and Legislative Assembly Ordinance, as I wanted to improve procedure, widen the franchise and arrange for more direct elections. The system of election by electoral colleges was regarded with suspicion by the intelligentsia, who thought that such a method gave the tribal authorities too much opportunity for rigging the results; but any amendments needed to be submitted to the Co-domini, and I feared the long period of negotiation and disagreement which would follow. The last month of the first session was a busy one, and some important matters were debated. The Marshall Report on Local Government (see below, pp. 127) interested the tribal leaders and was somewhat contentious. I had to pilot this Report through the House and had some dificulties. However, I was able to secure a unanimous vote accepting the principles of the Report, but agreeing that the pace at which it should be implemented should vary according to local conditions. The Legal Secretary's Bill amending the Code of Criminal Procedure also had points in it to which objections were raised, but after discussion and some amendments, workable compromises were reached and the value of parliamentary methods was shown. The Workshops and Factories Bill was passed, and rounded off a programme of labour legislation which I shall discuss later. Other important debates were on the education plan for the Northern Sudan, on the teaching of Arabic in the South, and on a proposal to create a new Ministry of Social Affairs.

During these years, when so much attention was being devoted to external political affairs and to the steps towards self-government, I was also occupied with three other major problems, the first of which concerned Egyptian propaganda in the Sudan. From the opening of negotiations by Egypt in early 1946 for a revision of the Anglo-Egyptian Treaty of 1936, until the ultimate decision in 1955 by the Sudanese to become independent, Egypt both officially through government agencies as well as through the press, radio and personal contacts, kept up continuous pressure on the Sudanese. This was strongly resisted by the independents, Sayed Abdel Rahman el Mahdi and the Umma party, and welcomed by the Ashigga and the 'Unity of the Nile Valley'

* *Abdel Salam el Khalifa.* Son of the Khalifa Abdullahi. Sudanese administrative officer. Later Under-Secretary for the Interior 1948-53 and as such member of Legislative Assembly.

supporters, many of whom were subsidised from time to time by Egyptian funds. The Sudan Government was put in an awkward position by this propaganda, because of the fact that Egypt was one of the Co-domini and therefore had the undoubted right to persuade the Sudanese of her interest in their future. The trouble was that much of their support was given to Sudanese who worked against the Sudan Government, which was constitutionally the agent of the Egyptians as much as of the British Government. These Sudanese with Egyptian support stirred up demonstrations which often turned into riots, and stimulated discord and indiscipline in schools and colleges. Youths who were dismissed from Sudan schools, no matter for what reason, were pretty sure of being found a place in schools or colleges in Egypt. If pro-Egyptian Sudanese were to be tried for breaches of the law, Egyptian lawyers were almost certain to propose coming to the Sudan to plead in the courts, although there were already adequate barristers in the country, and the Egyptians were not trained in Sudan law. Practically every Egyptian who came to the Sudan seemed to work against the Sudan Government in some way or other, and of course with the Egyptian army battalion, an Egyptian secondary school, and numbers of businessmen and officials in the Egyptian Irrigation Department, there were plenty of agents for propaganda.

It was therefore a more or less continuous exercise, and there were many incidents, large and small, which could be mentioned, but perhaps the following were the most notable. There was hardship in parts of the Northern Sudan in 1949 as a result of poor rains, and a semi-famine ensued in parts of the Kassala and Northern Provinces. This was not an abnormal occurrence and in such cases the Sudan Government had an organised procedure. I myself distributed imported Indian grain to White Nile people in 1926, while one of our Sudanese names for 1914 was 'the year of the Indian corn'. However, the Egyptian Government heard of the shortage in 1949 and, without consulting the Sudan Government, voted a large sum of money – £E.50,000 – to buy food and clothing for the 'famine-stricken' population. They proposed setting up an independent organisation to distribute this in order to by-pass the steps which the local authorities in the affected provinces were already taking. However, we thought that there should be co-operation of effort, and that the Egyptians should not set up a rival organisation. I was ultimately successful in persuading the Egyptian staff officer to agree that they would not purchase grain in the Sudan but import it, and that they would not import cloth and cotton-piece goods from Egypt, but buy from the big stocks of the local merchants, who were finding it difficult to dispose of them. The Egyptians made use of our committees for distributing their contribution and it all worked reasonably well, although a number of Egyptian officers toured the affected areas ostensibly to see that the distribution was being properly done but also to point out how very generous the Egyptian people had been.

An annual trouble was the offer by the Egyptian Ministry of Education of a number of scholarships in the Egyptian universities to Sudanese students. We were disturbed when lads who had been selected for our own University College, which was in its formative stage, were seduced away to Egypt during their first year, leaving their places in Khartoum vacant. But as the University College began to find its feet, and its educational standing came to be better realised, this handicap gradually lessened, and the numbers of those who left grew smaller.

Another cause of friction was the pillorying of Sayed Abdel Rahman el Mahdi, the leader of the independence movement, by the Egyptian press and radio, Some of the press comments were scurrilous, causing great offence to the Sayed, and the Umma party – of which he was the patron – was often enraged. The Egyptians occasionally realised what damage this was doing to their cause and for a short time would endeavour to woo the Sayed, but soon the old attacks were re-started. The Sayed would then ask me for a meeting and I would be pressed to ban the import of the offending papers and clamp down on the Sudanese papers that sided with the Egyptians, action which I was very loth to take.

The unrest and uncertainty caused by the prolonged negotiations about the Sudan, and the continuous Egyptian propaganda, reacted on the students in the University College, the pupils in the secondary schools, the artisan and labouring classes, and the tenants on the Gezira scheme. Demonstrations were frequent, and although usually good-tempered, on occasions they became violent and the police were forced to take strong measures to restore order. Some Sudanese newspapers fomented the trouble by critical and usually ill-founded attacks on the Government. All this of course had a background of nationalism and dislike of colonial rule, but in some measure it became just a habit and an outlet for youthful exuberance.

There was, however, no evidence of animosity against individual Europeans and during the eight years or so of repeated political disturbance, with excitement at fever pitch on many occasions, no European was attacked or injured. Perhaps the most sustained series of demonstrations was at the time of the elections for the Legislative Assembly in the autumn of 1948 when in the three towns of Khartoum, Khartoum North and Omdurman there were numerous small riots, and my telephone rang more or less continuously telling me of new outbreaks or the end of earlier ones. But again little damage was done and few people were seriously hurt. The most unfortunate incident occurred at Atbara where the police used tear-gas bombs to disperse a large crowd of strikers who were marching on the General Manager's office. Whether the bombs were old and had deteriorated was never discovered, but the cases splintered into thin strips of metal, which did great injury to a number of people, of whom several died from loss of blood. This was tragic because we had introduced these smoke bombs to try and avoid serious injuries, which had seemed much more likely if baton charges or shooting were ordered.

My second major concern was the growth of labour unrest. Before the war the Sudan had no labour legislation except for a Workman's Compensation Ordinance. This was out of date, and after the war it soon became clear that conditions had changed and that it would be necessary to get some labour legislation on to the statute book. Our first fear was over demobilisation, for the Sudan Defence Force had been expanded from a strength of 7,500 men to four times that number, somewhere in the region of 30,000. The troops had been well paid by Sudan standards. Many had served in the Middle East in Cyrenaica, Eritrea and Tripolitania and while under British army control had enjoyed rations and amenities far higher than those they had known at home. They had seen Egypt and learned ways of life unknown in the country districts of the Sudan. Two or three thousand had learned technical trades, as motor drivers, fitters, telegraphists, etc., and we wondered how they would settle again into their old ways of life. The Demobilisation Committee, composed of both military and civilian representatives, did good work; the release of men from the army was phased and the number demobilised at any one time was strictly controlled. They were given travel warrants and transport facilities to their homes and then gratuities and arrears of pay were issued to them at their own District Headquarters; in order not to cause inflation by throwing too much money on the market at any one time, they were paid in instalments. A number of the technically trained were found employment in the civil departments, especially in the new mechanical crop production scheme at Gedaref and in the Gezira. So this exercise, about which we had been anxious, was carried out easily, and the great bulk of the men settled down happily in their own districts; only the technicians and a number of clerical staff proved difficult, some of them appearing to encourage the labour agitation which began shortly after the war and continued for several years.

Atbara, the headquarters of the Sudan Railway Administration, was the centre of most of the labour agitation. Here was the greatest concentration of labour in the country, with all living and working together for the same organisation. In the Three Towns, more persons were employed, but they worked for many departments and commercial firms and had not the cohesion of Atbara. At Atbara there were a number of labour hotheads who, it was suspected, were financed from outside the Sudan, either by the Egyptians or by communist sympathisers. There was something to be said for labour's dissatisfaction with their conditions; skilled craftsmen, after many years experience of using machine tools and doing work requiring considerable technical ability, received less pay than their more academically educated young relatives who had obtained employment in the Railway's clerical cadres. Dissatisfaction increased and Government was slow to act, disliking a piecemeal attempt to rectify the situation and wishing to await a comprehensive review of all official salary scales which was to be carried out by a special commission. The railway workers refused to wait; they set up an association which was joined by almost the whole work force, and staged a series of strikes.

Meanwhile Ernest Bevin, the doyen of British trade unionists, and Foreign Secretary in the British Government, encouraged the Sudan Government and colonial governments to set about the creation of trade unions and to enact a series of labour laws to cover the whole field of labour relations. I was very much implicated in this, for labour was one of the Civil Secretary's responsibilities. In 1945 we had no labour officers or departmental organisation of any kind, and we had to build up from scratch at a time when labour unrest was growing and workers were uniting without any guidelines or legal basis, but with a tremendous power to cripple the activities of the country. The general atmosphere of political unrest also gave our enemies an opportunity to spread trouble for us in the new labour associations. Mr. Bevin had appointed a labour adviser to the British Embassy in Cairo, a Mr. Audsley,* who had served in the British Ministry of Labour, and I was able to call on him for advice and help in getting a trade union expert to draft the necessary legislation. Between 1948 and 1951 a number of Bills were presented to the Legislative Assembly and, after due debate, were passed into law. They consisted of a Trade Union Ordinance, a Regulation of Trade Disputes Ordinance, a Trade Union (arbitration and enquiry) Ordinance, a Workshop and Factory Act, a new Workman's Compensation Act, and an ordinance covering details of employers' and employees' relations. When completed they were comprehensive, and if they had existed in 1946 we could have

---

* *M. T. Audsley*. British Government civil servant. Ministry of Labour 1912–45. Counsellor (labour) British Embassy in Cairo 1945–56.

been saved a great deal of trouble; but coming as they did after strikes
and labour troubles, they seemed to prove to the hotheads that nothing
succeeds like forcible protest.

Even the new legislation did not satisfy the trade union leaders.
However, after an outcry about the Trades Union Ordinance, which
regulated the formation and registration of unions, Abdulla Bey Khalil
held a conference with the union leaders at which he went through the
ordinance with them and persuaded them that it really was what they
required. The wording was difficult and the Arabic translation of
technical trade union terms was often obscure and inaccurate. Mohammed Ahmed Mahgoub, who was trusted by the unions, was a great
help at this conference with his very conciliatory and constructive
attitude. Eventually it became possible to get the various associations
registered and put into some sort of legal form. However, so long as
the Government was not wholly Sudanese, but still half-European
in membership, it was easy for trade union leaders to struggle against
'colonialism'. Unfortunately, both in the Sudan, and afterwards in
Nigeria, the habit of striking against the European employer – governmental or private – had been formed, and independence did not
eradicate it. I think it is also true that trade unionism in Africa tended,
to begin with at least, to give power to trade union leaders and officials
who were not usually competent to exercise it, and the ordinary trade
union members were not sufficiently educated or experienced to know
what they were being asked to support by striking. Another mistake
in the Sudan was not to remove causes of strike before strikes occurred,
but to do so afterwards, which made the members think that striking
paid dividends. The slow meticulous procedure of the Finance Department seemed often much to blame for this.

My third major concern was with the establishment of democratic
local government. The Administrative Conference, which Sir Hubert
Huddleston set up in 1946, had made recommendations on the development of local government, as well as on the advances in responsible
government at the centre, and the recommendations of the local
government sub-committee under the chairmanship of Mohammed
Ahmed Mahgoub followed lines which had been generally accepted.
I describe above (pages 29 ff.) the way in which, under the impetus
imparted by Sir John Maffey, the administrative staff set up native
administrations throughout the country based largely on the tribal
chiefs, whose traditional authority was used to build up Native Courts
with considerable powers, and around which were devolved further
administrative and financial duties. The process was always suspect
to the educated and urban classes, who looked down on the 'illiterate'

country leaders and thought that their own superior education entitled them to rule the country.

In 1937 a Local Government Ordinance had been passed which created a system of local authorities, municipalities, townships and rural districts, and defined the powers which could be assigned to each of them. A local government authority from this time onwards was the administrative authority in any area. Where no council existed which could be appointed as the authority, its powers were vested in the District Commissioner, who thereby acquired legal powers for many of the actions which he had previously taken in running his district without formal authority. Thus there already existed a framework on which to build, but there remained the major problem of fitting the tribal chiefs into the local government authorities. By heredity and by the consent of the bulk of the tribesmen the chief was their leader and should be the head of the new body. But this was disliked by the intelligentsia and by Sir Sayed Ali Mirghani, the leader of the Khatmia, while the chiefs themselves feared the possible loss of dignity which standing for election might bring them.

These and other questions were raised by the report of the Administrative Conference and there was also the major question of organisation. Was there to be a tier system with junior authorities responsible to senior bodies and those perhaps responsible to a Province Council, or should each council be fully autonomous within its own sphere with its powers laid down in a warrant emanating from the Central Government? To inquire into all these questions it was decided to consult a recognised expert in local government, and we were fortunate in interesting Dr. A. H. Marshall,* the City Treasurer of Coventry, in our problems. He spent several months in the Sudan in 1948 and 1949 and provided the Sudan Government with an excellent report, which answered many of our questions and laid down foundations on which we could build. When I presented his report to the Legislative Assembly there was considerable debate, for country members did not agree to the immediate introduction of election for all council members. The Assembly agreed that this should be the goal, but that progress towards it would be determined in every case by the wishes of the people, and in fact by the degree of political sophistication of the area. Some of the tribal leaders were also suspicious of the role of the council's executive officers, fearing that they might usurp the power of the new authorities. After discussion and debate, the main principles of the Marshall Report were accepted with the understanding that their implementation should be gradual. The decisions reached by the

* *A. H. Marshall.* City Treasurer Coventry 1944–64. Adviser on local government to Sudan Government 1948–9. Many public appointments.

Legislative Assembly proved to be lasting, and they formed the basis of the system of local government which remained in operation throughout the country until 1971.

In most ways the system appeared satisfactory, but there was one important disadvantage: the District Commissioner's general responsibility for all aspects of his district would disappear, while the local government authority would have powers limited solely to local affairs. With the disappearance of the District Commissioner there would be no central government officer to co-ordinate all government activities in the district, and the police and technical officials would be responsible to departmental heads at the distant centre, which would lead to less co-operation and cohesion locally. How far the Sudan succeeded in finding a remedy for this difficulty I cannot really guess, for I had left the country before the new system was properly established. By 1949 warrants had been worked out and issued for five municipal councils, nine town councils, three urban councils, twenty rural district councils, six rural councils and seven local authorities, all of which had their independent budgets.

Ever since I first arrived in the Sudan I had intermittently been involved with aspects of the Gezira Scheme. In 1924 I had admired the newly constructed Sennar dam; in the 1930s I had encouraged White Nile people to move to the Gezira; while during the war I had been closely involved with the management of the Scheme. The Scheme, unique in the world, was a partnership between the local population, the Government and a commercial company – the Sudan Plantations Syndicate. The land was compulsorily rented by the Government from its owners who were paid a fair rental for it, calculated on average prices applicable before development began. The landowners had certain rights to tenancies, and they and other local inhabitants were allotted areas of 40 feddans each, ten of which were under cotton each year, five under millet and five under a bean crop; the remainder was fallow. The tenant received the whole of the grain and bean crops, and 40 per cent of the value of the cotton crop, in addition to which he paid no taxes. In bad cotton years he still had a guaranteed food supply for himself and his animals. The Government received 40 per cent of the value of the cotton crop to cover its expenditure in renting the land, paying the interest on the loans by which the dam at Sennar and the canalisation had been financed, and on running the irrigation control of the Scheme. The Syndicate received 20 per cent of the cotton crop for its managerial work and for ginning and selling the cotton. Under this system the Scheme developed from its start in the 1920s with varying vicissitudes until in the mid-1940s it was an established economic institution on which the Sudan as a whole largely depended for its revenue and food. The Syndicate's concession was due to end in 1950, and in the years before that date much thought was given to planning for the future, once Government had decided in 1944 that the concession would not be renewed. This decision was reached after considerable difficulty: the Syndicate was efficient, its management costs were cheap, its inspectors and staff were generally popular with the tenants and the Scheme was working well.

There was, however, much political feeling that a private foreign company should not have so much control over a national asset of this kind, and in the atmosphere of the times when public corporations were being formed to take over railways, coal mines, electrical and gas supplies in Britain, it seemed best to form a public corporation to take over from the Syndicate when its concession came to an end. A number of questions then arose. How was the new corporation to be formed? How would the percentages of profit be decided? Should the tenants not receive more? How would the management be responsible to Government without allowing too much political interference in the day-to-day working of the complicated irrigation and agricultural processes necessary to secure good crops? First the Advisory Council and then the Legislative Assembly debated the whole matter and set up advisory committees. After some hesitation I produced a memorandum advocating that part of the money, which had previously gone to Syndicate shareholders, should be used to improve social services in the Gezira area; local authorities in the Gezira itself went further and advocated a sort of Tennessee Valley Authority, whereby profits arising from the Gezira Scheme should be used in the Gezira. The Advisory Council recommended that while the Scheme should benefit the country as a whole, it should more particularly cater for the Gezira area. The Financial Secretary, however, pointed out that the Scheme had been supported by the general taxpayer in bad years when it had made no profits, and in the payment of the interest on the loans which financed the dam and the canalisation, and these would not be finally paid off until the 1970s. In the end the Legislative Assembly held a long and lively debate on the final Bill. This was listened to by a large body of Gezira tenants in the Strangers' Gallery, and they returned home considerably impressed by the freedom and privileges of the Assembly.

The Bill, as eventually worked out by the Financial Secretary and approved by the Legislative Assembly, allocated a percentage of profits to social development and was accepted by the Assembly with a number of minor amendments. Arthur Gaitskell,* the previous Syndicate's

* *Sir Arthur Gaitskell*. Sudan Plantations Syndicate 1945–50. Member of Executive Council and Legislative Assembly 1948–50. Chairman and Managing Director Gezira Board 1950–2. Colonial Development Corporation 1954 onwards.

chief executive, generously agreed to carry on for a year or two and was appointed Chairman and Managing Director of the new Gezira Board. Gaitskell had worked in the Syndicate for many years and I had known him since about 1924. He had been a protagonist of devolution in the Gezira to the Sudanese, and as a leading citizen had been appointed a member of the Executive Council and Chairman of the Khartoum University College Council after George Bredin's retirement. Arthur Gaitskell was the author of a comprehensive account of the Gezira Scheme after he retired, and I need make no further references to the Scheme here, as my connections with it after 1950 were mainly in connection with the development of the social service side. This was in the charge of administrative officers in whose work I was naturally keenly interested.

The Civil Secretary's duties and responsibilities were manifold, and it is impossible to deal with them all here, especially since in the eight years that I held the office there was an immense range of development in the Sudan with which I and my staff were intimately connected. One innovation which I found rather surprisingly fell within my range of responsibilities was the establishment of an airline. Sudan Airways started modestly when we bought two or three de Havilland 'Doves' and introduced internal services from Khartoum to Malakal, Wau and Juba, to El Obeid and Fasher and to Kassala and Port Sudan. For me it was a wonderful way of getting about, and I found that by using the air I could manage to get round the vast Sudan easily, see the Provincial Governors and learn of their problems. Combined with road transport, it also allowed me to make tours within provincial areas, and this kept me in touch with the men in the field, and gave me welcome changes from the continuous heavy office and political work of Khartoum.

Of course, air travel had its exciting moments. I shall never forget one return journey to Khartoum when a 'Dove', in which I and several equally large and heavy passengers were going to Merowe for the district agricultural show, lost the power of one engine about eighty miles north of Khartoum and our pilot turned back: the doubt was whether with only one engine functioning and such a heavy load the aircraft could keep in the air till we reached Khartoum. How glad we were to see the Shabluka Gorge on our port side, and then the Wadi Seydna airstrip below, and to land safely at Khartoum Airport, where fire-engines and Land Rovers were dashing about to aid us if necessary. Another exciting trip was south-eastwards to Gambeila to see that peculiar enclave which the Sudan Government leased from Ethiopia. We flew to Malakal, and then up the Sobat river, but when we neared the place where our pilot thought Gambeila should be, the country seemed to be blotted out by the smoke of countless grass and forest fires. We went up river and down again and circled round, and were more than a little relieved to touch down in the small town before our fuel ran out.

The Sudan Government had a D.C. at Gambeila to administer this tiny enclave which was only a mile square. Jack Maurice,* who had been there for many years – Newbold called him 'the oldest D.C. in Africa' – knew everyone in Western Ethiopia. His job was to run the enclave and help the Sudanese and Middle Eastern merchants in their trade in Western Ethiopia. He was a charming and congenial soul, and who did much for the Sudan Government's prestige in the neigh-bourhood. His little house was a hospitable resort in the evenings for people of all nationalities. It was said that when rationing of imports was started in the war, and we were all asked to say how many bottles of Scotch we needed each month, Jack answered the questionnaire: 'Some months 30 bottles and others 31: only 28 in February.' Jack retired very shortly after my visit to Gambeila and went to live in Cyprus, but his heart was in Africa and he did not long survive away from it.

Another air adventure I experienced was on a trip to Cairo. To show that the Sudan Government was kindly disposed to Egypt, I travelled by Misr Airways, the Egyptian state line. All went well till we got to Almaza Airport and the air hostess, a sweet little Egyptian girl, told us to fasten our seat-belts. The aircraft came down, and we shot along the runway without touching, and up again into the sky. I asked the little air hostess what had happened, and she said, 'He forgot to put down his undercarriage', so on we went round the airport, and our pilot made a second attempt. This time we hit the runway two or three times rather hard, but again took off into the sky. My girl friend said, 'He didn't know the undercarriage had come down.' The third time we were lucky and we taxied up to the airport building, where I was ushered out to be embraced and given a bouquet of flowers by the Director-General of Misr Airlines.

The need to hasten Sudanisation led to the faster growth of all educational facilities. Expansion of secondary schooling included new government schools at Wadi Seydna near Omdurman, Hantoub near Wad Medani and Khor Taggat near El Obeid. Two secondary schools were also established in the South at Atar near Malakal and Rumbek. At the same time the post-secondary higher schools which previously had had no corporate existence were combined into a new college, founded in 1944. This new college, which occupied the build-

* *J. K. Maurice.* Sudan Political Service 1927–49. At Gambeila 1928–49.

ings of the old Gordon College Secondary School, became a university college in 1951 and a full university five years later.

In 1944 the new college was governed by a council of thirty members of whom a number were Sudanese, presided over by Sir Douglas Newbold, while the first principal was Dr. Tothill, formerly the Director of Agriculture. When I succeeded Douglas Newbold I asked the Governor-General to appoint someone other than the Civil Secretary to chair the council as I already had enough work and I felt that I was not academically up to the appointment. Bredin was the next chairman, and he was succeeded in 1948 by Arthur Gaitskell. The amalgamation of the higher schools into the college was not always easy, the Kitchener School of Medicine was jealous of its independence and there were legal difficulties with regard to endowments, but gradually the unified college began to take shape. The school which had for years trained young Sudanese police and administrative officers became an important part of the college, and it was there that the young men who were later to take on the duties of the Political Service studied.

The growth of the college was unfortunately affected by the political unrest of the period, and as I mentioned earlier, a number of students were seduced away by the Egyptian universities, and others sometimes took part in noisy demonstrations in the city. The early years of Lewis Wilcher's time as principal* – he succeeded Tothill in 1947 – were much disturbed by these troubles. As the Civil Secretary was responsible for law and order I found myself involved and tried to steer a middle course, which inevitably brought criticism from both those who wanted a firm line taken and others who felt we were too harsh. In spite of these difficulties the College gradually developed; standards were maintained by good professors and lecturers, with visiting examiners from abroad; and by 1953, when I left, it was on a reasonably even keel, and as a sign of female emancipation there were already several girl undergraduates.

Towards the end of 1950 I had my fifty-first birthday and I told the Governor-General that I thought I should retire. The general rule in the Sudan was that the Government had the right to retire officials at the age of fifty, or they could choose to leave at forty-eight if they wished. The Government had almost always exercised its right and very few people were retained after the age of fifty. We had made arrangements for the succession to the office of Civil Secretary; Duncan

---

* *Lewis Wilcher*. Rhodes scholar, Balliol College. Lecturer University of Melbourne 1934–40. Asst. Director Army Education 1942–7. Principal University College, Khartoum 1947–56. Warden Queen Elizabeth House, Oxford 1956–68.

Cumming,* who had had a most successful career in the administration of occupied enemy territory during and after the war, came back and after a year as Governor of Kordofan had come into the office as my Deputy. However, early in November 1950, the Governor-General asked me to stay on for a further period. He said that in his view it would be for the good of the country and it would assist him if I would agree, but it put me in a very awkward position, as Cumming had been more or less promised the succession and I did not want to let him down. However, shortly after this Ernest Bevin asked the Sudan Government if they could suggest an official to take on the post of Administrator of Eritrea for a year or two until the future of the territory had been settled. Cumming accepted this appointment and made a great success of it, restoring law and order, and handing over the territory to the Ethiopians in a much better state than he had found it. Meanwhile I was to continue for another two years.

I quote here a passage from one of my monthly letters to governors, heads of departments and certain other senior officials and members of the Syndicate. I was told that these letters were referred to by some recipients as 'Uncle Jimmy's soothing syrup'. I started writing them when I was appointed Civil Secretary in 1945 and continued until I left the Sudan. They attempted to give an account of the general situation in the country during the previous month and the work of the C.S.'s office, and to let senior officers in the provinces know something of what was going on at the centre. This particular quotation is from a letter dated 4 January 1951 and, re-read more than twenty years later, it may seem rather prosy and avuncular, but it does convey some idea of the policy the Sudan Government was following and gives the lie to the accusation that British officials in the Sudan were working only for British imperial interests.

> In this my first letter for 1951, I should like first of all to wish you and your staff a very happy New Year. The year cannot be said to be opening with much appearance of peace and goodwill throughout the world and no one can prophesy what will happen to us all during the next twelve months. Communist influence seems to be spreading; the 'cold war' is warmer than it was. The shadow of a real war seems closer and darker. Here in the Sudan political and labour movements are increasing their activities, and the future here too seems to be obscure. But when we look at the gloom about us there

* *Sir Duncan Cumming*. Sudan Political Service 1925–51. District Service 1926–34. Civil Secretary's Office 1934–40. Seconded to OETA 1941. Chief Administrator Cyrenaica 1942–3. Chief Civil Administrative Officer Middle East 1945–8. Governor Kordofan 1949–50. Deputy Civil Secretary 1950–1. Chief Administrator Eritrea 1951–2.

are rays of light to cheer us up. I shall not attempt to describe the world scene, but here in the Sudan we can take courage from many signs and factors: we have probably never had stronger support in our policy from H.M.G., the British Parliament and the British people, than we have today. There is an immense fund of goodwill towards the British throughout the Sudan and even the most ardent Sudanese independent leader cannot visualise the administration of the country being carried on without British staff and British advice. We have a prosperous country after good rains: there is plenty of grain and water, and our exports of cotton, gum and the like command excellent prices. The Government budget is more than buoyant, and the Financial Secretary is wisely conserving his surpluses to build up reserves for a rainy day, and to limit the inflationary process.

Of course there are doubts and fears about the future – are political irresponsibility and impracticability going to make chaos out of good administration? Are the labour hotheads with their communist tendencies going to upset the economic advance of the country? Are the stooges of Egypt going to succeed in their continual denigration of British influence? No one can give a firm answer; no one can foresee how long we shall be wanted here, but one thing which is quite certain is that we are following the policy which is the British contribution to world political history and to go back on which would be a denial of all that the British Commonwealth stands for.

We have no alternative but to go on with our task, and not to give it up or to be chickenhearted at the difficulties which loom up in our path. I have quoted before in this connection from the Book of Joshua, Chapter I, and make bold to do so again: 'Only be thou strong and very courageous, that thou mayest observe to do according to the law . . . Turn not from it to the right hand or to the left, that thou mayest prosper whithersoever thou goest.' We need to recapture our mission, and to remember what we came to this country to do: to work for the wellbeing and progress of the Sudanese: to do justly and walk wisely: not to seek too much for ourselves, but to be the instruments of carrying out our country's policy loyally and tirelessly. And that policy is to lead the Sudanese onwards to govern themselves, and eventually to decide for themselves what their future status as a country is to be.

I have tried to restate what we are supposed to be doing, and what a difficult task we have ahead of us. But it is surely a task well worth doing, and one which, having begun, we cannot leave half-completed. We have instilled democratic ideals into these people; we have taught them to wish to govern themselves; the growth in political consciousness and in critical attitudes to the actions of government is what our education and our own outlook on life and affairs have given them.

## Appendix: Diary Notes on Provincial Tours

On my tours as Civil Secretary I would make notes in my diary of things which interested me or which were brought to my notice. Once back in Khartoum I would pass on these notes to the department or section of my office which was responsible, asking for information or pressing further action.

The following represent a selection from these notes.

## The Southern Provinces

### UPPER NILE

1945. D. C. Malakal complained about the lawlessness of the Blue Nile Arabs of Dar Muharib and Rufa'a el Hoi. What is D. C. Fung doing to stop them going South to U.N.P. to hunt game and shoot up Dinka? One *omda*'s brother-in-law, who shot at the police and killed a camel, is well known, but has not yet been arrested.

1948. Can Pawson take his wife to Waat? [Waat was a very remote H.Q. in the Eastern Nuer District with poor road communications and no telegraphic link.]

1949. Main need of the Province is roads and bridges: a ferry across the Bahr el Jebel [the White Nile] at Kilo 50 to link up the Western and Eastern Nuer. Is there no road making machinery available, as machinery can lessen the work infinitely? Schools, markets, trade and civilisation all follow the roads.

1950. Education of primitives: what result is likely to come of it unless economic advance is achieved at the same time? Detribalisation and loss of primitive virtues? This problem is being discussed at some length amongst the D.C.s, missionaries, etc., and they seem agreed that the present system of education is unlikely to do the people any real good. Longe [the Governor] has written a good note, which states the problem and gives a suggested answer. But I see no quick way of solving it.

1952. Local bon mot 'Unity of the Nile Valley under the common CLOWN of Egypt'.

### BAHR EL GHAZAL

1949. Missions – Bishop Mason of Verona Fathers at Wau discussed question of bush schools and assistance from local government councils. He said that Church could not hand over control of the schools to the Ministry of Education. I said I thought there should be a compromise and that he should discuss the problem with the Governor, the Director of Education and Mr. Hibbert* [Assistant Director South Education]. We also discussed religion

---

* *Denys Hibbert*. Sudan Political Service, Education Department 1929–39. Assistant Director of Education of Education, Southern Provinces 1945–50. Director of Education 1950–54. Headmaster Portsmouth Grammar School. Later served in the Solomon Islands.

in schools and his fears about it. Apparently some headmasters have general non-sectarian prayers and hymns and he thinks this is wrong. He complained about the sphere system [which allocated the missions particular areas] and the decision about Rumbek. He said he understood Archbishop David Mathew* had asked for the abolition of spheres. I said that this was correct but H.E. the Governor-General had not agreed.

1952. Dinka undoubtedly dislike education. It is also difficult to get teachers for them in the primary schools, as very few teachers can speak Dinka and practically no Dinkas advanced enough to teach. Bussere school has only 34 Dinkas instead of the 60 allowed for.

## EQUATORIA

1945. Arrived Juba 11 a.m. by air, five hours' flight. Met by Marwood [the Governor], inspected a guard of honour on the airfield: good turn out, but I dropped a brick by calling the Sergeant-Major *Bashawish*, and D.C. Bob Cooke reminded me 'no Arabic in the South'.

Medical service in Equatoria is very short staffed. Three major hospitals at Juba, Wau and Li Rangu, six minor hospitals and 82 dispensaries – clerical staff is insufficient for the volume of work. Take up with D.M.S. [Director of Medical Services], but I know he has no reserves.

1946. At Amadi: attended Moru Educational Council: good southern educationalist, Bartholemew Ragi. 87 boys in Amadi school with only one teacher. Visited experimental farm: dairy and workshop.

1948. Yambio – there is great delay in getting the Zande scheme going properly. Far too much apparent waste of cotton at the ginnery, and waste of labour and money in non-productive work, e.g. private housing, etc. Why does the Trading Section not use Zande shops? There is a lack of goods for sale and no purchase of exports. Agricultural Inspectors' time seems to be wasted, as they concentrate on buying cotton, and arranging cotton markets and exporting cotton, when they should be educating the people and encouraging better farming methods.

1949. Long talk at Rumbek with Ibrahim Bedri† [Sudanese A.D.C.] on Southern policy and Northern views on the South. Ashigga and Umma party rivalry. He is anti-Mahdist and anti-Egyptian. Quite reasonable about his own case – problem of finance and the education of his children. Inability to maintain two establishments [one in the South and one for his family in the North]. He would like to stay in the South, but can't afford it. The answer seems to be either an accelerated increase of pay (if it can be arranged) or a move North. He seems to have been pacified a bit by Abdel Salam el Khalifa [my Under-Secretary].

---

* *David Mathew*. Archbishop of Apamea. Assistant at the Pontifical Throne. Apostolic Delegate in Africa 1946–53. Bishop-in-Ordinary (R.C.) to H.M. Forces 1954–63.

† *Ibrahim Bedri*. Sudanese administrator. *Mamur* and later Assistant District Commissioner. Cousin of Dr. Ali Bedri. Founding member Sudan Republican Party 1951.

Benjamin Lwoki [a Member of the Legislative Assembly] told me that there was only slight interest in the Legislative Assembly among the people: all want union with the North, but no domination, and their own culture to remain. He also emphasised the need for agricultural advance.

1952. Dura is very dear in Juba – 26 Pt. a *keila*. There is a lot of theft of dura on steamers coming from the North. Some persuasion on Southerners to grow more food is needed, but it must not be real force. We need Inspectors of Agriculture whom the people know, who can guide and persuade. Grain levies are wrong. Persuasion not compulsion. No Inspectors of Agriculture available and Equatoria is now four short. D.C.s to do what they can to encourage more food production.

## Northern Sudan

### NORTHERN PROVINCE

1947. Atbara. Sudan Railways General Manager explained position regarding Joint Consultative Committees of railway workers and said he wanted legislation. Trade Unions had proved useful in Gold Coast and Nigeria but we would need a proper ex-Trade Union Official to advise and work out what is required.

1949. Berber. Big town with little to support it except cultivation and remittances. The people I met are keen to improve conditions and asked me about electricity and pumped water. I also met the hospital board, who want a new hospital. The present hospital is housed in the old dispensary and in an old building once used as a club. The latter is not very suitable, as rather delapitated and small. Dr. Ali Bakhariba* thought that the town could do with a 60-bedded hospital, and I certainly found present accommodation full up – pneumonias and a lot of women patients; and the out-patients department too is busy. Much struck by complaints of D.C.s everywhere that the Province Medical Inspector does not get round the dispensaries in the N.P.; one or two of the buildings seemed really very poor. Take up with D.M.S.

Madden† [the Province Governor] has written asking for the up-scaling of the D.C.'s post at Wadi Halfa on the grounds of the greater political activity recently and the need for Wadi Halfa to have a senior man there. I am not really convinced about this, because I don't think Halfa is at all busy or important for about 99% of the time, and as there is a telephone the D.C. should not really be left long without instructions or advice if he needs them.

* *Dr. Ali Bakhariba.* Sudanese medical officer, qualified 1929. Served at Ed Dueim and later at Berber.

† *J. F. Madden.* Sudan Political Service. Served in districts 1925–42. Civil Secretary's office (police) 1942–4. Deputy Governor Darfur 1944–6 and Northern Province 1946–8. Governor Northern Province 1949–51. Secretary Magistrates' Association 1952–65.

KASSALA PROVINCE

1946. At Gedaref: visited Leyla scheme for mechanised crop production. Boundaries explained. The dura has not come up to expectations and yields have been poor, due largely to badly spaced rains and grasshoppers. But obviously considerable potentialities. It is not fair to judge it on its first year. One of the troubles is personalities: X [Agricultural Inspector] is very anti-D.C. and of course there are endless troubles. The Director of the scheme also is sometimes stupid and doesn't improve things.

Left Kassala at 7 a.m. Breakfast at Aroma with Jock Young,* then by car through the Gash to Wagir Wells, where I visited the dispensary and the school. Then to Temintai. Gathering and discussion with Hadendowa and Beni Amer sheikhs. Arrived at Erkoweit Study Camp for University College students, etc., about 7.30 a.m. Cool and clear weather. After breakfast attended meeting of the camp, and discussed the group reports. Large number of questions about various subjects and general interest and aliveness, which is encouraging. Brains Trust in the evening.

KORDOFAN

1952. Arrived Lagowa about 12 noon from Abu Zabad. Interested to see progress of the village in sixteen years since I was D.C. Ginnery and cotton market in progress. Had tea with Sheikh Izzeddin Hemeida† and long talks with tribal elders. No special problems.

Nahud has changed little since I was here. Sheikh Muneim‡ a little stouter and less diffident now, but still a quiet nice little man. He had brought in a number of Hamar notables to meet me, most of whom I knew from 1936 days. No grouses or special problems.

DARFUR

1946. What about the liquor laws? Darfur has not been observing them at all. I told the Governor that I could not wink at the law being broken and that he must bring things into line with the law, as soon as he can.

Mohamed Effendi Bukhari (who was my clerk at Kamlin 23 years ago) asked me about his future. He would like a place in local government in Western Kordofan and has had correspondence. He is a nephew of the present Shartai of Sa'ata. Take up with Governor Kordofan.

Abu Bukr Ali el Tayeb, clerk in the Western Arab Corps office, wanted

---

* W. C. Young. Inspector of Agriculture Blue Nile Province for many years. Gash Delta 1942–8.

† Izzeddin Hemeida Nazir (head sheikh) of the Messeria Zuruq. Succeeded father (p. 62) in 1942.

‡ Muneim Mansur. Nazir of the Hamar tribe appointed in 1928 and still nazir in 1962. A small quiet unassuming man who gradually won great respect from his unruly tribe for his honesty and determination. Very religious: when we drove together and I halted, he always got out, and I never knew if it was because he really wished to pray or because he didn't trust my driving.

me to interfere to cancel a transfer arranged by the Director of Pay and Records at the clerk's own request, which he now wishes to have cancelled because Sayed Abdel Rahman has given him £E.200 to be the Umma agent in Fasher. I refused to interfere.

Sub-*mamur*, Mohd. Hassan Omer, has been drinking to excess again. He has been warned by the Governor against being drunk in public. He was drunk at Kas in front of Pumphrey* [D.C.]. He should be left at Zalingei District H.Q. until we see how he gets on. He must have done quite well over last three years: no major atrocities have been discovered and he seems honest.

1948. There seems no doubt that in many ways the administration of the District [Northern Darfur] is in a backward state. This will take some time to make up. The forms and shape of administration are needed, as a framework on which progress can be built. Without a court-house, a decent dispensary, a lock-up and offices it is difficult to see how the institutions of local government, which we seek to found, can be built up. The district will therefore need money for some time to make up the lee-way.

Charles† seems to be doing grand work: is keen and conscientious, but will get frustrated if he doesn't get tools and money to work with. The chief economic and social need of the District is more water. Mellit Dam has shown what can be done, and other similar schemes should be attempted, if good sites can be found.

[Newbold's prayer for the peoples of the Sudan copied out in my diary:]

'Almighty God, the fountain of all wisdom, whose divine providence ordereth all things upon earth, we pray Thee in Thy infinite mercy to preserve the peoples and tribes of this land. Let the shadow of Thy protection be on them in town and countryside, in mountains, forest and desert. Guard them, we beseech Thee, from all disasters, of famine, sickness and bloodshed. Pour into their hearts and minds Thy most precious gift of understanding so that they may bring peace into their feuds, justice into their councils, loving kindness into their homes and may cast away the works of darkness from their lives.'

* *M. E. C. Pumphrey*. Sudan Political Service 1930–48. Served in Western Kordofan 1931–4. Darfur 1944–6.
† *Sir Arthur Charles*. Sudan Political Service 1932—56. Served in districts – seconded to Palestine 1938–41. Equatoria and Darfur. Finance Department 1951—3. Director of Establishments 1953–5. Served in Aden. Assassinated as Speaker of Aden Assembly, 1966.

# CHAPTER IX

# THE RUSH TOWARDS SELF-GOVERNMENT
## 1951–1953

The establishment of the Legislative Assembly in 1948 had heralded if not a quiet period, at least one during which politics had not been virtually my sole preoccupation. However, towards the end of 1950 political excitement began to build up again and once more the Egyptians were involved.

The speech from the throne at the opening of the Egyptian Parliament in November included a deliberate reference to the unity of the Nile Valley, a statement which was calculated to raise the political temperature in the Sudan. The Umma party held a political rally in Omdurman and denounced Egypt and her policies. During this rally three ministers spoke publicly and Abdel Rahman Ali Taha was so outspoken that an official protest was telegraphed to the Governor-General from Nahas Pasha, the Prime Minister of Egypt. The Umma party then protested to the Governor-General about the Egyptian attitude and demanded speedy self-government. There was much propaganda by the party among members of the Assembly and even the ministers and the Speaker himself exerted a good deal of pressure on them. A motion was tabled for debate calling for immediate self-government, a demand which posed a difficult problem for the British members of the Assembly. We could not antagonise the ministers or their Umma supporters too much or we would lose their co-operation, but at the same time the country members and the Southerners were worried and thought that they were being swept along too fast in the tide of independence. I had more or less continuous meetings for several days with all the leaders but was unable to persuade the Umma to withdraw their motion. Eventually I myself produced an amending motion which, while agreeing with the aim of self-government, proposed that it be delayed.

The House was very crowded during this debate, with the public galleries filled until late at night. Not a voice among the many who spoke was raised against the ultimate goal of self-government for the Sudan, but the Southerners and many of the Northern country members were strongly of the opinion that the present time was premature. The debate on 14 December 1950 lasted from 9.30 a.m. until 1 p.m., resumed again at 4.30 p.m. and was not concluded until 1 a.m. next morning. My motion for delay was defeated by 41 votes to 40, and the Umma party motion carried by 39 votes to 38.

This debate caused quite a stir in the councils of the Co-domini, as the Egyptian Foreign Minister was in London at the time and about to have talks with the British Foreign Secretary. The Egyptian Prime Minister telegraphed the Governor-General demanding an explanation, and the British Foreign Secretary expressed his annoyance at the awkward time at which this debate had been permitted. But it would have been terribly difficult for the Governor-General to have stopped such a debate in what was after all a parliamentary body, and would have risked the Umma party taking offence and their possible non-cooperation in government.

There were some good results from the debate. The Southerners and country members were relieved to see that the British members did not support the Umma line whole-heartedly, while the narrow majority for the motion showed that many Sudanese did not support too hasty a policy, and also made it unnecessary for the Governor-General to take any action on the motion. At the same time the size of the Umma vote showed the Egyptians and the pro-Egyptian Sudanese that the independence party was not just a figment of the imagination, but that there was a strong urge in the country for self-government and subsequent independence. It was something of a relief to find that, following the debate, relations fairly quickly reverted to their previous smoothness. Both Sayed Abdel Rahman el Mahdi and Abdulla Bey Khalil assured me that the motion did not mean that they wished to embarrass the British officials in the Sudan Government, and that the exercise had really been an internal political one to reassure the young men of their party that they were not holding back in their objectives. I was further relieved that we were able to resume at once the collaboration with the ministers at the informal council meetings.

However, in spite of the maintenance of good relations it seemed essential not to sit back but to keep advancing and thus maintain the initiative. The Legislative Assembly's third session was opened by the Governor-General on 7 April 1961 and his speech foreshadowed quite a large programme of legislation, in addition to the Budget, a Bill to turn the University College of Khartoum into a fully-fledged independent university instead of being affiliated to London University, a Bill to lay down a code of military law for the Sudan Defence Force – it had previously been governed by the Egyptian code of military law, which was somewhat inappropriate as well as out of date – and the Local Government Bill which I mentioned earlier. A largely Sudanese committee had worked out a five-year development plan visualising an expenditure of about £E.20 million, of which 9·5 million were allocated to agriculture, irrigation, water supplies, veterinary service, aviation and other transport; 4 millions each to education and health, and 2·5 million for unforeseen expenditure. The money was expected to be raised mostly from budgetary surpluses. The Financial Secretary brought forward these proposals as a corollary to his Budget, and of course both the Financial Bill and this Development Bill gave splendid opportunities for every member of the Assembly to emphasise the needs of his own constituency. The session was a busy one, and went on until the adjournment on 19 May.

It was in June 1951, when I was Acting Governor-General, that I had the most anxious few days that I experienced during all my time as Civil Secretary. Towards the end of May I went on a tour of the Northern Province and got back to Khartoum on 6 June, to be met at the station by Louis Chick, the Financial Secretary, who had been stand-in as Acting Governor-General during my absence. He told me that all the police in the three towns of Khartoum, Khartoum North and Omdurman were on strike, and were occupying their barracks, in which lay the armouries containing their rifles and ammunition. With practically all the police striking and only a few troops available for mobile patrols, any looters, hooligans and criminals could have had all their own way. Incidents like the one at Khartoum North where a crowd of scallywags set a lorry on fire and broke into shops were only a tithe of what might have happened, but fortunately the District Commissioners had enlisted some special constables and hired enough vehicles to keep up a steady patrol.

After various discussions with the provincial and police authorities, I decided to bring in more troops, and the *Kaid* ordered in companies of the Camel Corps from El Obeid and of the Eastern Arab Corps from Gedaref. The troops came in very speedily, those from El Obeid making almost record time across country, and we were able to increase the mobile patrols, while the Governor and police officers continued their efforts to get the rank and file back to work. It appeared from these conversations that the self-appointed 'Police Committee' was quite intransigent and though they did not openly advocate violence, were being addressed and influenced by young Communists such as Mohammed Sayed Sallam and Sheikh el Shafia, who nightly appeared at the West Barracks and addressed the police in truculent and seditious language to an accompaniment of slogans and shouts. None of the police officers or administrative staff was allowed to speak to the rank and file, who were kept completely in the dark by the committee.

On 9 June the troops entered the barracks in the afternoon, while most of the mutinous police were asleep, and removed the arms and ammunition to the military armouries. After this I issued an ultimatum to the mutineers to return to their duty within a short period or consider themselves dismissed, and ordered the arrest of the committee. This was duly done on the 10th and a few police began to return to work. By the 13th the Khartoum trouble was more or less over. We took back nearly 1,000 men and discharged about 250. The committee members and a number of others who had instigated and encouraged the strike were tried by the magistrates and imprisoned, among them the President and Secretary of the Trade Union Federation. There were reactions sympathetic to the strikers among the police in Port Sudan, Atbara and Kassala, and troops were flown to Port Sudan where a breakdown of public security in the port might have been serious. A number of men who had been ringleaders at these places were discharged. By the end of the month law and order had been fully re-established and the police force had recovered much of its previous morale.

The mutiny in the police was a serious business, and I thought we were lucky to get out of it so easily. The Sudan Police had until this incident been most reliable and we had always counted on their remaining loyal. During all our service in the districts we had relied on the loyalty, devotion and friendship of this splendid body of men, and this mutiny was contrary to all experience. It seemed to me that with the greater sophistication of administration and growth in the volume of paper work, senior police and administrative officers had not been able to maintain the old personal contacts between officers and men, discipline had been too rigid and remote, and necessary improvements to housing, barrack accommodation and amenities had been too long delayed. I also wondered whether the appointment to our Sudan Police Force of officers from the British police with their professional outlook and standards had not inhibited the District Commissioners from taking the personal interest in their police, which had always been such a marked feature of our administration.

As Acting Governor-General, I appointed a commission, with Judge Watson* as Chairman, to enquire into the origins of the whole incident. The commission reported some four weeks later, and I referred the report to the Executive Council, which approved various recommendations put forward for improving the general police organisation in the Three Towns and agreed that the Commandant of the Khartoum Police at the time of the mutiny should be asked to

* *J. R. S. Watson.* Sudan Political Service 1935–55. Provincial service 1935–44. Joined Legal Department. Police magistrate, district judge and judge of the High Court 1944–55. Called to the Bar (Grays Inn) 1947.

resign, as Council agreed that his strict and remote administration of the force had been at least partly to blame for the trouble. He was well treated financially and received due compensation for his uncompleted contract.

During these months I had been trying to get agreement to an all-party commission to examine the constitution of the Executive Council and Legislative Assembly and to make recommendations for its development into a self-governing constitution. This would give complete power in internal affairs to a Sudanese Cabinet and Parliament, subject only to the Governor-General's overriding veto, which was necessary to conform with the Condominium Agreement, under which he was responsible to Britain and Egypt for the good government of Sudan. I thought that this commission, to win general support for its recommendations, should include representatives of all shades of opinion in the country, but negotiations to achieve this aim were difficult and frustrating. I proposed that an expatriate judge should be the chairman, and the Legal Secretary released Judge Stanley Baker* for this onerous job. The secretary was Mr. Keen, the Clerk to the Assembly, and then I had to try to persuade the various groups of Sudanese to be represented. There were difficulties at first about the terms of reference, but these were eventually surmounted when I succeeded in obtaining agreement of the parties to a commission composed almost entirely of politicians and townees, but neither the Umma party nor the other parties would agree to an adequate representation of tribal leaders or Southerners. This made things extraordinarily difficult, for I felt it wrong to overlook these provincial groups, but on the other hand had the Commission failed to get off the ground it would have been a real victory for the Ashigga, who were boycotting it, and for the Egyptians.

Another difficulty was that while all the leaders agreed privately that the Sudan Government could not properly support a constitution which was contrary to the Condominium Agreement, and that the Governor-General's reserved powers and veto could not constitutionally be abolished except with the agreement of Britain and Egypt, no Sudanese had the courage to say so in public. After two months argument and discussion, the Commission was at last formed, but its composition in my view was unbalanced and weighted heavily in favour of the urban areas. I did not foresee an easy passage for the Commission: it had to take into account the views of the Umma party, as contained in their resolution in the Legislative Assembly, and statements made

* *Judge Stanley Baker*. Sudan Political Service 1937–55. Provincial service and Civil Secretary's Office 1937–44. Joined Legal Department 1944. Barrister (Grays Inn) 1946. Judge of the High Court 1948.

subsequently by two other parties, the National Front and the Ittiha-diyan. It seemed clear that it would be bound to recommend an increase in the powers of the Assembly, the establishment of an upper house and the complete Sudanisation of the Executive Council; and I was anxious about the position of the South if decisions were taken to which its representatives were not a party. However, it seemed useless to pro-pose changes in the parliamentary set-up, unless these stemmed from the advice and recommendations of a truly Sudanese body. The Com-mission held its first meeting towards the end of April: it decided to tackle the major constitutional issues first and to leave the questions of electoral procedure, the number and boundaries of constituencies, and the size and powers of the proposed Senate until later. Further meetings were held in May and June, and the Commission then closed down for the summer, when the chairman was asked by the Commission itself to go to the U.K. to consult constitutional lawyers there on points which had worried it. As far as I could ascertain the Commission had done useful work; the extremists had had to climb down a little and be more practical, and above all it was still together and in being, which was quite an achievement on the part of Judge Stanley Baker, the chairman.

Throughout 1951 the pro-Egyptian groups were busy. Ismail el Azhari* issued a manifesto declaring that the Ashigga would never agree to participate in any constitutional bodies set up under the existing Condominium arrangements; and agents were sent out to tour the country and whip up enthusiasm for the Unity of the Nile Valley. The Egyptian Government, according to *El Ahram* – a news-paper thought to be in close contact with Government agencies – announced that Egypt was proposing to spend £E.450,000 on work of social welfare in the Sudan, and the Egyptian Government sent the Sudan Government a request for land in Omdurman on which to build a hospital. There were suggestions from the Egyptian Ministry of Education for opening more schools, especially Islamic schools in the Southern Provinces, and its Controller of Education in the Sudan spent a fortnight at Juba and Malakal reconnoitring. It appeared that 113 mosques and Islamic trusts – *Wakfs* – were receiving grants from Egypt. Egyptian visitors flocked to the Sudan – among them rotarians, doctors, irrigators, bankers and students.

* *Ismail el Azhari.* Teacher Sudan Education Department. Leader of Ashigga party and President Graduates' Congress 1943. Prime Minister of Self-Governing Sudan 1954. Declared Independence December 1955. Resigned 1956. Appointed President 1964. Died 1971.

There had been rumours for some time that the Egyptian Government, having failed to persuade the British to hand the Sudan over to them, proposed to abrogate the 1899 Condominium Agreement and the 1936 Anglo-Egyptian Treaty unilaterally. I was told about this in June 1951 by our Sudan Agent in Cairo, but it was correctly foreseen that with the King away on a honeymoon cruise and Nahas Pasha, the Prime Minister, off on a holiday trip to Europe, nothing was likely to happen until later in the year. The Governor-General was in Cairo in May and heard nothing. I visited the Egyptian Minister responsible for Sudan matters, Ibrahim Fareg Pasha, at Alexandria in late July on my way to the U.K. and got no indication from him, during a talk which lasted nearly two hours, that anything special was in the wind. He seemed pleasant and friendly, but I noted in my diary that the talks were of 'little real use'. However, the rumours persisted, and in the Sudan it was thought possible that the zero hour would be 21 September – 'Unity of the Nile Valley Day'. The Egyptians had made so many statements and tied themselves so tightly to this policy that it was difficult to see how they could avoid implementing it. So it was no very great surprise when on 8 October the Egyptian Prime Minister, Nahas Pasha, announced to a loudly cheering parliament in Cairo the unilateral abrogation of the 1936 Treaty and the 1899 Agreement concerning the Sudan. King Farouk was proclaimed King of the Sudan, and a Bill was introduced in the Egyptian Parliament to set up a Constitutional Assembly in the Sudan, and a Sudanese Cabinet to be appointed by King Farouk to govern the Sudan with certain subjects reserved for the Egyptian Government, including foreign affairs and defence.

The Governor-General and I were in Britain, and after meetings at the Foreign Office we hurried back to the Sudan where the Egyptian actions had caused considerable excitement. The Sudanese as a whole, including even the Ashigga, did not support the actions of the Egyptians. Many were glad to see the end of the Condominium Agreement, but the imposition of a constituent assembly, the proposed appointment of ministers by the King of Egypt, and the reservations of certain matters to the Egyptians were bitterly resented. They had been decreed without consultation with the Sudanese. The announcement by the Foreign Secretary in the House of Commons that the British Government did not recognise the unilateral abrogation of the treaties, would continue to support the administration of the Governor-General, and looked forward to the institution of a self-governing constitution by the end of 1952, was welcomed generally in the Sudan. The Legislative Assembly passed a motion almost unanimously on 25 October thanking the British Government for their stand, and deploring the Egyptian

Government's attempt to impose King Farouk's sovereignty and a constitution on the Sudan without consultation with the Sudanese.

There were other results in the Sudan. I have been told on credible authority that as soon as the Egyptian action was known in Omdurman, Sayed Abdel Rahman el Mahdi was pressed by many of his followers to take advantage of the end of the Condominium to declare the Sudan independent, and it was only the opposition of Abdulla Bey Khalil and one or two others which prevented him attempting to stage such a coup. Abdulla Bey is said to have told the Sayed that he had promised Sir James Robertson that the Umma party would take no unconstitutional action, and this apparently brought Abdel Rahman and his hotheads back to reality.

More important was the effect on the Constitutional Commission, which broke up on the grounds that, with the abrogation of the 1899 Agreement by Egypt, there was now no constitutional basis for the existing administration. The question which worried some members was the theoretical one, namely where did sovereignty reside during the period until the Sudanese could exercise self-determination and sovereignty was finally transferred to the people of the Sudan? This did not seem to me to matter very much from a practical point of view, so long as the British guaranteed the defence of the country and its advance towards self-government, but to the more logical minds of Derdiri Mohamed Osman* and Mohamed Ahmed Mahgoub it was important. Before they broke up, the Commission sent a telegram to the Secretary-General of the United Nations asking for the appointment of a U.N. Commission to supervise the administration of the Sudan during the intervening period. No reply was received to this message and after a few days' waiting the Commission disintegrated. It seemed most expedient that we should try to save as much as possible of its work and that the Government should prepare a new draft constitution based as far as possible on the agreements reached by the Commission before it broke up. Judge Stanley Baker was therefore asked to prepare a report of the Commission's work, which would bring out as far as possible their agreed recommendations for the new constitution.

On the receipt of a very able report by the Judge, it was decided to have it printed and laid on the table of the Assembly. It would then be necessary to have certain questions arising put to the House, to obtain their views before the legal draftsmen could get on with their task of producing a Bill amending the existing constitution to cover

* *Derdiri Mohamed Osman.* Sudanese district judge. Supporter of Khatmia and strong critic of Condominium Government. Member of the Constitutional Commission 1951–2.

F

the alterations proposed. The Assembly discussed these matters and slowly and laboriously we waded through the various points on which guidance was sought, spending ten days on these debates. Generally speaking the atmosphere was friendly and co-operative, though I thought that some of the difficulties about the Governor-General's legal responsibilities to the Co-domini were brushed aside rather irrationally. But we did obtain answers to the questions that had been raised, and the next step – the drafting of the Amendment Bill – could be started.

The draft constitutional Bill was presented to the Assembly in April 1952 and finally passed in May, after which the Assembly was adjourned at the end of what proved to be the last sitting. I think that the failure to seek the extension of the Assembly's life was probably one of the greatest mistakes I made as Civil Secretary, for it resulted in there being no representative body for about fifteen months. The Assembly's legal life was originally three years, and when this term ended in December 1951, it was extended for a further six months and then for another four until October 1952. It was hoped that elections for the parliament proposed under the new constitution could be held before the rains of 1952, or at least before the beginning of 1953: but, as it turned out, we could not ignore General Neguib's negotiations with the Sudanese political parties which were followed by fresh Anglo-Egyptian talks, and the agreement of February 1953. It was the autumn of 1953 before elections were held, and early 1954 before the new parliament met. From October 1952 until January 1954 there was no representative body in existence which could speak for the Sudanese as a people, and because of this lacuna the Southerners, and country people generally, lost any opportunity of influencing events.

I think that I should have realised, after the delays in 1947 and 1948 when we tried to get agreement between the Co-domini about the Legislative Assembly proposals, that it was most unlikely for them to agree speedily to the new proposals, and we should therefore have extended the Assembly's life further. It was in my mind, however, that to lengthen the life of the old Assembly and Executive Council might well be taken by Sudanese politicians to show that the British members of the Government were dragging their feet and were not going ahead fast enough with the elections under the new constitution. Nevertheless, it ought to have been easy to persuade them that a further extension of the life of the Assembly, as a guarantee in case of delays, would be a harmless insurance, and only be used if the unforeseen happened. Up to July, when the *coup d'état* took place in Egypt, there seemed no likelihood of Egypt agreeing to the new constitutional Bill and we had an assurance from the British Foreign Secretary that we should not be held up a second time. As things turned out it was a major error not to have kept the Assembly alive as a mouthpiece for the country people and the Southerners.

The unexpected events which were totally to alter the situation were taking place meanwhile in Egypt. There were serious riots in Cairo and in Ismailia on the canal, which resulted in the Wafd Government under Nahas Pasha being dismissed; Ali Maher Pasha formed a new administration, but this in turn lasted only a few weeks. These troubles in Egypt led to renewed attempts, chiefly on the part of the U.S. Embassy in Cairo, to find a way out of the unsettled situation, and they revived the old Sidki-Bevin idea of King Farouk's symbolic sovereignty over the Sudan. In the Sudan, however, this still appeared impossible, and the only way out was to press on with the election of a truly representative parliament, which could be asked to consider whether King Farouk's claim could be admitted. After Ali Maher's government fell, Hillali Pasha took over, and he had the idea of trying to conciliate Sayed Abdel Rahman to the idea of Egyptian sovereignty. However, his government also fell and Hussein Sirry Pasha was Prime Minister when the army *coup d'état* took place in July 1952. King Farouk abdicated and left the country, and General Neguib became the ruler of Egypt.

General Neguib was known to many Sudanese. He had lived in the Sudan when his father had been serving there, and had for some time been a pupil at the Gordon College Secondary School where many of the leading Sudanese politicians had been fellow schoolboys with him – in fact it was difficult to meet any Sudanese in the first days of his rule who had not been at school with him. His brother, Ali, had been the Egyptian A.D.C. to the Governor-General at the Palace, and had been popular in Khartoum society. Neguib before long turned his attention to the Sudan problem and immediately won great esteem among the Sudanese Independents by giving up the previous unbending Egyptian claim to sovereignty over the Sudan, and agreeing that the Sudanese should be allowed complete self-determination, including independence from Egypt if they should want it. He held a number of conferences with the Sudanese political parties and signed separate agreements with them all in the course of two or three months, based on variously amended versions of our new self-government statute; and he was then able to start negotiations with the British Government through the Ambassador in Cairo, Sir Ralph Stevenson. I was asked to go to Cairo to see the Ambassador and General Neguib, and flew down on 15 November. I went over the whole ground in discussions with the Ambassador and his staff, and also saw Mr. Caffery, the American Ambassador, who had been strongly pressing the British

Embassy to settle with the Egyptians, even at the price of selling the Sudan. He told me that I was not such a 'foul fiend' as he had imagined me; but it was obvious that he, like many of the U.S. citizens who had come to the Sudan, could not appreciate our concern for what one of them described as 'ten million bloody niggers'.

But I made no progress with General Neguib when I told him that the Sudanese were not yet ready to run their country without a considerable amount of outside help – and that I feared great troubles in the Southern Sudan if the Southerners were handed over to be ruled by the Northerners without any safeguards. He had already had his meetings with the political parties and was obviously in a strong position. I found him a pleasant man to talk to: he had a nice shy smile, smoked a pipe, and was friendly and easy. But unfortunately I was unable to persuade him of the difficulties I saw about the South if all the British administrative staff left as quickly as he proposed.

The talks between the British and Egyptians went on for a couple of months: we were kept informed by a constant stream of telegrams between the Foreign Office and the Embassy, as well as between both of them and the Governor-General; and the Governor-General of course had to comment and reply with copies to both. The flow was so constant, and our cyphering staff so overworked, that we often got behindhand, and a reply from London to Cairo to a telegram would arrive before we had seen the original from Cairo to London, and vice versa. For two months or so a small committee consisting of myself, the Attorney-General, my political assistant and the Governor-General's Private Secretary met morning and evening to deal with the inflow and prepare draft replies, which the Private Secretary then cleared with the Governor-General before they were despatched. We struggled hard to prevent including in the agreement the clauses which laid down the complete and almost immediate Sudanisation of the administration, army and police and any other posts likely to have political influence, as we thought that this would mean deterioration in standards of administration, for Sudanese replacements of adequate ability and experience could not immediately be found for so many posts. We also tried to have retained in the statute the safeguards for the South, which the Legislative Assembly had accepted. But it was all to no avail and in January 1953 all the Sudanese political parties signed a further agreement with General Neguib's emissary, Major Salah Salim,* who had come to Khartoum. The final signature was that on behalf of the

* *Major Salah Salim.* Member of General Neguib's Egyptian Government. Visited Sudan January 1953. Signed agreement with Sudanese political parties During trip to the South gained notoriety by performing native dances very lightly clad. Retired August 1955.

S.R.P.* by Derdiri Nugud and Zein el Abdin Saleh, in spite of opposition by most of the sheikhs. I noted in my diary on 10 January: 'What
then do we do? There seems little point in struggling, if all the political
parties are with Egypt. But would we desert the South or the *nazirs*,
if we gave in? Have we the power to stand out any longer?'

On 11 January, Abdulla Bey Khalil came and discussed the whole
position with me. He was not at all happy, but it did not seem to me
that we could continue to carry on our opposition any longer, especially,
as his party, the Umma, had signed with the other parties. The two
main objections to the proposed agreement were the question of the
South, as the Southerners had not been consulted in any way by the
political parties or by the Egyptians and were bound to feel that their
wishes and interests had been ignored. They had no political party of
their own at the time, and by the dissolution of the Assembly their
representatives had nowhere to voice their views about the South or
about objections to the clauses dealing with compulsory and rapid
Sudanisation before the Sudanese could exercise the right of self-
determination.

As far as we British in the Sudan were concerned, we did not object
to Sudanisation; we had pushed ahead with it as fast as seemed possible,
and had certainly promoted to senior posts some Sudanese who were
hardly up to the responsibilities which they had to assume. Too rapid
Sudanisation of top posts would mean that some of them would be
filled by persons who could not carry out the work, and would also
mean a gap somewhere down the line, as the number of candidates
suitable for selection who were coming forward was inadequate to
fill all the vacancies that would occur if every British administrative
official left within a short time. I suppose an administrator is bound to
overemphasize the importance of good administration just as the politician underestimates its value; but reasonable standards of official
ability, integrity, experience and devotion to duty seem essential if the
happiness and good government of the common people are to be safeguarded. Our representations along these lines were brushed aside in
the negotiations in Cairo, and it was decided that the Anglo-Egyptian
Agreement should be signed in Cairo on 14 February.

* *Sudan Republican Party* was formed by a number of the educated class and of the
tribal leaders who, while supporting the movement towards self-government and
independence, wished to dissociate themselves from the Umma party and Sayed
Abdel Rahman el Mahdi, whose supposed ambition to be king led to the 'Republican' aim of the party. The Civil Secretary's Office was accused of sponsoring the
party's inception, but this was untrue. When asked about the proposal I had said
there was no objection to anyone who wished forming a party. The two men mentioned were educated townsmen who acted without consulting their tribal fellow-
members.

This was clearly going to be a most important day for the Sudan, and one immediate question was how we, as the expatriate rulers, were to greet it. We had fought against much in the Agreement for reasons which seemed valid to us, but I felt that we should identify ourselves with the great majority of the Sudanese and that to accept the Agreement with some show of enthusiasm would make the next year or two until the hand-over much easier than if we sulked in our tents and did not, for all our misgivings, participate in the Sudanese rejoicing at this milestone in their history. The Governor-General agreed with this attitude and arrangements were made for a ceremonial gathering outside the Secretariat on the 14th, which was declared a public holiday. H.E. agreed to give an evening party in the Palace Gardens on the same day.

On Saturday the 14th, enormous crowds gathered at the Secretariat: the grass lawns were thronged with cheerful milling people who engulfed the three guards of honour, composed of Sudanese, Egyptian and British troops. The verandahs, stairs and roofs of the Secretariat building were crowded with people and one could not help wondering whether they could safely carry such a load. A platform had been erected in the shadow of Kitchener's statue, and on this places were found for the members of the Executive Council, some other notables and the Governor-General, who made a suitable and friendly speech. The proceedings went off safely enough; there were no incidents and, as I noted in my diary, 'no harm done'. When it was over the crowds dispersed quietly and I held a press conference in my office, where we had coffee and soft drinks. The Palace party in the evening was also successful. The band of a battalion of the King's Own Yorkshire Light Infantry beat retreat, marching and counter-marching on the lawns in first-class style, and a most cheerful party ensued, at which hundreds of people came to shake me by the hand and congratulate me on the Agreement.

Criticisms were afterwards voiced by some of the expatriate staff, especially in the Southern Sudan, against the way in which we had taken part in these celebrations of an agreement which was far from satisfactory. I was accused of having sold the pass, and handed over the South to the Egyptians and the Northerners contrary to the promises repeatedly made in the past, and one rather hysterical lady asked my wife how she could continue to live with a man who had betrayed the South and his own staff. In all it was an unhappy time. General Neguib, speaking in Egypt on 16 February, was frank enough about Egyptian hopes that the Sudanese, when they came to choose their final form of government, would decide to join Egypt. He also declared that though the Sudanese could choose independence for their final status, this did not mean that they could join the British Commonwealth if they so wished. The British Foreign Secretary in the House of Commons later said that independence did include the right to ask for entry to the Commonwealth – but this idea was never pursued.

Neguib's speech caused Sayed Abdel Rahman and the pro-independence group considerable alarm. Fears of Egyptian infiltration and propaganda intensified, and on the 18th when Sayed Abdel Rahman and his son Sayed Saddik came to breakfast, I was treated to a long discourse upon British responsibilities. The Sayed declared that in spite of all the insults he had endured – including the lack of due precedence at the last Palace party – he remained loyal to the British. It was still the British responsibility to ensure that the Egyptians did not use the new agreement to fill the Sudan with Egyptians and dominate the country. He was not the only Sudanese to be obviously shaken by General Neguib's speech, for other visitors also arrived to voice their fears. Sheikh Babikr Karamullah* was disconsolate, and could not understand what Sayed Ali Mirghani's policy was. Sheikh Ali Idris el Kadi† thought the Government should help the Sudan Republican party, and Fateh el Bedawi‡ talked long and bitterly about Egyptian intrigues. It is never very wise to say 'I told you so'; but I did suggest that perhaps the political parties ought to have thought about these dangers before they made their party agreements with the Egyptians, for these after all had led to the Anglo-Egyptian Agreement. But I encouraged them to keep together and try to face the future in a more united way. Many times during these days I quoted Aesop's fable about the bundle of sticks being hard to break, while individual sticks broke easily.

On Friday the 20th the united political parties had a celebration in Omdurman to mark the Anglo-Egyptian Agreement, to which many British officials were invited. There were big but orderly crowds. We heard speeches from various leaders, and there was considerable enthusiasm. I was surprised at the very friendly way in which I and other expatriate officials were greeted by everyone, and at the complete absence of any anti-British feeling, at least as far as we were concerned as individuals.

Another stage in Sudanese history was now completed. The agreement laid down a timetable and programme for the eventual decision by the Sudanese on their future status; it provided for the replacement

* *Babikr Karamullah*. Elderly merchant from El Fasher who was a strong supporter of Sayed Ali Mirghani.
† *Ali Idris el Kadi*. Member of the Sudan Republican party. A sheikh from Sennar.
‡ *Fateh el Bedawi*. Ex-*mamur* promoted to Assistant District Commissioner. A follower of Sayed Abdel Rahman and an Umma party supporter.

of foreign officials by Sudanese, and it endorsed our self-government
constitution suitably amended to cover the new provisions for the
Sudanisation, Electoral, and Governor-General's Commissions.
If all we had fought for in the prolonged negotiations had not been
achieved, there were still hopes for the future – 'the unity of the Nile
Valley' had not been imposed upon the Sudan, and the Sudanese had
the promise of independence if they wished it.

## Last Weeks in the Sudan

The Anglo-Egyptian agreement had been signed, and the Sudanese
had been guaranteed the right of self-determination, for which we
British in the Sudan Government had fought for so long. It therefore
seemed to me that my job in the Sudan was done, and that it might be
embarrassing for the Governor-General and for the first Sudanese
prime minister if I, who had been prime minister to all intents and
purposes for so many years, still remained on the stage; furthermore
it was difficult to see what role I could play now. The new prime
minister, whoever he was and whenever he was appointed, would not
want me hanging about in the wings, and I could see no appointment
for which the Governor-General would want me.

So I told him early in February that I thought that I should retire
in April, and that A. C. Beaton, my deputy, should carry on as the
Civil Secretary until a prime minister was appointed, when the post
of Civil Secretary should be abolished, and Beaton or another should
become the Permanent Secretary for the Ministry of the Interior.
The political side of the Civil Secretary's office would disappear entirely, but until the Sudan became independent or was absorbed by
Egypt, the Governor-General would require a senior political officer
to advise him on the internal and external trends of political thought
and action. I suggested W. H. T. Luce* for this appointment. Sir
Robert Howe agreed with all this; the officers concerned were informed, and I began to make my preparations to leave about the middle
of April.

During the next two months there were still some final jobs to be
done, and among these were two major problems. One was to find
suitable Sudanese members of the three commissions which had to be
set up under the terms of the recent agreement. In all three were
to be non-Sudanese representatives, but there were also to be Sudanese
members, and without the Legislative Assembly, and with the un-

---

* *Sir William Luce.* Sudan Political Service 1930–56. Provincial service 1930–41.
Private Secretary to Governor General 1941–7. Governor Blue Nile Province 1951–3.
Adviser to Governor-General 1953–6. Governor Aden Protectorate 1956–60. British
Resident in Persian Gulf 1961–6.

compromising attitude of some of the Sudanese political parties, it was not easy to get agreement on the Sudanese members. The three commissions were first, the Governor-General's Commission of five members, to advise him on matters requiring his decision; secondly, the Sudanisation Commission, to review the senior posts in the Civil Service and arrange for the substitution by Sudanese of all foreigners – mainly British, of course – in the administration, army and police. It was also to consider posts in other government departments, and recommend which of these had such political importance that they might influence voting in the forthcoming elections and the final decision about the long-term future of the country. Thirdly, the Electoral Commission was to revise the electoral arrangements made in the Ordinance, to decide in which constituencies voting could be by direct ballot, and which by electoral colleges or indirect voting; then to conduct the elections as soon as they had made all the necessary preparations.

The British and Egyptian Governments lost no time in making their appointments, and by the beginning of March, barely a month after the agreement had been signed, foreign members of the Commissions began to arrive in Khartoum. My main recollection of the arrival of the Commissions was the importance expressed by the individual members about their housing and office accommodation. Housing was already scarce and difficult in Khartoum, and the arrival of several foreign representatives with quite lofty ideas of their own and their country's prestige was a headache for the Civil Secretary's office, which acted as government landlord. However, these problems were all surmounted and by April, when I left the Sudan, they were settling down to supervise the transitional period.

The second major problem was the future of the British officials who were serving in the Sudan Government. By the terms of the Anglo-Egyptian agreement all administrative, police and army officers had to be removed before the Sudanese could decide upon their future, and the same applied to any others in the departments whose influence might affect the votes in the forthcoming general election, which had to be conducted 'in a free and neutral atmosphere'. Until the final stages of the negotiations, too little attention had been paid to this article, but the Senior Civil Servants' Association was now seeking a statement from the British Government about their rights and expectations, and representatives of the Association sought interviews with me and the Governor-General. Many of the British were serving on contract, and these would not be so difficult to deal with, as most contracts included a clause covering their premature ending with some element of compensation. The difficulty was how to safeguard the future and the pension rights of those officials who were serving on pensionable terms. Many were comparatively young or in mid-career, and if they left the Sudan, as compelled so to do by the Agreement, what other occupation would be found for them? If they were retired on the pensions they had earned plus some element of compensation for the cutting short of their careers, what guarantee would there be that the future Sudan Government would honour the undertaking made by the Governor-General under the terms of the existing Pensions Ordinance?

The situation in the Sudan was very different from that which I later had to deal with in Nigeria, for in Nigeria there was no compulsion on the British officials to retire; they could serve on under the independent Government, and many did so for a considerable time under schemes which the Colonial Office, with great experience of handing over, had devised. In the Sudan many had to go under the terms of the Agreement, while others were required to go by the Sudanisation Commission. Some time later the Foreign Office set up a committee to help those who retired from the Sudan Service to find alternative employment, and the great majority found reasonably suitable and lucrative appointments. The proposed agreement between the new Sudan and British Governments to guarantee the payment of pensions came to nothing, but the Sudan Government has continued to pay all the pensions earned most conscientiously and regularly ever since independence. The British Government eventually agreed to treat Sudan pensions similarly to those of other overseas services by granting them pension supplements from the Treasury to make up for the rise in the cost of living and the drop in the value of money; it also gave reassuring guarantees should the Sudan default.

After the anxieties and hard work of the recent months I thought I should have one last trip into the real Sudan, away from the Khartoum political atmosphere, and I arranged to go to Darfur in the middle of March to attend the Eastern Darfur tribal gathering. K. D. D. Henderson* was provincial governor at El Fasher, and I flew there on 14 March. We set off in the middle of the day for Um Kedada where the meeting was to be held, but half-way down the road the car broke down and we had to transfer to a lorry, and only reached our destination at about 11 p.m. My diary has the comment 'A dreadful day'. Next day was the gathering: some 3,000 tribesmen were on parade, and in the accustomed style we mounted our camels and rode round the great circle; and then stood on the dais while the parade

* *K. D. D. Henderson.* Sudan Political Service 1926–53. Served in Provinces 1927–38 and 1944–6. Civil Secretary's Office 1938–44. and 1946–9. Governor Darfur 1949–53. Secretary Spalding Trust from 1953.

marched past us. The Berti tribe is not one of the big Sudan tribes, but they did their stuff and it was a happy and successful morning. In the afternoon the new Rural District Council offices were opened, and I made a speech in Arabic. Then followed the customary tea party with the *nazirs* and sheikhs, and later in the evening I had a more difficult job – to speak to the British D.C.s about the Anglo-Egyptian Agreement and what it meant for them in the future. Next day followed the usual pattern at these gatherings. I spoke for some time with the notables from Dar Hamar in my old district of Western Kordofan; lunched with the senior officials; attended the races and sports, and watched the Governor give away the prizes. What fun it all was, and how many similar earlier gatherings came to mind! Then next day back to Fasher in an open car, when I got rather burnt by the sun, and there I found my wife who had flown up from Khartoum to join me, and we set off on the 18th to go up to Sunni, that charming little rest house on the side of Jebel Marra, a huge volcanic mountain in the centre of Darfur. Jack and Anne Wilson* (D.C. Nyala) had come up to meet us there, and we had two lovely quiet days with them: bathed in a pool in the stream and walked up the hill to see the scenery and the cultivations, irrigated by little runnels opened up by the local farmers from the stream which came down from the mountain. But the rest was brief, for on the second evening a message came out from El Fasher saying that I must go back to Khartoum as the Governor-General wanted me to meet Mr. Selwyn Lloyd,† Minister of State at the Foreign Office, who had just arrived. So next morning we packed up and went off back to El Fasher, six hours' journey, and the next day caught an aeroplane to Khartoum.

It turned out that Mr. Selwyn Lloyd had come to find out for the Foreign Office what the situation in the Sudan was after the Anglo-Egyptian Agreement of February. We had meetings at which he met the Southern provincial governors and got some idea from them about the depressing effects of the Agreement on the South. The more educated Southerners felt that the Agreement had let them down, and they feared that they had been handed over to the Northern politicians without the safeguards they wanted. Then he saw the representatives of the Senior Civil Servants' Association and discussed with them the new position of British officials, and what should be done about their contracts of service now that they were to be forced to retire. I noted

---

* *J. H. T. Wilson.* Sudan Political Service 1936–54. All his service was in the Provinces.

† *Selwyn Lloyd.* Minister of State, Foreign Office 1951–5. Foreign Secretary 1955–60. Speaker of House of Commons 1970–.

that this meeting went on for two and a half hours and 'we didn't really get very far'. He came twice to see me in my house about my own position, and said that the British Government wanted me to stay on a bit longer and not leave the Sudan so quickly. I was given many flattering reasons why I should delay my retirement and I replied with many reasons why I should not. I also told him that I was responsible to the Governor-General – not to H.M.G. – and if the Governor-General wanted to reopen this matter, it was up to him. I said that other people were concerned and had been told of their future appointments and I could not change if it meant their being done down. So he went off to consult H.E., and a day or two later said that he had discussed it all again and the programme I proposed had better go ahead. It was thought that my knowledge and influence, as a result of my long tenure of the Civil Secretary's office, might be a steadying factor in the next few months, which were bound to be difficult; but I was not at all sure, for many reasons, that this out-balanced the need for a change in the very different circumstances. I was confirmed in this belief about a year later when there were serious riots and some bloodshed in Khartoum on the occasion of General Neguib's visit for the state opening of the new parliament. To my astonishment, I heard on the wireless in British Guiana, where I then was, that the Egyptians accused me of instigating these disorders though I was 5,000 miles away and had not been in the Sudan for ten months. It seemed clear that after the long fight to prevent the Egyptians taking over the Sudan, with which I was personally identified, my presence during the transitional period might have made relations between the Sudan Government and the Egyptians more difficult.

Our last fortnight in Khartoum was an orgy of farewell parties given by Sudanese and British friends, and we were inundated by invitations which lack of time did not allow us to accept. There were also presentations from various bodies; the British in the Political Service subscribed to give us a wonderful silver tray with the crests of the provinces engraved on it, and the Sudanese administrative officials were equally generous with a set of nine silver ashtrays, each one having inset in it the badge of a province. Individual friends gave us keepsakes. We were given a farewell dinner at the Palace by the Governor-General, and on the evening that we took the train to Port Sudan the Sudanese members of the Executive Council gave us a large farewell cocktail party, and hundreds of people went on from it to the station at Khartoum North where the Sudan Defence Force Band played, ending up with 'Auld Lang Syne' as the train moved out. There were similar farewells at Ed Damer, Atbara and Port Sudan, and people seemed genuinely sorry to say 'good-bye'.

So ended more than thirty years in the Sudan which had been intensely interesting and worthwhile. About this time I wrote:

There have been immense changes in the Sudan during the eight years in which I have been Civil Secretary, and the country has had an exciting and wonderful history. My main memory of these years is the long Anglo-Egyptian dispute about the future of the country, and ever since 1946 this had been one of the main problems with which I have had to deal. The reactions of the Sudanese to these prolonged negotiations have also been a major factor and it has, I think, been one of the successes of these years that on the whole thay have been so peaceful and the Sudanese have shown their confidence in our direction of affairs: the country has remained remarkably quiet and we have got ahead with developments of all sorts. Perhaps one of the reasons for this was the success of the Legislative Assembly as an institution; for from difficult beginnings it gradually obtained a reputation and an assured place in the life of the community.

During these years we have had our labour troubles and the promulgation of much labour legislation. There has been some criticism of what was done, but my feeling is that we have had more success in our labour relations than many other African and Colonial territories and that, as a result of patience and determination, the labour problem is easing now, and there is a real hope of better relationships in future. The prosperity of these recent years; the work put in on development plans; the expansion of water supplies; the opening up of the South and the economic and educational expansion there; the consolidation of local government with the Marshall plan and the new Ordinance have all been little triumphs in themselves and together have meant an immense amount of hard work and real achievement.

Looking back on it all: realising the mistakes and the successes, my abiding memory will be the helpfulness and co-operation which I have received from all my colleagues, and especially the loyalty and backing given me by the Political Service. Anything that has been achieved has been due to this wonderful teamwork.

Looking back to over thirty years of service in the country, what stands out particularly is the friendliness and patience of the Sudanese: their toughness and their ability to stand up to the harsh climatic conditions: their cheerfulness in adversity and their underlying decency and common-sense. Without these characteristics among the ordinary people, our task would have been far less congenial.

When I left the Sudan, it was the thought of leaving the ordinary people that was saddest. It was probable that in the future I would meet many of the leaders again in London, or in the Sudan itself if we ever had the chance of revisiting it. But the policemen I had known and trekked about with in harsh circumstances and difficult country, the motor drivers, the servants, the gardeners and other workers, the village sheikhs and little shopkeepers – I was unlikely ever to meet any of them again. I could not help wondering how they would fare in the new self-governing regime, and whether the new Sudanese rulers would look after them as we had tried to do, and put the peoples' interests before their own.

Several years later I met a young Sudanese in one of the Sudan's embassies abroad and we talked about the past and what the British had tried to do in the Sudan. He said that whatever people might say about the Condominium Government, it had done four things for the Sudan. It had obtained for the country the right of self-determination, allowing it eventually to choose independence. A well-trained non-political civil service with high standards of duty and honesty had been established. The rule of law applied to everyone, however exalted, and politics did not interfere with it. Finally, it had prevented foreigners speculating in land and so preserved the country for the Sudanese. I thought that if this was what the new generation of Sudanese thought about us, it augured well for the future, and was a fine testimonial to our less than sixty years of rule in the Sudan.

It would be impossible for me to end this account of my time in the Sudan without referring to the support and encouragement which I was given in these last six years by the Governor-General, Sir Robert Howe. He came as successor to Sir Hubert Huddleston, a soldier who had long experience of the Middle East with administrative experience and a decisive mentality. Howe was a diplomat, with little experience of administration, and as a newcomer into a fairly closely-knit society he must sometimes have felt very much alone. I found him always accessible and interested in all that was happening. He learned Arabic, and made a practice of meeting and talking to Sudanese of every rank and class. He was hospitable and kindly, and entertained generously at the Palace. He travelled round the country and came to know a great deal about it and its people; and even in difficult times, when there was danger of demonstrations and disorder, he did not cut down his touring. He did not take as decisive a part in administration as Huddleston had done, and left things much more to the three Secretaries, so that I often felt after discussing a problem with him that he had not really told me what he thought should be done. As the hand-over became nearer, the Governor-General's position became more difficult and Sir Robert Howe rose to the situation. The following comments made at the time are very appropriate:

The handover had to come, and once the trickle started the flood-gates were bound to burst. If Howe had tried to hang on and delay matters there would almost certainly have been riots and possibly a lot of bloodshed. Goodwill on both sides would have been strained to breaking point, and the final handover tarnished with bitterness and enmity. As it was governors were seen off with guards of honour, and all the right courtesies and ceremonials were observed, with politicians of all persuasions maintaining the utmost friendliness all through the last two sad months. Howe must take a lot of credit for that and his training enabled him to hold the reins with the necessary velvet glove. His detachment was more apparent than real, despite his long leaves and his cold reception of much that one might have expected him to enthuse over.

It was largely because of Sir Robert Howe's success in making friends with Ismail el Azhari, the first Sudanese Prime Minister, that relations remained friendly and courteous: and El Azhari, who had always been in opposition and had not co-operated with the Government, was grateful for his friendly reception by the Governor-General, who put him at his ease and helped him as best he could.

The difficulties we experienced during these years of preparation for independence from the squabbling and dissension among the political parties and the individual politicians still seem to continue today, and the succession of coalition or military governments and lack of firm policies promoted by a major party under strong leadership has prevented the Sudan from making greater progress, and in my view has been one of the reasons why their Government was for so long unable to show decisive statesmanship in settling the Southern problem.

Lord Cromer's condominium constitution, enshrined in the 1899 Agreement with Egypt, solved the problem of the Sudan temporarily, though from the very beginning, as Sir Reginald Wingate* himself told me, there were troubles with the Egyptians, who did not willingly accept it. But it only worked as long as the British were in a situation to dominate Egypt. Once the Egyptians began to throw off British control in Egypt there were repercussions in the Sudan, and with the two different views of the Co-domini about the future of the Sudan – self-determination or incorporation in Egypt – the task of the Sudan Government was gradually made nore and more difficult. Perhaps it would have been better to allow the Egyptians a great share in the administration of the Sudan at an early date, but difference in ultimate aims would have made co-operation almost impossible. The administration

* *Sir Reginald Wingate.* Governor-General of the Sudan 1899–1916. British High Commissioner in Egypt 1916–19.

of Egypt itself, as we saw it right up to King Farouk's abdication, with the graft and corruption that was so obvious and the appalling differences between the pasha class and *fellahin*, made all of us who hoped for better things in the Sudan resist any proposals to allow the Egyptians a share in the administration. We advertised vacancies in the Sudan Civil Service conscientiously in Egypt, but no Egyptians were ready to join the Sudan Service on equal terms of entry at the bottom of the ladder. They could have joined and would have been accepted on Civil Service terms, but they wished to come in at the top of our cadres, and this was impossible without lessening the intake of Sudanese and prejudicing the prospects of British already in the junior ranks.

Reading the present-day comments on colonial rule, with their accusations of exploitation of the local inhabitants and the exaggerated stories of imperial oppression, it is far from easy to recognise such a picture in the Sudan as I knew it. The British administrators as a whole was imbued with a sense of service, knowing that we were there to administer the Sudan for the benefit of its peoples. We were adequately but not extravagantly paid – £40 a month for a new entry to the political service was not a big salary by any means even in 1922 – and the top Civil Service posts were also modestly remunerated. Economic exploitation is often alleged – 'the Sudanese grew cotton for Lancashire' is a frequent charge – but the independent Sudan still exports cotton, while the division of profits is only marginally altered since the early days, and the Gezira tenants are now little better off proportionately than they were before. When the British went to the Sudan after Kitchener's victory at Omdurman the country was in a sorry plight: poverty and indigenous oppression were everywhere, and starvation was not infrequent. Between 1898 and 1956 – in less than sixty years – it was developed into a modern state with all the government machinery and appurtenances of civilisation. Schools and a university; dispensaries, hospitals and a school of medicine; railway, steamer and airways systems; postal and telegraphic services; a new port on the Red Sea; vast areas of irrigated land; a system of local government apreading all over the country; a central parliamentary authority and a council of ministers – all had been created where nothing of this kind existed before. A system of law courts and a country-wide police force kept the peace, and where once it was unsafe to go far from home without armed protection it was now possible to travel anywhere in safety without arms or any protection. Sudan cities were as safe or safer than cities in the United Kingdom to walk about in at night. As one old man in Rufa'a said: 'These young men criticise the Government, but I can go out safely by day now and sleep in peace at night, whereas in the first thirty years of my life, I never

2. The Author and Lady Robertson outside the Governor's house at Wad Medani, *c.* 1940.

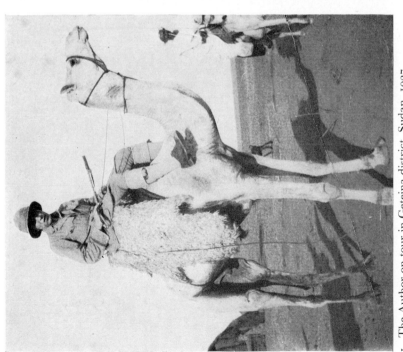

1. The Author on tour in Geteina district, Sudan, 1927.

Three of the Author's homes in the Sudan: 3. District Commissioner's house, El Nahud (1934–6); 4. Nile river steamer on which he lived when Jebel Aulia Commissioner (1936–7); 5. Khartoum, 1946–53.

6. The Author as Civil Secretary, 1950.

7. The Author (centre) and District Commissioner fording the Chell River, Bahr el Ghazal province. on the way from Aweil to Raga, 1951.

8. Crowds in front of, and on top of, the Secretariat building, Khartoum, at the ceremony to commemorate the Anglo-Egyptian agreement of 14 February 1953. Kitchener's statue in centre. Abdulla Bey Khalil is speaking; the Governor-General, Sir Robert Howe, is seated between him and the policeman; the Author is to left of the policeman with hands to face.

knew when I woke up in the morning if I would be alive in the evening.'

It was in building up these structures of civilisation that we were engaged, and it was to this aim that we gave our energies and our devotion. Was this a bad thing to do, as is alleged by our critics now? Was Virgil wrong in his definition of the colonial ideals – *pacisque imponere morem, parcere subjectis et debellare superbos?*

# PART THREE

# GOVERNOR-GENERAL
# OF NIGERIA

# CHAPTER X

# ON TO NIGERIA

## Via British Guiana

My wife and I got back to the U.K. from the Sudan at the beginning of May 1953, and I took about six months' holiday before beginning to look for something else to do. We had quite a task getting our house in order for permanent residence and there was the garden which was probably a little too big to cultivate on our own, and for which help was not easy to find. I had also people to see and was invited to give talks about the Sudan to a number of different bodies. The Foreign Office asked me to keep in touch with them in case they wished to consult me about Sudan matters, and I was invited to sit on a committee set up by the Foreign Office to help members of the Sudan service, who had been made redundant by the Anglo-Egyptian agreement, to find other employment. Geoffrey Hawkesworth,* who had been Governor of Kordofan, was later appointed to carry out the work and was most successful in finding suitable posts for the great majority. I was greatly pleased to be made a K.C.M.G. in the Birthday Honours and also to be appointed an Honorary Fellow of Balliol. Previous Civil Secretaries in the Sudan had been awarded the K.B.E., but I was the first to be awarded the K.C.M.G. as well. To be made an Honorary Fellow of Balliol was something I had never expected and it seemed to me a wonderful distinction. I could only suppose that the Dean, my old and close friend Alastair Rodger,† had been responsible for this mark of approval by my old College. As it turned out, these two appointments were announced in the same number of *The Times*, on 1 June 1953. I had never received the accolade for the K.B.E. which had been awarded on 1 January 1948, so when I attended an investiture at Buckingham Palace in July 1953, I was duly dubbed by Her Majesty and given the insignia of both these knighthoods at the same investiture. H.M. remarked that I looked like a Christmas tree.

By October I had begun to think that I had better try to get some further employment, so I let the Colonial Office know that I would be

---

* *Geoffrey Hawkesworth.* Sudan Political Service 1926–54. District service 1927–45. Deputy Governor and Governor Kordofan 1945–54. Re-employment Bureau London 1954–6. Chairman Federal Public Service Commission Nigeria 1958–63.

† *A. B. Rodger.* Fellow of Balliol 1924–61. Tutor in History. Dean 1933–52.

available if they had anything suitable for me and before long I was invited to call and see some of the senior officials. There was a vacancy in the East Africa High Commission – which supervised the common services in the three East African territories of Kenya, Uganda, Tanganyika – for someone to take control of Transport and Communications, and the suggestion was that I might consider that. However, I did not think that I had any real qualifications for railways and harbours, and I asked if I could see Oliver Lyttelton,* the Colonial Secretary, to explain why I wished to decline that office, and inform him about the sort of thing which would interest me – something more constitutional and political.

It happened that the British Government had suspended the constitution of British Guiana in October 1953, and this action had been the subject of considerable criticism and comment in the House of Commons and also of course in British Guiana itself, where the suspended ministers and their party were indignant at the return to direct colonial rule after the comparatively advanced form of representative government they had been given under the suspended constitution. This had been based on the report of a commission headed by Sir John Waddington in 1951, and gave elected Guyanese ministers a majority in the Executive Council. The elected ministers were all members of the People's Progressive Party under the leadership of Dr. Cheddi Jagan.† They had proved unwilling to accept the limitations imposed on their powers by the constitution, and had actively worked against the authority of the Governor as well as heading agitation against the Government of which they were members. After debates in the House of Commons, the Colonial Secretary announced that he was going to set up a commission with the following terms of reference: 'In the light of the circumstances which made it necessary to suspend the Constitution of British Guiana to consider and to recommend what changes are required in it.'

When I saw Oliver Lyttelton in November and told him that I was looking for employment but had turned down an offer which his staff had made, he asked me if I would be prepared to go as a member of the Commission to British Guiana. At that time he contemplated, I think, that a judge should chair the Commission, but he later changed his mind and invited me to be chairman, with Sir Donald Jackson,‡

* *Oliver Lyttelton*. Conservative M.P. and Colonial Secretary 1951–4. Subsequently Viscount Chandos.

† *Dr. Cheddi Jagan*. Guyanese of East Indian descent, Marxist. Leader of the People's Progressive Party 1953–7 and a minister in British Guiana Government of 1953, suspended by H.M.G. Dentist by profession.

‡ *Sir Donald Jackson*. Born in British Guiana 1892. Called to the Bar (Middle

Chief Justice of the Windward and Leeward Islands, and George Woodcock,* then Assistant Secretary of the Trades Union Congress, as members. I accepted, and the composition and terms of reference of the Commission were announced in the House of Commons on 2 December 1953. The report of the Commission (Cmnd. 9274 of September 1954) gives a full account of our work and recommendations, and I need not repeat what is detailed at considerable length in the report.

I found British Guiana a very interesting country and thoroughly enjoyed the two months which the Commission spent there. The people were friendly, and although we had difficulties at the start of our visit, as a result of the boycott of our Commission by the People's Progressive Party and the contention of a committee of right-wing citizens that our terms of reference were too restrictive, the size of the Commission too small and its members not sufficiently important, we managed to overcome them and got down to work quickly. We held a press conference three days after we arrived at Georgetown, and the next day I broadcast a general message explaining our plans and inviting anyone who wished to meet us to do so. We did not succeed in getting the People's Progressive Party to withdraw their boycott and so we never met the party's leaders; but a number of party members did come to see us, a few in secret, and we promised not to disclose their names.

To allow time for would-be witnesses to prepare to meet us or to write their memoranda, we spent a few days travelling round the country and were fortunate to see much of it and many of its people. My main impression was of the natural difficulty of the territory: most of the population lived on the strip of land ten miles wide along the sea coast where the original Dutch settlers had protected the fertile low-lying plains by a sea wall behind which lay the towns and cultivated lands producing mainly sugar cane and rice. Native housing seemed generally poor, consisting chiefly of wooden shacks and 'ranges', many in a dilapitated and miserable state, though the sugar firms had begun a big scheme of replacement on their estates. The population was mixed, mainly of East Indian and African origins. We thought that there were signs that the racial differences were beginning to

---

Temple) 1927 and practised in B.G. Chief Justice, Windward and Leeward Islands 1950-7. Speaker of Legislative Council B.G., 1957-9. Justice of Appeal, Federal Supreme Court of West Indies and British Caribbean Court of Appeal 1961-6. Chairman or member of many commissions and committees.

* *George Woodcock.* 1st-class Hons. P.P.E., Oxford 1933. Civil Servant 1934-6. Joined T.U.C. 1936. Assistant General Secretary 1947-60. General Secretary 1960-8. Privy Councillor 1967.

become a serious problem and that there was latent hostility, chiefly because those of African origin had progressed faster than the East Indians, and were monopolising posts in the civil service, the police and the junior white collar grades in trade and education. This division of the population, which originated from the import by the British of indentured labour from India after the liberation of the slaves, later became much more marked, but in 1954 opposition to colonial rule no doubt acted as a unifying force.

Behind the coastal plains lay the forest country, mainly unpopulated, but growing much fine timber and in places providing bauxite deposits, which were being mined at Mackenzie on the Demerara River and on the Berbice River up from New Amsterdam. Beyond the forest belt lay the Rupununi, an open savanna country, where there were a few cattle ranches, and small numbers of primitive Amerindian tribes, the remnants of the indigenous population. I thought that the greatest handicaps to the development of the country were its great rivers, the Pomaroon, Essequibo, Demerara, Berbice and Corentyne, with their broad estuaries and rapid currents. Bridging seemed out of the question except at vast expense, while in spite of their size they unfortunately provided no easy waterways into the interior, as they were obstructed by rapids and falls at varying distances inland. There were no roads joining the interior with the coast, and the forest tracks were hard and difficult. It was therefore impossible to move easily about the country, and communications could certainly not be improved without much capital investment. Even the wide Rupununi plains, though green and pleasant looking when we were there, did not provide good grazing, and cattle raising was not as profitable as it should have been. There was also the difficulty of getting the products down to the centres of population. An abattoir had been established at Letham, and when we flew from Letham back to Atkinson Field near Georgetown we shared the Dakota aircraft with a load of beef being exported to the coast. The falls at Kaieteur on the Potaro river are magnificent and certainly surpass expectations. Our amphibious aircraft landed above the falls on the river which is about 200 ft. wide and we walked down half a mile to see them. The top fall is almost 750 ft. and the lower one 82 ft., but they seem to be united to form one continuous fall, which plunges down and down into a narrow gorge. It is a magnificent and awe-inspiring sight, with the spray billowing up in fine clouds, and the view is enhanced by the marvellous trees and shrubs of the forest all around and along the sides of the gorge. When our Grumman 'Goose' took off again, we came straight down the river and appeared to become airborne just where the river left us and plunged over the precipice – rather a terrifying experience.

Georgetown, the capital, where we did most of our work, is on the sea coast, several feet below sea level, on the east bank of the Demerara river, which must be a mile broad at its mouth and which is navigable for fifty or sixty miles by ships of 5,000 or 6,000 tons exporting bauxite from Mackenzie. Georgetown has some fine broad streets laid out originally by the Dutch in the eighteenth century, but it also had sordid and miserable slum quarters, and the climate when we were there was humid and unpleasant – not unlike that of Lagos, where I was to be stationed later. The Chief Justice kindly allocated us his spacious and well-equipped court-room for our meetings and we began our hearing sessions on 18 January. We held these inquiries on twenty-eight days in Georgetown and on nine days at other places. Almost all were held in public, but a few people preferred to speak in private and we agreed to meet their wishes. Most of the witnesses had little to tell us. To emphasise their views publicly, 160 came forward out of the 220 who had presented memoranda, and in addition we saw eighty witnesses who had not presented written statements. We found considerable interest in the constitutional problems among all classes, and some of the documents sent to us were carefully and intelligently written, but the great majority of the witnesses seemed to me only to emphasise their widespread feeling of frustration at the conditions of life in the colony. Education and acquaintance with life in the U.S.A. and in the U.K. by men who had served in the forces during the war made them realise how poor and mean were conditions in British Guiana and led them to support almost any political solution which would give a promise or some hope of economic and cultural development. It was for this reason that the People's Progressive Party had obtained such a large following, and by the end of our inquiries my colleagues and I had come to the conclusion that in any general election the mass of the voters would support any party which promised radical improvement of living conditions in the country, however impossible fulfilment would be. It was not going to be easy to make radical changes for the better in a few years, and the natural difficulties of the terrain could obviously not be surmounted without immense expenditure of capital and a long, slow slog. The British connections which had lasted for over 150 years had done little to make the country prosperous, and without a great sustained effort on the part of Her Majesty's Government, the Colonial Government and the people generally, it seemed to me that the feelings of frustration and discontent were bound to continue and intensify. The greatest assistance that Britain had given British Guiana and other Carabbean territories in recent years had been the Commonwealth Sugar Agreement of 1951, which guaranteed the sale to the U.K. of about 75 per cent of Guiana's sugar production at a reasonable price, which could be reviewed from time to time to meet changes in costs. But this did not provide riches to the sugar companies or to the workers, though it stabilised a reasonable return, and there was still discontent on the sugar estates. This seemed to me partly due to a general assumption that 'from a bottomless source all things desirable should as of right be provided', and I had the impression of a lack of self-reliance and of little realisation that all must play a part in the advancement of the country. One would have liked to see a little enthusiasm for self-help and more personal initiative, though in truth it required more than any or all the local population could do to raise the level of material wellbeing as far as they would wish.

It also seemed to me that in comparison with the Sudan, the only backward territory that I had known well, British Guiana, with its tiny population of about 450,000 people and its small economic potential, tried to support too imposing a structure of government; Governor, Chief Secretary, Chief Justice, Financial Secretary and Directors of Departments all existed with junior staffs and in as considerable a style as we had had in the Sudan, which was twenty times bigger in every way. I thought this unfortunate and that the administration could have been cut down to fit the circumstances. In spite of this heavy top layer, administration seemed slow and inefficient, due partly to excessive centralisation but also to a lower standard in district officials than that to which I had been used in the Sudan and was afterwards to find in Nigeria. The District Commissioners appeared to have little initiative and drive, and to depend too much on instructions from H.Q. With the poor communications in much of the country, this was bound to lead to delays and misunderstandings, and the lack of discretion allowed to the district officers, when taken with the lower rates of salary in British Guiana compared with other colonies, led to good men seeking transfer to other more remunerative and less frustrating posts in other territories.

The great majority of our witnesses were simple people, obviously not well off and often living at a bare subsistence level. They were happy by nature, but felt that they should have better conditions of livelihood and had no idea how to achieve them. They were pathetically loyal to the British connections and to the Queen, but felt that the British Government should do more to help them. It was only a few months after the Coronation and one could see pictures of the Queen and the Coronation procession everywhere. One People's Progressive Party supporter who came to see us sported a wonderfully coloured tie depicting the Queen's coach and horses moving through the crowds and finally through a P.P.P. brooch at his collar. We got rather tired of hearing the same story from most of the witnesses, but having invited everyone to meet us and promised to hear them, we could not turn them away and spent many weary hours going over the same ground.

I was lucky in my colleagues on the Commission. Sir Donald Jackson was himself a Guyanese who knew almost everyone of any importance in British Guiana, which was of tremendous value. He was a wise, sensible, imperturbable man with a great sense of humour. Woodcock and he were keenly interested in cricket and soccer and followed the fortunes of their favourite teams devotedly with many an argument and discussion. George Woodcock's knowledge of trade unionism was of immense value to the Commission, as much of our inquiry concerned the rivalries in British Guiana of the two big unions on the sugar plantations, the Guyana Industrial Workers' Union and the Man Power Citizen's Association. Woodcock had a very alert and intelligent mind and took a leading part in questioning our witnesses and probing into the facts behind their evidence. I thought that on occasions he was a little hard on senior government officials and representatives of big business, and he sometimes obviously seemed to them to be unnecessarily critical of their actions and motives. This led such witnesses to be suspicious of the Commission, especially when we put to them unnecessarily generous interpretations of P.P.P. ministerial actions, just to see how they reacted to such versions. But in our discussions on the P.P.P. and in the assessments we finally came to about the Communist slant of some of the ministers, Woodcock found far less excuse for them than appeared likely from his examination of our governmental and commercial witnesses.

We were in Georgetown when the M.C.C. touring cricket team played a test match at Bourda Green, and were present when the famous 'bottles' incident took place there on 27 February. We were invited to the pavilion that day and sat through the afternoon watching the West Indians bat. Scoring was slow and there were one or two umpire's decisions which the crowd did not like, and the climax came when a local Guyanese hero – McWatt – was run out. As far as I could see from where we sat, there was no doubt at all that he was well out of his ground, but for the local crowd, already peeved by the previous decisions, and having been sitting for hours imbibing their rum and feeling bored, this was the last straw and a shower of bottles, cushions and some chairs rained on to the field. No one was hurt, police reinforcements arrived just in case, and order was soon restored. Some of the leading Guyanese on the pavilion roof with us apologised for the incident: 'This would never have happened before Jagan's Government had let law and order deteriorate – all the result of the Communist influence of Jagan', and so on. I am afraid I annoyed some of them by saying that it all seemed pretty harmless, and by asking if they had ever seen Celtic play the Rangers in Glasgow: 'There we don't throw bottles: we hit one another on the head with them.' I was thought to be taking their troubles far too flippantly.

After one of our trips to hear evidence, I was sitting on the pier at New Amsterdam waiting for the rowing boat to take me out to the amphibian when a very dark young Negro, dressed in a green shirt and khaki shorts, came up to me and asked if I was Sir James Robertson. When I said I was, he told me that his name was George Robertson and his grandfather had come from Scotland to work at Blairmont, and he wondered if we were cousins. I said that Robertson was a common name and that I couldn't claim this relationship, but at any rate we were fellow-clansmen. Another dark-skinned Robertson had given evidence before the Commission as representative of a sports club. I was given to understand that when the slaves were freed, many took the surname of their owners, and only a small percentage of those with English or Scottish names are actually descended from British ancestors.

After two months in British Guiana we thought we had heard and learned enough and that any further stay would be valueless. We decided to spend a couple of days in Trinidad to see how things worked there and to inquire from the Governor, Sir Hubert Rance,* and the Colonial Secretary, Maurice Dorman,† about the Trinidad constitution and their methods of dealing with problems similar to those of British Guiana. They were very helpful and the visit was useful and interesting, but of course Trinidad was rich compared with British Guiana and had much greater resources in its oil and asphalt. There was a mixed population in Trinidad too, though the East Indian element was not so big a proportion as in British Guiana. It seemed to me to be much more viable than British Guiana in every way, and has certainly been more stable and settled in its recent history. We then went to Barbados and stayed there for three weeks reading up our evidence and discussing how we should frame our report. We had useful discussions and found ourselves in complete agreement. I was happy about this, because we were a very diverse trio, with altogether different backgrounds. I, a Scotsman, had been a Sudan administrative and political officer, with considerable experience of a people who, like the Guyanese, were seeking self-government and independence. I had served out in the country districts and had experience both of the uneducated and illiter-

* *Sir Hubert Rance*. Major-General. Army service 1916–46. Governor of Burma 1946–8. Governor Trinidad and Tobago 1950–5.

† *Sir Maurice Dorman*. Colonial Service 1935–56, Tanganyika, Malta, Palestine, Gold Coast and Trinidad (Colonial Secretary). Governor Sierra Leone 1956–62. Governor-General Malta 1964–70.

ate but often wise country people, and of the townsfolk, who had some education and had been in touch with Western and liberal influence. Sir Donald Jackson, a West Indian, brought up and experienced in legal affairs, rather conservative and *laudator temporis acti*, was a Guyanese himself and knew far more about the actual conditions than did either Woodcock or myself, but perhaps he was therefore less inclined to consider rapid changes and the upset of the society and standards he had known. George Woodcock, an Englishman from Lancashire, was a left-wing radical who had left school at fourteen, worked in a factory and educated himself at night school till he obtained a scholarship to Oxford where his abilities had won him a first-class honours degree. He had been a civil servant and then a T.U.C. man. In spite of our varied experiences we thought alike on this problem, and had no difficulty in agreeing on what we wished to say, both about the past and about what we recommended for the future.

It seemed clear enough from all we had learned that the suspension of the constitution in 1953 had been inevitable, given the fact that the People's Progressive Party ministers had determinedly refused to play according to the rules of the game, which the British Government had developed in their past experience of the transition from direct colonial rule to responsible national government. This policy involved a gradual and orderly advance, with the devolution of more power to the local people step by step as they learned how to exercise it. The P.P.P. ministers were unwilling to progress gradually, were resentful of any of the checks and balances which were the essence of a limited constitution, and from the start refused to accept any curb on their power. They would not take advice from the *ex officio* members of the Executive Council and were insolent both to them and to the Governor himself. We were convinced that some of them, if not members of a Communist party, were actively influenced by Communist theory and doctrine. It seemed that until a party could evolve that was prepared to accept the thesis that, before full self-government was granted, some powers must be reserved for H.M.G. and some restrictions placed upon the elected representatives of the people, British Guiana could not make much constitutional progress. We saw little hope of such a party soon emerging in sufficient strength to win a general election in the country, for the ordinary people, dissatisfied with conditions and anxious for sweeping improvements, would vote in a new election for the P.P.P. once again, and we did not think that the party leaders, fortified by a new mandate, would accept and co-operate in any constitution short of full self-government on their own terms. So we came to the conclusion that so long as the P.P.P. retained its existing leadership and policies, there was no measure of partial self-government which could be restored at once without the certainty of renewed constitutional crisis, and went on to recommend a period of marking time in constitutional advance. We also gave our recommendation that energetic action should be taken to improve social and economic conditions in order to remove some of the frustrations and despair of the masses and thereby to make the people generally less susceptible to the empty promises and vague dreams of the P.P.P. leaders.

I quote here our main conclusions, as printed in our report:

We are satisfied that the setback to orderly constitutional progress in British Guiana was due not to defects in the Constitution but to the fact that those in control of the People's Progressive Party proved themselves to be relentless and unscrupulous in their determination to pervert the authority of Government to their own disruptive and undemocratic ends.

We are, therefore, drawn to the conclusion, that so long as the People's Progressive Party retains its present leadership and policies there is no way in which any real measure of responsible government can be restored without the certainty that the country will again be subjected to constitutional crisis.

We have no doubt that British Guiana with its precarious economy cannot afford another crisis of the kind that developed in 1953 and we can, therefore, see no alternative but to recommend a period of marking time in the advance towards self-government.

We cannot estimate the length of the period which should elapse before the advance towards self-government is resumed. Everything will depend upon the extent to which the people of British Guiana, including the leaders of the People's Progressive Party themselves, can be brought to the realisation that the futile and deliberately disruptive policies for which the People's Progressive Party at present stands are no basis for the future constitutional progress of their country.

Although we reached these conclusions at Barbados in our three weeks there, it took a considerable time to produce the final report. We each took sections of it to draft, and our secretary began to prepare other parts, all based on the outline of these conclusions. We then had numerous meetings in London – twenty-four in all, according to my diary – to go through the drafts and get the final wording to our liking. I finally presented the Report to the Permanent Under-Secretary, Sir Thomas Lloyd, at the Colonial Office on 3 September.

I look back on that visit to the West Indies and British Guiana with a great deal of pleasure. I gained much from it, and it opened a new hemisphere to me. Whether our Commission was at all useful to British Guiana, and to the future of its charming people, is hard to assess; but I suspect that the British Government was not sorry to have our unbiased approval of their suspension of the constitution, and that the present more placid and prosperous state of affairs in the independent state of Guiana may in a small degree be due to our conservative recommendations. I sincerely hope that we did something to help the people whom I got to like so well.

## Arrival in Nigeria

Following the work of the British Guiana Constitutional Commission I thought I was going to settle down to life at home. I did a certain amount of lecturing on the Sudan and British Guiana, wrote numerous testimonials for former Sudan officials, and also sat on final interview boards for the Civil Service Commission. When I left the Sudan in 1953 and had, as I thought, retired from government service, I was invited by General Buckley, the charman of the Uganda Company, to join its board of directors. I met General Buckley through Bill Gordon who had been billeted in our house in Khartoum during the war, and after retiring from the army had been appointed the company's general manager in Uganda. I agreed to join the board and, except for the years when I was in Nigeria, remained a director until the end of 1969. Shortly after joining the board I was most interested to have an opportunity to see its work in Uganda at first hand.

Towards the end of February 1955 I was asked by the Colonial Office if I would return to the Caribbean and prepare a scheme for the establishment of a civil service for the new Federation of the West Indies, which was about to be set up. I had been interested in the Caribbean during my work on the British Guiana Commission, and agreed. My appointment to this new post – it was a one-man commission – was announced in the House of Commons on 9 March, and I began my preparations, intending to leave about a month later. A secretary from the Trinidad Civil Service was appointed with whom I had some correspondence about our plans, and I arranged to meet him at Barbados about the middle of April. However, all this fell through after I was summoned to see Mr. Lennox-Boyd,* the Colonial Secretary, on 29 March. I thought he was going to talk about the task I had undertaken in the West Indies, and advise me about what was required. But this was not what he wanted at all, for he offered me the appointment of Governor-General of Nigeria. He said that Sir John

---

* *Lord Boyd of Merton.* Conservative politician who held various ministerial posts from 1938 onwards. Colonial Secretary 1954–9.

† *Sir John Macpherson.* Colonial Admin. Service 1921–55. Governor and Governor-General Nigeria 1948–55. Permanent Under-Secretary of State, Colonial Office 1956–9.

Macpherson† was retiring and I should be required to go out in June to take up the appointment for three years. This was a flattering if somewhat frightening offer and I asked if I could have a day or two to think it over and discuss it with my wife.

I suppose there was really no doubt that I would accept. Nigeria was the largest British colonial territory at that time and, once India and Pakistan were independent countries, the biggest and most important job that remained. I had had no experience of West Africa, and was ignorant about the general situation in Nigeria, but it was bound to be exciting and I was proud to have been offered it. I was fit and not worried about my health. My Sudan experience and knowledge of Arabic would help me in my dealing with the Northern Muslim people; and I hoped that the fact that I had started at the bottom as an Assistant District Commissioner in the Sudan would perhaps make me, although an outsider, more acceptable to the members of the Nigerian administrative service than someone who had been brought in from politics or some occupation unconnected with colonial administration. I met my wife that afternoon in Regent Street outside Garrards, where we had a date, and she said 'What did he want?' When I told her that he wanted me to go to Nigeria as Governor-General, our immediate reaction was 'Let's go and have a drink!' This was not easy at 3 p.m., so we went to Paddington and took the train home. Of course, after a day or two I wrote to Mr. Lennox-Boyd and said I was ready to go to Nigeria. The appointment was announced on 9 April on the B.B.C., but the national newspapers were on strike, so it was some time before many of my friends heard of it. But I was almost immediately involved with the Colonial Office, being briefed on the situation in Nigeria, meeting people who would be able to help me, and others who hoped that as Governor-General I should be able to help them. I was advised that I had better go to Nigeria by sea, as I should be able to get some idea of the general atmosphere by meeting people on the ship, so I agreed to do this and arranged to sail on the liner *Aureol* on 2 June from Liverpool.

I met leading Nigerians who happened to be in London and we were given a slap-up dinner at the Hyde Park Hotel by Chief Michael Okorodudu, the representative in Britain of the Western Regional Government. Chief Okorodudu, in his speech proposing our health, told us how there had been many conflicting rumours as to who would be the new Governor-General: X was suggested, and Y, and it was thought that Z was a possibility, 'but in the end, a rank outsider won'! Barclays Bank D.C.O., Shell, the Boy Scouts, St. John Ambulance, the British Council, the British Bank of West Africa, the Church Missionary Society, the Colonial Development Corporation – all wanted to give me luncheons, and of course I had to see all the various sections of the Colonial Office. Each departmental head impressed on me the vital importance of the side of the work with which he was concerned. I met Nigerian students, British commercials and all sorts of people with Nigerian contacts. Finally my wife and I went for a week's holiday in Cornwall, where we had good weather and explored a part of England we had never visited before.

As was customary, I had to go to Buckingham Palace to see the Queen, and kiss hands. Her Majesty told me that she wanted to visit Nigeria but that there were some difficulties. It was not clear to Her Majesty's advisers whether the various governments in Nigeria would welcome a visit and, if they did, whether she could go to Nigeria without also going to the Gold Coast, where the political situation was thought to be too unstable to permit a visit. I made it my first duty when I got to Nigeria to go into the feasibility of a royal visit.

When I undertook the Nigerian assignment, the Colonial Secretary gave me no precise instructions about the policy I was to carry out. It was clear that Nigeria was on the road to independence, but no date had then been set, and I was not led to think that the day would come before I had completed the three years for which I was appointed. It was left to me to interpret policy from past correspondence and from my assessment of the situation as it developed following my arrival in Nigeria. It was obvious that I should continue to make preparations for independence, and especially to work for the unification of the country as best I could. Naturally I read as many files as possible in the Colonial Office as well as a number of books on Nigeria. It seemed a much more complicated country than the Sudan, and if its area was smaller, the population was at least four times greater.

During 1953 and 1954 there had been conferences on the constitutional future of the country, as a result of which the federal character of Nigeria had been strengthened. The three main regions of the country – North, East and West – had their separate areas of power enlarged. A number of specified subjects were made federal or concurrent responsibilities, but all residual matters were to be under regional authority. To encourage national awareness, there was to be a federal legislative body directly elected by the whole country, rather than through the regional assemblies. Half the total seats were to be filled by representatives of the north, and half by men from the southern regions of the country. Each of the regions would be under a British governor, but effective authority was largely devolved on the Nigerian regional premiers and their ministers. On the Central Executive, chaired by the Governor-General, there were three *ex officio* members, but the remain-

G

ing ten were Nigerians, three from each region and one from the Southern Cameroons.

The country's civil service was split up, with each region having its own independent service separate from that of the Federal Government. The judiciary was similarly divided along regional lines under a Federal Supreme Court, which had the power to hear appeals from the high courts of the regions and of Lagos. After some resistance from the Western Region representatives it was finally decided that Lagos would be made a federal enclave, like Canberra and Washington D.C. While the Regions provided many of the local services, the principal collector of revenue was the Federal Government and under the 1953 arrangements the money was to be divided among the regions in proportion to the contributions made. This federal structure was due for review by 1956, and at the same time it had been agreed that any of the regions could then request full internal self-government in all matters for which they were responsible.

It was clear to me that the main problem, even at that early stage, was the difficulty of getting the North and the South to work together, and from what I read this appeared to apply just as much to the British officials in the two parts of the country as to the Africans. I saw an extract from a Colonial Office pronouncement of November 1954 which said: 'It remains H.M.G.'s firm policy to preserve the unity of Nigeria in the interests of all her peoples. At this critical juncture it is more than ever necessary that all British officials in the North and especially those in positions of authority or influence, should do all in their power to discourage separatist or secessional tendencies amongst the Northern Nigerians.' I was to learn much more about this problem when I reached Nigeria.

My wife could not come out at this time, so I set off on the *Aureol* for Lagos by myself and had an uneventful passage out. I met numbers of Africans and Europeans on board. I gave a few small drinks parties for Nigerians and expatriates, and everyone was very friendly and easy to get on with. There were few people on board from the North, for with the direct air service from Kano to Europe it was now much easier for Northern officials and their families to travel by air, and this of course prevented the British from the two parts of the country meeting as much as they had done previously. We called at Bathurst, Freetown and Takoradi, and I was greeted at all these places by senior officials who made me feel welcome. At Takoradi, Mr. Phelps,* an official from the Secretariat at Lagos, joined the ship to help me with the speech

---

* *A. J. Phelps.* Colonial Administrative Service, Chief Secretary's Office Lagos 1955. Later in Ministry of Finance and on retirement from Nigeria appointed to the British Treasury. Under-Secretary 1972.

which I had to make after being sworn in as Governor-General on arrival at Lagos.

We reached Lagos Harbour at mid-day on 15 June and I disembarked immediately, took the salute from a guard of honour, and crossed the harbour to Government House in a launch. There a reception had been arranged for about fifty people including the three Regional Premiers, Dr. Azikiwe,* Chief Awolowo,† and the Sardauna Al Hadji Ahmadu Bello;‡ the Federal Ministers and senior officials, both British and Nigerian, as well as the Sultan of Sokoto, the most senior of the Northern Chiefs. After photographs they dispersed and I had lunch with Sir Hugo and Lady Marshall.§ Sir Hugo had been Acting Governor-General since Sir John Macpherson had left two months before. He was himself about to retire after long service in Nigeria, which had ended by his being Lieutenant-Governor Western Nigeria and then for some months Chief Secretary of the Federation. I learned much from him and Lady Marshall during the six weeks before they left on final leave.

The same afternoon I had to don my new Governor-General's uniform for the first time, complete with medals, and to drive in state with my A.D.C. to the Supreme Court where, after inspecting a guard of honour, I was sworn in as Governor-General by Mr. Justice Jibowa,¶ the acting Chief Justice of the Federal Supreme Court. This was apparently the first time that the oath had been administered by a Nigerian judge on such an occasion, and it was taken as an omen of rapid Nigerianisation to come. Some remarks that I made in my address about the role of Governor-General vis-à-vis his ministers were well received, especially when I said that I saw my duty as that of adviser and guide to my ministers, who would be mainly responsible

* *Dr. Nnamdi Azikiwe.* Born 1904 – Ibo tribe. Educated Nigeria and U.S.A. Journalist, newspaper owner and politician 1934–53. Founded N.C.N.C. party 1944. Minister, Eastern Nigeria and Premier 1954–9. President Federal Senate 1959–60. Governor-General 1960–3. President of Federation 1963–6.

† *Chief Awolowo.* Born 1909 – Yoruba. Barrister 1946. Founder and leader of Action Group party. Premier Western Region 1954–9. Leader of Federal Opposition 1959–62. Imprisoned for alleged attempted plot 1962. Commissioner for Finance 1969–71.

‡ *Sardauna Al Hadji Ahmadu Bello.* Member of royal family of Sokoto. District head at Raba and Gusau. Member of Northern Region legislature 1952–66. Minister of Works and later of Local Government. Premier Northern Region 1955–66. Assassinated 1966.

§ *Sir Hugo Marshall.* Colonial Administrative Service in Nigeria 1928–55. Lieut.-Governor Western Nigeria 1952–4. Chief Secretary, Federation of Nigeria 1954–5.

¶ *Mr. Justice Jibowa.* Nigerian barrister from Western Region. Member Supreme Court and Acting Chief Justice 1955. Chief Justice Western Region 1957–60. Died 1960.

for the formulation of policies. I called for mutual respect and trust between the ministers and their expatriate civil servants, and emphasised that this was a two-way attitude requiring give and take on both sides. It all appeared to go down well, and the local press next morning was complimentary. The day ended with a formal dinner party at Government House for the ministers and high officials.

Once I had settled in I made it my first aim to get around the country to obtain a rapid view of it as a whole and to meet as many people as I could. Sir John Rankine,* Governor of the Western Region, was due to go on leave quite soon after I reached Nigeria, so I paid a preliminary visit to Ibadan shortly after my arrival and met most of the leaders of the Western Regional Government. Chief Awolowo, the Premier, presided at a big reception for me at which he spoke well. I had met him previously in Khartoum when he had visited the Sudan on his way to India some years before, and as I had given a luncheon party for him in my house there, I had got to know him a little. He returned the compliment by giving me lunch at Ibadan in his house, and afterwards I had an interesting talk with him and his ministers. We discussed the next constitutional conference, and most of the points which they wished to make sounded reasonable. The ministers all expressed delight at the idea of a royal visit. At Ibadan I also visited the University College which was a federal institution and was shown round by Dr. Alexander, then Vice-Principal. The College was on holiday and the Principal in England, but I was given information about its progress, and ideas for the address which as Visitor I should have to make to the Congregation on Founder's Day. I saw the unfinished teaching hospital on which the Federal Government was spending some £5 million.

Early in July I set off on a two-week tour of the other Regions. I went by train from Lagos to Kaduna, the capital of the North, where I stayed with the Governor, Sir Bryan Sharwood-Smith,† and met the Northern ministers and leading officers of the Northern Government. The Premier, the Sardauna of Sokoto, welcomed me to a meeting of the Executive Council, during which we had a general discussion about federal and regional matters. I was left in no doubt that they were in no great hurry for independence and that they preferred to delay until they had more educated Northerners for their civil service so that

---

* *Sir John Rankine.* Colonial Administrative Service 1931–66. Served in Uganda, Fiji and Barbados. Chief Secretary Kenya 1947–51. Resident Zanzibar 1953–4. Governor Western Region Nigeria 1954–60.

† *Sir Bryan Sharwood-Smith.* Colonial Administrative Service 1920–57. Served in Cameroons and Northern Nigeria 1920–52. Lieut.-Governor Northern Nigeria 1952–4. Governor 1954–7.

they would not be so dependent on Southern staff. The Sardauna said that they would far rather retain expatriate officers than have to accept an influx of Ibos or other Southerners. They did not want the Federal Government to be too powerful, and would prefer to see some sort of agency on the lines of the East Africa High Commission rather than a federal authority with overriding powers. The Executive Council welcomed and seemed genuinely delighted at the idea of a visit by the Queen and the Duke of Edinburgh.

While in the North I also visited Zaria and Kano before flying to Sokoto to meet the Sultan who, as Seriki Muslimin, was head of the Muslims in the North. He struck me as a wise and sensible man, perhaps a little jealous of his young cousin the Sardauna who, as Premier, now wielded so much power. I next went to Maiduguri to meet the Shehu of Bornu, one of the most important emirs in the North. Maiduguri was a pleasant place, with fine woods of neem trees. The Shehu was very elderly and rather deaf, but he obviously had great prestige among his people. When I paid my official call on him, gaily caparisoned horses and camels appeared with their riders wearing shirts of mail, wonderful turbans and bright clothes, while some were clad in the Mahdist *jibba* – patched shirt – once the uniform of the Khalifa's armies in the Sudan. The Kanuri leaders whom I met seemed able and intelligent, and it was here that I first encountered Shettima Kashim,* then the Waziri of Bornu, who later as Sir Ibrahim Kashim became Governor of the Northern Region after Sir Gawain Bell left Nigeria in 1962. After Maiduguri we flew to Jos on the Northern plateau, the centre of the tin-mining area, to which I was to pay frequent visits during my time in Nigeria, and then on by train to Makurdi on the Benue, the provincial town of the Tiv country.

I was struck by the similarity between the Northern provinces adjoining the Sahara and the central Sudan. There were the same long parched vistas I remembered from Kordofan and Darfur, with baobab trees in plenty. The country was thickly populated, especially around Kano, and the people were very similar to the Sudanese. Though Muslims, their Arabic was confined to a knowledge of the Koran and I did not find that they had much more comprehension of my Sudanese colloquial Arabic than I had of their Hausa dialect.

I went directly from the North to the Eastern Region, beginning my

---

* *Shettima Kashim Ibrahim, Alhaji.* Minister of Social Services, Central Government 1952. Regional Minister Social Development 1955. Waziri of Bornu 1955. Chairman Nigerian College of Art and Science and Technology 1957–62. Governor Northern Nigeria 1962–6.

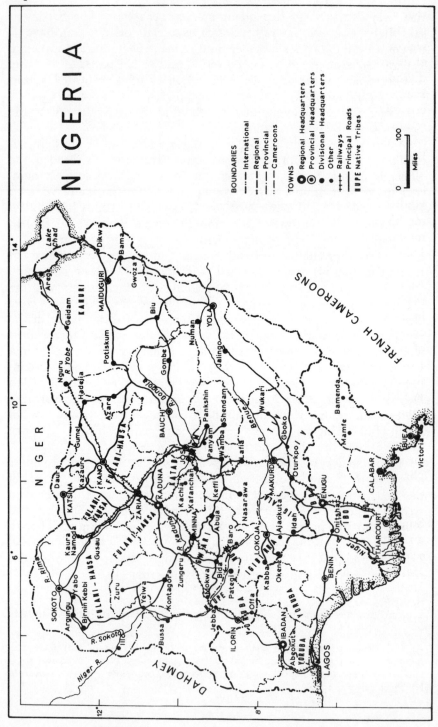

tour at Enugu, the capital. There I met the Governor Sir Clem Pleass,* the Premier Dr. Azikiwe, and the Executive Council. They warmly welcomed the proposal of the royal visit, but had a number of points of difference with the Federal Government and complained about the division of revenue between the federation and the regions. They seemed keener on maintaining the unity of Nigeria than the Northern or Western ministers, and I received the impression that they would wish to retain or even increase federal authority at the next constitutional conference. They did not want to increase the number of states in the South, unless the vast Northern region was also divided. They told me about the search for oil, and the revolution in financial circumstances for the East if exploitable quantities were found. Dr. Azikiwe very kindly gave a cocktail party for me at his house that evening, and showed me his excellent library of which he seemed very proud. There were many books in it about local government and administration which I should have enjoyed reading.

Next morning I went on by train, and after calling at Umuahia and Aba, where I met officials and notables on the station platforms, we reached Port Harcourt in the afternoon in a storm of rain. I had to inspect a guard of honour at the station and went on through damp crowds in pouring rain to the Roxy Hall where I was greeted by parades of Boy Scouts and Girl Guides, and by the time I had inspected them I was just as soaked as they were. Then, in the Hall, there were speeches, singing and introductions to the leading citizens of Port Harcourt. We had a large dinner party that evening, and next day I was shown round the town and the port and had the various problems of town planning and port expansion explained to me. After a lunch for administrative officers I took the afternoon off and had a game of golf on the Port Harcourt course, which I always thought was the best in Nigeria. But in the evening I was on the job again with a visit to the sports club, and a dinner party at the Residency for leading personalities.

Calabar was the next stop, a journey of about forty minutes by air. Some four or five thousand schoolchildren lined the route from the airfield to the Residency and very nice they looked in their various school uniforms. There the usual programme: a reception at the Council Hall, a luncheon party for local notables, a visit to the Hope Waddell Institute (a secondary school which, being run by the Church of Scotland, interested me), a drinks party followed by a dinner party, and after that a visit to the club where there was a dance. Next morning I was taken into the country to see rubber estates and visited a palm oil plantation and factory, returning in time to call at the Calabar Africa

* Sir Clem Pleass. Colonial Administrative Service, Nigeria 1924-56. Lieut.-Governor Eastern Region 1952-4. Governor 1954-6.

Club where there were speeches and dances, and then back to the Residency to give lunch to the Nigerian and expatriate administrative officers. In the afternoon I flew on to Tiko in the Southern Cameroons, and after the usual guard of honour and meeting with ministers, motored up to Buea, the capital of the Southern Cameroons.

The Cameroons had been German territory until the 1914-18 war, when it was occupied by British and French forces. It was then divided, and about two-thirds became French mandated territory and the remainder British. The British part was administered by Nigeria, the Northern section as an integral part of Northern Nigeria, while the southern section by 1955 had become a separate region with a Commissioner and an Executive Council. As Governor-General of Nigeria I was the High Commissioner, and was responsible for the government of the British Cameroons, through the British Government, to the United Nations. The Southern part was economically more developed than the North, with a considerable area of banana and palm oil plantations, and seemed the more important of the two sections. I made many visits to the South, but only went twice to the Northern section. The Southern Cameroons seemed a most interesting territory with its varied and beautiful scenery and lush vegetation. The great mass of the Cameroon Mountain, still an active volcano, towered nearly 14,000 feet over the plains between Victoria and Kumba, and further north the Bamenda plateau was a delightful part of the country, though its communications were still poor.

On this first visit I could not go far afield and from Buea visited only Victoria and Bota to see the headquarters of the Development Corporation and some of its activities. The Schloss where the Commissioner lived was built in the 1890s by a German governor of the Cameroons: it is quite different in its architecture from the British colonial style, looking rather like one of the castles on the Rhine. Sited 3,000 feet up the slopes of the mountain, it has magnificent views, and with the fertile volcanic soil is surrounded by beautiful trees and gardens, plentifully watered by the heavy rainfall enjoyed by the Cameroons. I had a meeting with the Commissioner, Brigadier Gibbons,* and his Executive Council, and visited the House of Assembly to address its members. We had long, interesting talks about the country and its problems and I got to know some of the leaders, Messrs. Endely, Muna and Mbile. They were thrilled at the idea of a visit by the Queen, though in the event they all had to come to Lagos to meet her, as the Cameroons airport at Tiko was not considered very safe.

* *Brigadier E. J. Gibbons.* Colonial Administrative Service 1929–56. Seconded to Army 1941–6. Eastern Provinces, Nigeria 1948. Commissioner for Cameroons 1949–56.

I flew back to Lagos on 21 July and settled down for a week or two to do some work and to sort out my impressions of Nigeria. This tour was perhaps too concentrated and too brief to allow me to come to any real conclusions, but I had certainly obtained impressions of the size and variety of the country and of the major problems which faced it. My private secretary calculated that we had travelled 2,040 miles by air, 1,220 by rail and nearly 1,000 by car, and that I had spoken personally to, and shaken hands with, over 3,000 people, all in seventeen days – so it all took some sorting out. One thing I had ascertained was that the Regional Governments, like the Federal Government, received the proposal for the Queen's visit with considerable enthusiasm, and I was assured that the visit would be popular in Nigeria. There was still the difficulty about the Gold Coast, and I thought that the best way to find out about that was to discuss it with the Governor. So I invited Sir Charles Arden-Clarke* to Lagos. He still thought the political situation in the Gold Coast too unsettled for a Royal visit there, but agreed with me that there was no reason why Nigeria should not be visited separately, and I undertook to inform the Colonial Secretary of this view.

Although my tour round the country had been brief, it had made me realise the need for swift action, especially on the relations between North and South. The Federal Constitution, introduced in September 1954, did not seem to be working smoothly and difficulties involving the Federal and Regional Governments had already occurred.

Throughout the country as a whole tribalism remained strong, although in secondary schools and colleges, as well as in the Federal and Regional Assemblies, people of different origins mixed without ill-feeling. The political parties themselves represented the largest tribal groups in the three Regions; the Northern People's Congress was Fulani–Hausa dominated, the N.C.N.C. in the East mainly Ibo, while in the West the Action Group was predominantly Yoruba. There were instances of members of other tribes playing an important part in the parties, such as Kola Balogun, a Yoruba from Oshogbo, in the N.C.N.C., but in general tribal loyalties appeared paramount. There seemed to be no strong ideological differences in the policies of the parties; perhaps the N.C.N.C. under Dr. Azikiwe's leadership was a little more left-wing than the Action Group – one of my N.C.N.C. Federal Ministers told me that the Action Group was a fascist organisation – while the Northern People's Congress was clearly more conservative than the

* *Sir Charles Arden-Clarke*. Colonial Service. Governor Sarawak 1949–53. Governor Gold Coast (Ghana) 1953–7.

other two parties. However, the only interest of all three seemed to be that of maintaining their power in their own tribal areas and thereafter spreading their influence into other regions. It was natural that the opposition to the Ibo-dominated Government in the Eastern Region should ally itself with the Action Group, and that the two opposition parties in the North should support the N.C.N.C. and the Action Group respectively. During my first few months in Nigeria the chief difficulties were in the Western Region where the Action Group Government was taking strong measures against the Alafin of Oyo, a leading Yoruba chief, who had shown sympathy with the N.C.N.C. in the recent Federal Elections. The Action Group had won the earlier Regional Election, and had a considerable majority in the Regional House of Assembly, but in the Federal Election for the House of Representatives, held some months later, the N.C.N.C. had obtained a majority in the West and under the constitution the three Western ministers in the Federal Council of Ministers had to come from the party from that Region which had the most seats in the House of Representatives.

My first council was therefore composed of six N.C.N.C. ministers, three N.P.C., one Cameroonian and the three expatriate officials, but had no Action Group representatives. One of the Federal ministers, Adelabu,* a Yoruba, who lived in Ibadan but supported the N.C.N.C., was also bitterly disliked by the Action Group, and this involved the Federal Council of Ministers in the regional squabbling. The leader of the N.C.N.C. in the Federal Council of Ministers was Dr. Mbadiwe,† and I tried to persuade him and Adelabu that Federal ministers should be more careful in their dealing with the regions. Clearly, as politicians, they could not get away altogether from their party responsibilities and allegiances but they should be reasonably moderate in their language, should maintain the dignity of the Council of Ministers and should not give the opposing political parties the opportunity of showing them up in a bad light. By accepting office in the Council of Ministers, I told them, they had agreed to refrain from the grosser forms of party antagonism, and they should remember that hatred of them was bound to lead to hatred of the Federal Government of which they were members, and this would not benefit the unity of Nigeria in which they professed to believe. I do not think that my lecture did much good, but we survived these troubles partly, I believe, because Dr. Azikiwe, leader of the N.C.N.C., exercised a sensible moderating influence.

The main weakness of the Federal Government was that none of

---

* *Adelabu* – a Yoruba from Ibadan, outspoken and tactless. Federal Minister. Killed in motor accident 1956.

† *Dr. Kingsley Mbadiwe* – Ibo. Minister in Federal Government, 1955–66. Led N.C.N.C. party in Federal House of Representatives. Educated U.S.A.

the political party leaders was himself a member of the House of Representatives. They preferred to remain in the Regions as the heads of the Regional Governments. This meant that in the Federal House of Representatives the parties were led by the second strings, and they had to accept political rulings and dictation from the heads of their parties in the Regional capitals. This led to indecisiveness and in many cases to failure in co-operation. On one occasion later on, when I went to Kaduna and the Premier of the North came to call on me, I asked him, after the usual polite salutations, if there were any matters he would like to talk over with me, and got the cold answer that he was fed up with the Federal Government and did not wish to discuss anything. Eventually I discovered from him that the Federal Government had refused to allot him a number of police outrider motor-cyclists as a permanent escort, and that he was sulking. He used later to ask me how his 'lieutenant' – the Prime Minister – was managing.

My main channel for influencing the regions – and, as I hoped, advancing the federal cause – was through the Regional governors. In theory their responsibility for regional matters should not have impinged much on mine for Federal affairs, but in practice the problems of the Federation were such that we came into contact a great deal. Sir Bryan Sharwood-Smith in the North had served for many years in that region and had absorbed much of the Northern attitude; but he combined this with a realisation of the need to hold Nigeria together, and he had a difficult job persuading the Northern politicians from being too parochial and unresponsive to the need for unity. He and I kept closely in touch and he was meticulously conscientious in ringing me up and informing me of what was happening in the North.

Sir Clem Pleass, Governor of the Eastern Region, had also been many years in Nigeria. He had a difficult time with his Premier, Dr. Azikiwe, who was primarily a nationalist and in speeches and writings had taken the lead in pressing for the speedy end to colonial rule. Azikiwe had been educated in the U.S.A. and had a good mind and a retentive memory. He was interested in athletics and boxing, and often surprised me by his knowledge of records and record-holders. At the same time he seemed an odd, variable character, with great charm on occasions, but on others difficult and unpredictable. Pleass found it far from easy to follow his changing moods.

In the West matters were no easier for Sir John Rankine. His Yoruba Premier, Chief Awolowo, was a lawyer who had been called to the Bar in London, and was a man of great energy and ambition. He was seldom ready to be advised by the Governor or to recognise the limitations on a Regional government under a Federal constitution;

with the result that there was considerable friction between the Regional and Federal ministers, which involved Sir John and myself.

At the Federal level, one of my main responsibilities was that of presiding over the Council of Ministers. The Council at this stage was composed of three expatriate officials, the Chief Secretary, the Financial Secretary and the Attorney-General (the Secretary was also a British official) and the Nigerian ministers. It was not until two years later in August 1957 that the officials disappeared and their places were taken by a Prime Minister and a Minister of Finance. To begin with, therefore, the set-up was very similar to that which I had known in the Sudan where, as Acting Governor-General, I had presided on many occasions over the Executive Council, and the level of discussion was very similar. After the Council of Ministers became all Nigerian, it was easier to manage: the expatriate officials sometimes seemed to rub the Nigerians up the wrong way and we had more acrimony in our discussions in the early days than later when I was the only non-Nigerian present. I think this was because I never pressed a point on which my Nigerian ministers disagreed with me, unless the matter at issue was of real importance, whereas sometimes expatriate officials would continue to argue their ideas in the face of ministerial opposition, even though the question was of no great moment.

I was also involved in meetings of the Privy Council. This body, consisting of the Chief Secretary, the Attorney-General and four Nigerians (two ministers and two senior officials) met from time to time to advise the Governor-General whether, in cases of a murderer being condemned to death, he, on behalf of the Queen, should confirm the sentence or commute it to life imprisonment. In the Sudan we had had a different system: the Chief Justice there advised the Governor-General directly in writing and it seemed to me that this was a simpler and better method than having to get the advice of a Privy Council. If I disagreed with the Chief Justice in the Sudan, on the occasions when I was acting, I could talk it over with him and then make a decision. If I disagreed with the Privy Council, I had to report the matter to the Secretary of State. I also found that the Nigerian members of the Privy Council were much less inclined to show clemency than I would have been in cases where, for instance, there had obviously been provocation or other extenuating circumstances, and I sometimes had to argue strenuously to get their agreement to commutation.

The civil service was another subject in which I quickly involved myself. From my early inquiries and reading of the files it seemed to me that, for a country so far advanced politically towards self-government and independence, there were far fewer Nigerians in senior posts in the civil service, the police and the army than there should have been, and that the Sudan had gone much faster ahead in African-isation than Nigeria. One of the first important minutes I sent out after my arrival was to the Inspector-General of Police asking him to let me have proposals for a rapid expansion of the Nigerian senior officer strength and for the development of more officer-training facilities. Some steps forward had been taken in the army where General Whistler* (who had been our commander-in-chief in the Sudan, before coming to West Africa) had started an officers' training school at Teshie near Accra, but the number of Nigerian officers who had passed out and taken the subsequent training courses in the U.K. was very small. It was difficult to get the army moving, as the R.W.A.F.F. was still under War Office control, but I had conversations with Major-General Inglis† who commanded in Nigeria, and with Lieutenant-General Herbert,‡ G.O.C. West Africa, and considerable progress was soon made. The situation in the civil administration was not dissimilar, but, as the civil service had now been divided up among the Regions and the Federation, I had responsibility only for the Federal section. I tried to impress on the Public Service Commission that it was impera-tive to push on the capable Nigerians and get them into the higher segments of the service as soon as they could do the work and take responsibilities, and that risks would have to be taken. There seemed to be little realisation in many quarters in Nigeria that independence was not far away and that an independent Nigeria would demand that its civil service and security forces should be predominately Nigerian in composition.

Furthermore the division of the civil service between the Federal Government and the Regions had not been completed, and one of my first tasks was to get this job finished. It was not difficult because, although the service had originally been unitary in theory, most officers had in fact been confined during their service to one area, chiefly because of language difficulties. It would have been folly to send an Ibo- or a Yoruba-speaking officer to an area where only Hausa was spoken or vice versa, and so in most cases there was no difficulty in assigning officers to the Regions. It was not so easy in the case of secretariat officers, but again local knowledge was important. During the next few years some misfits became apparent, and in some cases Regional Governments demanded the transfers of a few officers who

---

* *General Sir Lashmer Whistler. Kaid el Amm* (G.O.C.) Sudan 1947–9. Had com-manded 3rd Div. from Normandy till end of the war. C.-in-C. West Africa 1951–3. Col.-Commandant R.W.A.F.F. and Hon. Col. Nigerian Forces 1959–62.

† *Major-General G. H. Inglis.* G.O.C. Nigeria District 1953–6.

‡ *Lieut.-General Sir Otway Herbert.* G.O.C. British troops in Berbin 1947–9. Home Commands 1949–53. G.O.C.-in-C. West Africa 1953–6.

had become unpopular with their ministers; I was usually able to find places for them in the Federal service, which in October 1955 was 662 under an approved strength of 2,443.

I also found that the carefully scheduled division of Federal and Regional functions of government enshrined in the constitution were not apparently understood by some of the ministers and their officials. Federal departments seemed to consider that they still had authority to dictate on Regional matters as they had done in the past, when the Lagos Government ruled the whole country. Some of the correspondence, which I read in files that came to me, between Federal and Regional ministries was far too stormy and bitter and did not make for friendly co-operation. I also found that Regional ministers and civil servants took it upon themselves to act in matters which by the new constitution were entirely Federal. The Sardauna's trips to the Middle East and his excursions into international affairs in Egypt and Saudi Arabia were trespasses on the Federal Government's authority in foreign affairs. The boycott of Israeli Boy Scouts at Kano and elsewhere in the North, as they went through on an organised visit to the Eastern Region, showed one facet of the problem of North–South relationships.

There were other difficulties in the working of the constitution. The police and the army were Federal bodies and under the ultimate authority of the Governor-General, but the Regional Governments could not be excluded from all dealings with them; the West in particular was keen to have some control over the forces. From the beginning I acted on the compromise that the Regional Governors were my local representatives in these matters, and the local commissioners of police and local battalion commanders would work in the Regions under the delegated authority, which I reposed in the Governors. Although it was never defined and was an 'understood' rather than a 'constitutional' practice, this on the whole worked reasonably well. Later, before independence, we came to a more official arrangement.

As the Regional Governments began to find their feet and realise their powers, it soon became clear to me that there was little co-operation in economic planning, or in the way in which each government dealt with its civil service. The former led to uneconomic rivalries in development projects, and it seemed essential that planning should be co-ordinated in some way. A mission organised by the International Bank for Reconstruction and Development, in a Report published in the second half of 1954, had recommended that representatives of the Federal and Regional Governments should meet from time to time and discuss their economic problems and proposals. To implement this we set up an Economic Council which first met in October 1955. There were four representatives from each of the Nigerian Governments and two from the Southern Cameroons. I presided at the regular biannual meetings which were held in the different capitals – Lagos, Ibadan, Kaduna and Enugu – and enjoyed the discussions which were usually friendly and co-operative. Although the Council had no executive authority, it had valuable results in helping to create a broad economic policy for the country as a whole. In 1958 the Council set up a joint planning committee, composed of officials under the chairmanship of Mr. R. Fenton,* the first Governor of the Central Bank of Nigeria. A year later this committee published an Economic Survey of Nigeria, which was a valuable synopsis, and showed that in some degree the Council had succeeded in becoming a unifying influence in the economic sphere.

Partly because of the success of this joint Council, I pressed later for the formation of a similar body to deal with civil service questions. The division of the service had created a situation in which there was some friction. The four Governments were free to deal with their civil services as they wished and to pay them whatever they could afford. Consequently former colleagues might find themselves on varying salary scales and with very different opportunities for promotion. A council to deal with matters of this kind was eventually established, and towards the end of my time in Nigeria it was usually presided over by the Prime Minister himself. It performed useful work and was another recognition of the need to keep the Governments in touch with each other and working on more or less similar lines. Perhaps it was especially valuable to the Federal Government, whose officials in the various country-wide services worked in close touch with Regional officals throughout Nigeria, and for whose contentment some co-ordination of salaries and service benefits with those of Regional officials was necessary. But I remember protests from Eastern Regional officers about promotions in the Federal service of men junior to unpromoted men in the East. At the start the Western Region, with its prosperous cocoa revenues, seemed to cause the most problems, but as in the economic field, discussion and cordial personal contacts helped to create an atmosphere of co-operation.

My chief impression of Nigeria during these early months was of the need to encourage a feeling of unity in the country. The rather weak Federal form of government did not make for unity, and I determined that my job must be to fly the Federal flag all round the country and try to make the Federation a living reality. Looking back now, it is

* *R. Fenton.* Served Bank of England. Governor Central Bank of Nigeria 1958–63. Chief Overseas Dept., Bank of England 1965.

clear that I did not succeed. Nigeria had an appearance of unity in October 1960 when independence was granted, but this unity was largely superficial. It was based perhaps on the need for the tribal parties to show some form of Nigerian unity in their relations with the colonial power; but this phantom of unity soon began to fade when the need for it disappeared. I was obviously too optimistic and did not appreciate the strength of the tribal ties and animosities. But the Royal visit in January 1956 seemed to show a Nigeria which was united in welcoming its Queen and the Head of the Commonwealth; this, too, possibly gave a false impression of the unity of the country.

In October 1955 I went to London for a week, partly to talk about the Queen's projected visit but also to discuss Nigerian problems with the Secretary of State and his officials. It was at this time that the decision was taken that the royal visit should take place at the end of January 1956 and would probably last until the middle of February. This did not give us a great deal of time for planning the programme and making any necessary alterations to the various houses where the Queen and her party would stay. We heard later that usually a year's notice was given, but we had only three months to prepare. However, everyone was enthusiastic and a great amount of work was put into the preparations. As Governor-General I had to co-ordinate the planning throughout the country, and it was difficult to fit in some of the wishes of Regional ministers with what seemed to me reasonable to expect Her Majesty to do. This led to considerable acrimony in telephonic exchanges, especially with the Western Region, where the Governor, Sir John Rankine, had to persuade his ministers that some of their ideas were simply not possible. I had arranged a steamer tour in the Delta area for November, so had to leave a lot of this work to Ralph Grey,* the Chief Secretary; he had a difficult time with many problems, which he reported to me by a very indistinct wireless telephone to the steamer. However, we got over this. Grey went to London to mull it all over with the Queen's staff and eventually a programme was agreed upon.

The Queen and the Duke of Edinburgh flew from London with their staff on the evening of 27 January 1956 and reached Ikeja airport at 10 a.m. the next morning after a non-stop flight. After the welcome at the airport, the inspection of the guard of honour and the introductions of the Federal Ministers and some of the leading officials, we drove the 11 miles to Lagos in procession through immense and wildly

* *Ralph Grey*. Born New Zealand. Colonial Administrative Service 1937–68. Chief Secretary Federal Government Nigeria 1954–7. Deputy Governor-General 1957–9. Governor British Guiana 1959–64. Bahamas 1964–7. Governor Northern Ireland 1968–. Lord Grey of Naughton 1968.

enthusiastic crowds. At the Lagos town boundary there was a short ceremony, when the Oba of Lagos welcomed Her Majesty and she made a suitable reply, and we then drove on over Carter Bridge to Government House, where my wife and I again greeted Her Majesty and Prince Philip and presented members of our staff. The next four days were busy and on the whole successful. There was a presentation of colours on the Racecourse, the Queen's speech to the Federal House of Representatives, a visit to the Law Courts, a large garden party and a number of formal and informal luncheon and dinner parties, a service in the Cathedral, and a very pleasant quiet Sunday at our chalet at Lighthouse Beach. We found that although the preparations for these various ceremonies had been onerous and a feeling of anxiety lest anything should go wrong was always at the back of our minds, our royal visitors were so relaxed and easy that the actual event was far less worrying than its anticipation. After the first day or two, when the success of the visit began to be obvious, the Queen, the Duke and their staff clearly appeared to be enjoying themselves and made our anxieties seem unnecessary. The Queen's sense of humour and the Duke's ability to make conversation with all sorts of people made the duty of presenting people to them easy and pleasant.

On 1 February the royal party left for Kaduna. I had wondered whether I should accompany them on their visits to the Regions, but had decided that it would be better if I did not go, as there were to be no especially Federal occasions in the North or the East, and I would perhaps be a bit out of place and in the way. As it turned out all went well: the Durbar at Kaduna was a great success, and the gathering of war canoes at Port Harcourt was a colourful spectacle. The royal party returned to Lagos from Enugu and Benin on the 9th, all in good form and again stayed with us at Government House. On Friday we had a lunch for the Cameroon ministers and notables and an evening reception for about a hundred Cameroon people who had come in. That afternoon there was a children's rally on the Racecourse when 29,000 children and thousands of spectators were present. The children marched, sang and danced and the royal visitors mingled informally and happily with them. This immense gathering was excellently organised; there were no accidents, and the children all reached home again safely with no one missing.

Next day was Ibadan's turn, and the royal party went by train from Lagos, stopping at Abeokuta on the way. At Ibadan the University College and the Teaching Hospital were Federal institutions and as I was the Visitor of the College it was incumbent on me to attend the royal visits to them. According to my diary 'The ceremonies all went off well and the students gave H.M. and H.R.H. fine receptions.'

This was another happy and successful day. We had lunch at the College and I had the privilege of sitting next to the Queen. I wrote in my diary: 'The Queen said quite a lot at lunch, has obviously picked up information about everything, and is very shrewd in her assessment of people.'

On Wednesday the 15th the royal party returned to Lagos and we had a final dinner party that evening for about thirty people, including the French Governor of Dahomey, M. Biros and his wife. After dinner the Queen made a farewell broadcast from my office and talked to the Federal ministers and the French Governor, and we then had a gay party in the billiard room where Prince Philip showed us how to play billiard fives and billiard cricket.

Next morning we saw them off on their way home, with a first stop at Kano. The tour with its excitement and thrill was over, and for some days we all felt flat and dejected. The visit had been a great success: the Queen had been warmly received, with pomp and pageantry but also with obvious friendliness and sincerity. As one Nigerian wrote, 'There were no animosities, no enmities, no recriminations, no hostile demonstrations.' I hoped that the visit would tend to unite the various parts of the country, as Her Majesty was Queen of all her subjects in Nigeria. Her Majesty's kindness and consideration to me and my wife personally will always be with us, and we cherish many happy memories of little personal incidents. At Lighthouse Beach at lunch on the first Sunday, I was congratulating myself that we had had no gate-crashers, when the Queen said 'It's so quiet and peaceful. No one to be seen, except one of your policemen, Sir James, under every bush', and if one looked one could see a white robe under quite a number of bushes. At the royal visit to the Nigerian Parliament, I went on ahead to welcome Her Majesty at the parliament building and on her arrival, after my salute, she shook me by the hand and said 'Here we are: on the job again!' – and then we went in and she read her speech to her Nigerian Parliament. When the lights all went out at dinner and my wife and I thought the world had more or less come to an end, the Queen eased the situation by saying, 'Oh well! we all know the way to our mouths!' I was especially honoured by being sent for, before she left for Northern Nigeria, and told by the Duke of Edinburgh in his shirt sleeves, wearing red braces, 'The Queen wants you.' The Queen said that as I had been largely responsible for arranging her visit to Nigeria and as she would be giving some decorations in the North and East before she returned to Lagos, she would like me to receive the first decoration of the tour. She then presented me with the insignia of the G.C.V.O. – I thought this a very kind and thoughtful act.

So it was a memorable time for us and made all the planning and hard work on preparations and rehearsals well worthwhile. Others had the same tale to tell: the American Consul-General; M. Biros, the French Governor; Nigerian ministers; all who came in contact with Her Majesty were charmed by her and will remember those days and her gracious friendliness as long as they live.

After the Queen left, my life resumed its normal course of attending meetings and entertaining. There was a stream of visitors following the royal visit, for its publicity had put Nigeria on the map, and most of them seemed to wish to come and talk to me about it all.

I had an argument with the Council of Ministers, who disliked the Information Office's film of the royal tour and wanted it to be remade to show them taking a larger part in proceedings. I agreed with them that perhaps there were too many white faces in the film, and that security measures had been overplayed; while the many informal incidents when Her Majesty and Prince Philip had met ordinary Nigerians were not given enough prominence. I told them not to be petty-minded and seek the limelight for themselves; but of course in the end we compromised, allowing the original film to be released while the visit was still of current interest, and asking for a second one to be produced showing more of the ministers.

I was soon out on tour again, and in the first half of 1956 went to both the North and East. The visit to the East and the Southern Cameroons was one of the most enjoyable tours we made in Nigeria, and I found the plateau at Bamenda in the Southern Cameroons one of the most beautiful and pleasant places I have found in Africa. The scenery was lovely, the climate cool and invigorating, and I found the local people most interesting. The Chiefs were oddities in some ways, yet they seemed to command the respect of their people. The Fon of Bafut (caricatured by Durrell) wore an incredible hat, and had a wonderful compound and rest house. The Fon of Bali put on a magnificent show for us with bands and dancing girls in a delightful little theatre. At Wum where we met the Fon of Bum (surprisingly pronounced 'Boom' as the Queen remarked after she had met him), I discovered that many of my guests at the drinks party had univited friends outside to whom they passed drinks through the windows. At Nkambe, the next stop on the road round the plateau, we stayed for a couple of nights and I was able to get some exercise by riding round the station on my hosts' ponies. On the Sunday we attended the Baptist Church at Ndu, which of course was crowded to the door. My diary comments: 'Full church, hearty singing in a very ranting style. I read the lesson, Galatians 6:1–10, and an African padre preached in English and the

vernacular. I don't know whether the lesson was intended to carry
a special message for me as Governor-General, verse 3 reads: 'For if a
man thinketh himself to be something when he is nothing, he deceiveth
himself'! After the service we went to the Baptist missionaries' house,
but were much delayed on the way by a parade of horsemen, dancers,
youths and girls in the football field. Men from the nomadic Fulani
tribes put up a splendid show, galloping their horses and firing their
guns.'

Then we went on to Nsau, where we called on the Fon, of whom I
commented: 'A rather wet little man who has no personality but is said
to be in good charge of his people.' The Roman Catholic Mission at
Nsau was a wonderful place, with its maternity home and orphanage
run by Dr. Plotzer and Mother Camilla, two remarkable women who
seemed to be doing magnificent work for the women of the area.
Mother Camilla had spent all her active life at this station, and her
maternity clinic was now dealing with the grandchildren of her first
patients. She was loved and respected for miles around. Another social
worker there was Miss Elizabeth O'Kelly who was trying – successfully – to raise the self-respect of the women: one of her most important
experiments was the introduction of simple corn mills to help them
avoid the continual drudgery of daily grinding the corn for their
families. The co-operative-owned hand mills were a tremendous boon
to them. Another dedicated woman whom we met on this tour was Dr.
Petit-Pierre at the large Basel Mission leper settlement at Manyemen
on the Mamfe-Kumba road. Seeing people like these at work and
observing the affection with which they were obviously regarded by
the people made one feel very humble, and I have often wished that the
intellectual and left-wing critics of missionary endeavour could have
seen the work they were doing and the happiness they brought to primitive people, who without them would have had no help or medical
attention at all. The opportunities that it gave to such work always
seemed to me one of the great benefits of colonial rule, though admittedly it only scratched the surface of an immeasurable problem.

Meanwhile a storm was brewing in the political world. The
N.C.N.C. Chief Whip in the Eastern Region, Mr. E. O. Eyo, had
quarrelled with Dr. Azikiwe, the Regional Premier. Dr. Azikiwe,
among his activities before becoming Premier, had established the
African Continental Bank, which had branches in various towns in
Nigeria and in which – though he was now a political leader and
Premier – he still retained a commanding holding of shares. His wife
and other members of his family also remained shareholders. It ap-
peared that with his cognisance – if not at his instruction – the Eastern
Development Corporation, an instrument of the Eastern Regional

Government, had made the sum of £2 million available to the Bank. Mr. Eyo demanded an impartial inquiry, and since he was Chairman of the Development Corporation, as well as N.C.N.C. chief whip, his allegations could hardly be ignored. We were put in a difficult position, for we had to take action, and it did not seem right that Dr. Azikiwe, with these allegations hanging over him, should take a leading part in the constitutional conference due to take place a month or two later. On the other hand there was certainly some doubt about Dr. Azikiwe's personal involvement in the transactions and about whether he stood to gain anything personally from them. In any case it seemed doubtful whether, even if he was held by an inquiry to have acted improperly. this would be thought by his supporters to be something which they themselves would consider wrong.

My point of view was that, so long as were ruling Nigeria, we could not shut our eyes and ignore actions which we thought were contrary to proper behaviour on the part of a leading minister, and I pressed this strongly upon the Secretary of State. It was finally decided that an inquiry should be made, and Mr. Lennox-Boyd announced in the House of Commons on 24 July 1956 that he was appointing a Commission, and that the constitutional conference would be postponed until the inquiry was completed. Dr. Azikiwe was at first indignant that the inquiry was being held. His party claimed that the Secretary of State had no constitutional right to appoint such a tribunal, and even alleged that the action constituted an attack on an indigenous bank on behalf of British banking interests in Nigeria. As far as I know, this accusation was entirely untrue. No such idea entered my mind when I pressed for an inquiry to be made; nor did I hear it mentioned in any of the many discussions which took place before the Secretary of State's final decision was made. However, before the hearing began, Dr. Azikiwe became reconciled to the idea and co-operated very reasonably, appearing before the tribunal and defending his actions as being perfectly justifiable. The Eastern Regional House of Assembly also agreed officially with the inquiry in August 1956.

Sir Stafford Foster-Sutton,* the Chief Justice of the Federal Supreme Court, was appointed chairman of the tribunal, which was sworn in on 25 August. A number of eminent lawyers came from the U.K. in connection with the inquiry. Bernard MacKenna,† now a judge, acted as the advocate leading the case for the Government (I would not call it

---

* *Sir Stafford Foster-Sutton.* Called to the Bar 1926. Solicitor-General Jamaica 1936. Attorney-General Cyprus 1940, Kenya 1944, Malaya 1948. Chief Justice Malaya 1950. Chief Justice Nigerian Federal Supreme Court 1955–8.

† *Sir Bernard MacKenna.* Called to the Bar 1932. K.C. 1950. Western Circuit. Judge of the High Court of Justice 1961.

prosecution), and Frank Soskice* was Dr. Azikiwe's advocate. Others implicated also briefed lawyers from Britain as well as Nigerian lawyers.

The tribunal sat from August till November and naturally its proceedings were followed with great interest among the politically-minded classes in Nigeria. I was greatly impressed by the way Sir Stafford Foster-Sutton presided over the tribunal and maintained the highest standards of judicial behaviour. The publication of the report in January 1957 was welcomed by Dr. Azikiwe's critics, who were glad to draw attention to the parts of it which concluded that his actions in connection with the deposit of so much public money in his own bank fell short of the expectations of reasonable people. But the N.C.N.C. and his supporters clearly thought that the report had exonerated him, and repeated their previous opinion that his actions had had purely nationalistic motives in order to break the monopoly of the two British banks in the country. As far as I could see, the evidence showed no criminal intention on Zik's part but a good deal of carelessness and some stupidity. His action in allowing so large an investment to be made in an enterprise in which he had considerable personal interest was far from wise, and certainly quite contrary to British ideas, although it did not appear that he had made any personal profit from it. A British politician would surely have disposed of his shareholding in the bank before taking ministerial office. In any case it made little difference to his position in Nigeria as, shortly after the report's publication, he asked for a dissolution of the Eastern House of Assembly, and at the subsequent regional Election, held in March 1957, his party won a greater number of seats than before. He was once more Premier of the East and thus able to lead the N.C.N.C. delegation to the forthcoming constitutional conference which was now fixed for May 1957.

The only casualty of the inquiry was Sir Clem Pleass, the Governor of the Eastern Region, who considered that in the aftermath his position would be very difficult, for he felt unable to continue on easy terms with his Premier and the N.C.N.C. Government of his region. In the discussions on the regional budget some months before, there had been difficulties with his ministers, who had cut out certain increases in the salaries of senior expatriate officials. Pleass had had no option but to use his constitutional power and insist on the pay increases being awarded: so the budget had been passed by the Governor under his reserved powers, and not by the Regional House of Assembly. Later, when the tribunal was set up by the Secretary of State, the blame

* *Sir Frank Soskice.* British Labour M.P. 1945–66. Called to the Bar 1926. Solicitor-General 1945–51, Attorney-General 1951. Home Secretary and Lord Privy Seal 1964–6. Lord Stow Hill 1966.

for this too was put locally on the Governor, who had in fact been rather opposed to it; and by the autumn of 1956 he was certainly unpopular in N.C.N.C. circles in the Region. I saw this for myself on a tour that I made in late October 1956. At Aba and one or two other places placards were carried in the crowds that met me, saying 'Pleass must go' and 'Welcome Sir James: Sir Clem must go.' When he himself said he thought he should retire, it was obvious that he was right, although I felt it was terribly unfair that a man of the highest integrity, who was intensely keen on his job and had the greatest regard for the welfare of his people, should be the victim of unreasonable public outcry against decisions which were not his or recommended by him. But he was obviously not going to be able to improve relations with his ministers and would therefore be unable to give them the guidance they required. His successor, Sir Robert Stapledon, arrived to take up his appointment in mid-December.

The Federal Council of Ministers, though kept informed of the reasons for setting up the tribunal, were not called upon to approve the decisions taken, and were only involved when it came to paying for certain of the costs. It seemed hopeless to expect the Eastern Region to pay these and I undertook to persuade the Federal Council of Ministers to accept the charge against Federal funds, the inquiry being for the good of Nigeria as a whole. I had some difficulty persuading the Federal ministers to foot the bill, but in the end they accepted my recommendation.

Dr. Mbadiwe, the senior N.C.N.C. minister in the Federal Government, for a time imagined that he might lead an anti-Zik breakaway in the N.C.N.C., and a considerable lack of harmony developed in the party. It came to nothing, as in the end Mbadiwe had to face the fact that he could not shake Zik's hold on the N.C.N.C., and after some months of almost solitary opposition to Zik, he ate humble pie and returned to the fold. His grounds for trying to get rid of Zik were that the tribunal had shown that he was not trustworthy and he had brought shame on the N.C.N.C., but Dr. Mbadiwe's own reputation was not such as to make this a very credible reason to the majority of the party's supporters.

During my years in Nigeria I found that the general local attitude to what we consider to be financial rectitude was very different from ours. The West African term 'dash' seems to cover all kinds of gifts, from the ordinary little waiter's tip to a large bribe by a firm to persuade a minister to award a government contract. A hospital nurse might even require a shilling before fetching a patient a bedpan. In my position at the head of the administration, I heard frequent rumours of such malpractice, and I remember several instances when I was pretty sure that some crooked work was taking place, but had no hard evidence on which to act. The permanent allotment of valuable crown land near the Denton causeway into Lagos to a firm of Greek merchants seemed to me improper, and I suggested to the Council of Ministers that Government should only dispose of it after an auction when all interested parties would have a chance of bidding. However, the ministers would not back me up, and confirmed their colleague's action in allocating it to the Greek firm. A more serious case was the grant of a contract to a German firm for the reconstruction of one of the harbours. I heard that a British firm had submitted the lowest tender but as they refused to give a 'dash' to the minister concerned, they lost the contract. The rumour was that the Germans had given the minister £20,000. I had a system whereby all telegrams issuing from the Federal Government under the name of the Governor-General were shown to me after they had been sent, and a few days after I had heard these rumours I saw a telegram from the minister in question to the Nigerian office in London asking the officials there to get the contract with the German firm signed at once, and not to delay matters longer in negotiating amendments suggested by officials in Lagos. This gave me the excuse to ask to see the file, and I was able to send it to the Prime Minister asking why the lowest tender had not been accepted. In the end the P.M. overrode the minister's decision, cancelled the grant of the contract to the Germans and gave it to the British firm, who had submitted the lowest tender. The P.M.'s action was facilitated by the fact that the minister had gone into hospital by this time, and we never knew if he had received the 'dash' or not.

Another bad case which I heard of was in connection with the acquisition of land at Ikeja for a Western Region industrial area. The land was valued reasonably generously by a lands officer of the Regional Ministry, and the agreement of the landowners to the sale was obtained. However, the minister concerned, in submitting the proposal to the Regional Executive Council, was alleged to have doubled the proposed purchase price. His figures was accepted by his ministerial colleagues and the enhanced price was paid by the Regional Treasury, though of course one never heard how much of the new price went to the sellers of the land and how much got diverted on the way. Again there was no real evidence; only rumours and allegations, on which it was impossible to act. However, by inquiries and vigilance we were perhaps able to keep this evil down to some degree, though a few of the ministers, both Federal and Regional, became well known in local gossip for their corruptibility. After independence this practice became more and more unrestrained, and the popularity of the first army *coup d'état* in 1966 was largely due to a universal hope that the army government would put down corrupt practices.

In March 1957 my wife and I went to Accra to attend the celebrations for the Independence of the Gold Coast, now renamed Ghana. I was leader of the Nigerian delegation to the ceremonies, which was composed of representatives from all the Nigerian Governments. We stayed with Robert Jackson* and his distinguished and charming wife Barbara Ward,† and were wonderfully looked after. I had met Kwame Nkrumah in Lagos two years before when he was enjoying a holiday cruise. I invited him to visit Government House, and on his return journey he asked if he could come again and continue our conversations. I had found him a pleasant and easy person, and at these celebrations in Accra he went out of his way to make us welcome. He had not acquired at this time the somewhat difficult manners and attitude which he was reported to exhibit later. He had a charm of manner which made one like him greatly, and although he caused some annoyance by being late for every engagement, he could smile it all off with the greatest ease. The best story that I have of the Accra Independence celebrations was about Vice-President Nixon, who represented President Eisenhower. The Governor, Sir Charles Arden-Clarke, gave a large reception one morning at Christiansborg Castle, to which we were all invited. I happened to be standing near when Mr Nixon greeted a big Negro whom he thought was a Ghanaian, shook him warmly by the hand and said: 'This must be the most wonderful day of your life: what does it feel like to be free?' To which the reply was, 'I can't rightly say, Mr. Vice-President: you see, I come from Alabama.' He was an American press correspondent. Even in 1957 I noticed that Mr. Nixon did unrehearsed stops of his car and would dash into the crowd to kiss a black baby or sign an autograph book. I liked Mr. Manley, Prime Minister of Jamaica, who seemed to have a fine sense of humour. I was sitting near him at one of the big shows dressed in my uniform, holding my cocked hat with its feathers, and medals duly in place, when he leant over and whispered, 'Solomon in all his glory?' Another Premier I liked very much was Garfield Todd from Rhodesia, a tall, fine-looking man, who seemed from our conversations to have ideas very similar to mine about African policies. What a pity it was that he could not continue to rule Rhodesia.

* *Sir Robert Jackson.* Director-General Middle East Supply Centre 1942–5. In charge of U.N.R.A.A.'s work in Europe 1945–7. Volta Dam Commission Ghana and Ghana Development Commission 1953–61. United Nations Development Programme from 1963.
† *Lady Jackson* (Barbara Ward). Author and economist.

I felt that I obtained some ideas about Independence celebrations at Accra, and was able to bring them into consideration when Nigerian Independence was celebrated three years later. It was about this time that the Secretary of State, Alan Lennox-Boyd, asked me about my plans for the future. I had signed on for three years as Governor-General, but he was good enough to say that it seemed a pity for me to leave when Nigeria was so close to independence. I agreed to continue until that time, unless for any reason I or the British Government felt I should leave. I could not have been given a fairer deal.

# CHAPTER XI

# CONSTITUTIONAL PROGRESS

At the Constitutional Conference in 1953 the then Secretary of State, Oliver Lyttelton, had promised a further conference in 1956 to review the Federal and Regional arrangements and discuss further steps towards self-government. I had been thinking about these matters ever since my arrival in the country, and from the autumn of 1955 began to make concrete preparations.

I had had meetings with all the leading politicians and was aware of what they felt to be the main issues. Chief Awolowo had said publicly that the existing relations between Federation and the Regions should be maintained, so the status of Lagos was unlikely to generate the argument which had developed in 1954. He preferred to raise the question of the control of the police and of a new Mid-West state based on Benin. The Eastern Premier, Dr. Azikiwe, and his ministers thought there should be a revision of the financial arrangements for revenue allocation, and they were opposed to more states in the South, unless the North were divided up at the same time. The Northerners were still in no hurry for self-government and independence. They still thought that they were unprepared but maintained their desire for self-government 'as soon as is practicable'. My Minister of Transport, Abu Bakar Tafawa Balewa,* who was the deputy leader of the N.P.C., told me they would oppose any move to break up the Northern Region, and wished to maintain all the existing regional boundaries. They would not agree to the Federal Government being given more powers, and in fact would have liked to see little more than some kind of central agency to hold the country together.

I called Governors and political leaders to Lagos on 5 January 1956, when we decided that the conference should be held the following May in London, away from the pressures of the Nigerian capital. I hoped that we would be able to settle some of the outstanding problems at this preliminary meeting rather than having to troop off to the Colonial Secretary in London with little decided. There was a good deal of argument on various matters between Drs. Azikiwe and

* *Sir Abu Bakar Tafawa Balewa.* Northern Nigerian. Minister (Works, Transport) in Federal Government 1953–60. Prime Minister of Federation 1957. Assassinated 1966.

Mbadiwe on the one side and Chiefs Awolowo and Rotimi Williams,* one of his ministers, on the other, while the Northern representatives were very restrained. However, I was disappointed with the results, feeling that little had been resolved, though the Regional Governors did not think the results had been bad. Perhaps the Nigerians were looking foward to the visit to Britain.

The investigation into the financial affairs of Dr. Azikiwe delayed the London Conference until May 1957, and fortunately the postponement itself caused little difficulty. By that time the politicians had realised that the British Government was conscientiously intending to give them independence before long, and that in the circumstances a brief delay was no serious cause for concern. At a meeting I had in June 1955 with the Western Regional Executive Council, Chief Awolowo had himself suggested that in order to keep Oliver Lyttelton's promise the conference could be convened in August 1956, but need not actually begin then, and he appeared to be in no great hurry for the actual meeting.

I used the delay for further preparation of the major issues, on which we in Lagos worked in conjunction with the Colonial Office in London. In view of the North's hesitation at the prospect of speedy independence, the question was raised of full self-government by the Regions in matters for which they were responsible. Such a move would mean that Regional Governors retained a constitutional position but no longer acted as executive officers, and we tried to visualise how the new system would work. Clearly the position of the Federal police force in the Regions would have to be considered, and the relations of the Regional Premiers with the local police commissioners defined. The Regional Governments obviously had heavy responsibilities for law and order and the question arose of how they were to exercise this if the police force in the Regions was outside their jurisdiction. Another difficult matter was the division of revenue between the Federation and the Regions. The existing arrangements, which had been recommended by Sir Louis Chick's† Commission at the beginning of the Federation, were not popular with the Regions, and both the North and the East thought that they had been unfairly treated in the existing allocation. Then there were many calls by the minority groups for a greater share in their own government, which they thought could be best obtained by the creation of more states. I had seen some of these peoples' representatives on my tours, and had no doubt that there were strong feelings in their minds that they should not be left in regions where the big tribal

---

* *Chief Rotimi Williams* – Yoruba from Lagos. Barrister. Attorney-General Western Region 1953–62.

† *Sir Louis Chick*. See above, page 82.

units, the Hausa-Fulani, Ibo and Yoruba, were in such a majority that the smaller groups had no chance of influencing policy. The chief complaints were in the so-called Middle Belt in the Northern Region, which consisted of the districts inhabited by the non-Hausa and Fulani peoples such as the Tiv and Birom; the Calabar, Ogoja and Rivers provinces in the East, where the Efik, Ibibio, Annang and Kalabari lived; and the Mid-West provinces of the Western Region inhabited by Bini, Ijaw, Ijekri and Western Ibo. Southern politicians were not averse to the possibility of new regions, especially as they were anxious to see the massive power of the North weakened. However, action of this kind would inevitably mean administrative difficulties, and the alterations might cause great tribal animosity and the breakdown of law and order at a time when peace was essential for the successful transfer of power.

Then there was the question of the structure of the Federal Government. With the regions becoming self-governing, it was time for the Federation to take a step forward and, with independence coming near, a prime minister was required to head the Federation, and he and his ministers needed to be given more control over affairs.

We wrote and argued on these and other problems; I suppose all this work was of value in helping us to get our thoughts straight, but I see that I commented at the time: 'The briefs for the Constitutional Conference are exceedingly intricate and difficult, and I can't believe that this is the right way to do things.' I think that at the time I was recalling my Sudan experiences, when the local people did all the planning without interference and only referred the finished article to the Co-domini for agreement.

The Nigerian delegations to the conference were also making their preparations. The Action Group documents drawn up by Chiefs Awolowo and Rotimi Williams had obviously involved a great deal of careful thinking and hard work. In contrast the N.C.N.C. papers did not come up to the standard I expected from them, while the N.P.C. produced very few written memoranda.

Armed with numerous documents, all parties eventually met for the promised constitutional conference on 23 May 1957 in Lancaster House, London. The opening session, with a host of reporters and broadcasters in the brilliantly lit and decorated rooms, was a fine spectacle, and the formal opening addresses of the Secretary of State and the Nigerian political leaders struck a friendly and businesslike note. Somewhat to my surprise I was invited to address the opening session, and I endeavoured to stress the role of the federal system of government in reconciling regional differences while promoting national consciousness.

I also reminded the politicians of the administrative difficulties their schemes might entail, and remarked: 'It is a sobering thought to remember that we have only just finished implementing the recommendations of the last constitutional conference. I think it is only four months ago since the final splitting of the Nigerian Civil Service into four different services was completed, and now we have made a start all over again.' Throughout the conference, which continued with hardly a break for about a month, the atmosphere was always constructive and co-operative.

However, outside the conference chamber there was cause for a certain amount of irritation. The Nigerians had asked for the London venue in order to avoid the political pressures of Lagos, but they found themselves exposed instead to a demanding social round. There were far too many invitations to evening parties, cocktail receptions and dinners, and I think that the great majority of the members of the conference found these tedious. The Northern Premier in his autobiography wrote of the 'nuisance of British hospitality' and the dislike which he and his colleagues felt for the parties given by business firms. He explained how he and his fellow-delegates managed to avoid most of them by taking turns to attend. This was unfortunately not possible for the Governor-General, and I spent far too much time at evening parties, which were mostly not at all useful, though one occasionally met interesting people at them.

Fortunately the conference proved more worthwhile, and we were soon making progress in our deliberations. We dealt with the constitution of a self-governing Region within the Federation and agreed that the Eastern and Western Regions should become completely self-governing in their regional functions by August. This was important because the constitutions agreed upon would become the model for the North as well as for any new regions that might be created; at the same time they would lay down the relationship between the federal authorities and the regional governments. We spent much time on these discussions, going into considerable detail, and the resulting constitutions were duly accepted by the conference. Dr. Azikiwe and Chief Awolowo, together with their respective ministers, became the real rulers of their Regions and the Governors were little more than figureheads. The Northern Region did not wish to have the same timing, but asked that their regional self-government should be delayed until 1959 when they hoped to be better able to cope with the new system. Their chief difficulty was the lack of trained Northern staff, for the leaders did not wish to depend on Southerners to fill administrative posts. However, some changes were made in the North: the posts of Civil and Financial Secretary were both abolished, and instead the

Premier became the co-ordinating member of the Council, and a Minister of Finance was appointed. The Governor retained his reserved powers and veto as well as continuing to preside over the meetings of the Executive Council. The conference thus made important changes in the Regions, and I think that the Premiers all appreciated the great increase in responsibility which now fell on them, and the new obligation to co-ordinate the work of their governments, which had previously fallen upon the Governors and Civil Secretaries. My impression is that they found this no easy task. Chief Awolowo, speaking shortly afterwards, said that 'This event carried with it very grave responsibilities.' Dr. Azikiwe saw in it 'a major achievement' which marked 'the end of the beginning of the struggle for freedom from political tutelage'.

There have often been criticisms of the final constitution worked out for Nigeria, and the British have been blamed for 'imposing' a federal and democratic constitution on a country which was not ready for it, and which in any case did not understand it. This view I consider to be wholly misplaced, for no constitution was imposed; the final form was worked out in complete harmony and freedom of expression between the British Government and the Nigerian political parties. It was Nigerian pressure in 1953 and 1954 that led to the establishment of the federal system, since the leaders of all the Regions were determined to deal with local problems locally, and not to continue to be ruled by a unitary government working from Lagos. The North probably felt this most strongly, but the East and the West were not far behind, and the speedy and intense reaction in the summer of 1966 to General Ironsi's intention to revert to government from Lagos showed how strong the feelings were, as they still are.

The arrangements for the Federal Government were also considered. It was decided that the three British senior officials on the Council of Ministers would step down. The post of Chief Secretary and Financial Secretary should disappear, to be replaced by a Prime Minister and Minister of Finance, while the Attorney-General would advise the Government from outside the Council. There was also to be a Deputy Governor-General to assist the Governor-General in matters remaining under his control, and the Financial Secretary became the Permanent Secretary in the Ministry of Finance. The Ministers would in future be appointed by the Governor-General on the recommendations of the Prime Minister, and no longer by the Governor-General on the recommendations of the representatives of the Regions. This made it possible for a Prime Minister to appoint a cabinet entirely from his own party or to form a coalition as he thought best. The Governor-General was still to preside over the Council of Ministers, and to have the power of veto over decisions taken in it, though of course this power was carefully restricted and use of the veto had to be reported to the Secretary of State. I never had to use it during my years in Nigeria.

I was very much concerned in the conference's discussions about the police, to which I have referred earlier. I could sympathise with the feelings of the Regional Governments that, as they were to be self-governing in the conduct of their functions, they ought to have some power to maintain law and order in their areas. If the Nigeria police remained wholly under Federal control, there would be a very anomalous situation, and the Regional Governments could disclaim responsibility for law and order. On the other hand, so long as the Federal Government was not self-governing, and the Governor-General remained responsible to the British Parliament for the affairs of Nigeria, he could not hand over the Federal police or army to the Regional Governments. The matter was complicated by the existence in the North and West of forces of local government police, who were administered and paid for by the various local authorities. There was some idea of the Regions taking over control of these forces and increasing their size and capacity. The objections to this were that the rank and file were only slightly trained and that they owed allegiance not to the community as a whole but to the local Emirs and Chiefs, who were all identified with the ruling political party. Furthermore, this solution would mean the existence of two forces – federal and regional – in each region, which might easily lead to difficulties.

The Nigerian representatives at the conference readily agreed that the police should not become identified with any political party, and the minority representatives were especially emphatic that the Regional Premiers, who were all leaders of political parties, should not have complete control over the Federal forces in their respective Regions. The Sardauna, Premier of the North, and Chief Awolowo of the Western Region, were especially interested in this problem, and at one time it looked as if the conference might break down over it. However, we succeeded in finding a compromise solution. The Nigeria police should remain a Federal body under the control of the Inspector-General,* who would be responsible directly to the Governor-General. The police commissioners in each region would be responsible to the Inspector-General for the administration of the police in their Regions, but would also keep in close contact with the Regional Premiers,

---

* *Sir C. K. Bovell.* Served in Colonial Police, Malaya 1935–56. Interned Singapore 1942–45. Appointed to Nigeria, Inspector-General 1956, served till 1962. Knighted 1961. Later Bursar Worksop College, Radley College.

whose instructions about the deployment and use of the police they should accept. However, if it appeared to them that these instructions contradicted general Federal police policy or were otherwise unacceptable, they would be entitled to refer them to the Inspector-General. A Police Council would be set up consisting of the Governor-General as Chairman, the Federal Prime Minister and the Regional Premiers and attended by the Inspector General and the Regional Commissioners of Police. This body would be the final controlling authority to which all police questions could be referred; it would also agree the annual budget and consider any proposals for alteration in establishment. In addition a Police Service Commission would be set up to advise the Governor-General on such matters as appointments, dismissals, promotion and pay.

The conference accepted these proposals and the new system was brought into force at once. It seemed to satisfy the Regions, and it certainly worked well enough until the country became independent. After that I cannot say, except that it is generally reported that during all the recent troubles in Nigeria the Federal police have done well and have proved a steadying influence. It was chiefly due to the good relations built up by the Inspector-General and the Regional Commissioners of Police with the political leaders that this compromise arrangement worked successfully for several years, and that in spite of some difficulties between the Federation and the Regions, especially at the time of the Federal General Elections in December 1959, there were no serious conflicts over the police.

Three problems which faced the conference led to the establishment of commissions of enquiry to report later to a resumed conference. One examined the fears of the minority groups which I described earlier and which were constantly repeated during the talks; another was established to look into the very complex question of revenue division; while a third was required to make recommendations about the electoral system for Federal elections. It was thought that there should be one seat in the Federal legislature for every 100,000 of the population, but that the constituencies should also conform to the existing administrative divisions as far as possible. This was not easy to arrange because of the varying size of the administrative units, and it was the problem of boundaries which the commission was to examine. Furthermore, it was agreed that the Governor-General should convene a further conference in Nigeria to work out the electoral rules and procedures for the next Federal elections, which were due in 1959.

The only subject on which the conference disappointed the Nigerian politicians was the fixing of a date for Independence. The Nigerians submitted a united application to the Secretary of State, for the

H

agreement of the British Government, that Independence should be granted in 1959. This was refused on two grounds, first that the reports of the commissions now to be set up had to be completed before a date could be fixed as they might affect the whole situation in the country, and secondly that until the Eastern and Western Regions had shown their capacity as self-governing territories, it was premature to assume that Nigeria was ready for Independence. So the conference was adjourned for a year, and the Secretary of State set about finding suitable people for appointment to the three commissions.

When we returned to Nigeria there were two main results of the conference. In August the East and West became self-governing in all their Regional functions; the Premiers now presided over the regional Executive Councils, and the Governors became purely constitutional heads of the Regions as representatives of the Crown. This made little difference in ordinary practice, since for a year or two the Eastern and Western Executive Councils had been in nearly complete control, though the Governors of the regions had retained their little-used power of veto.

Although the attainment of regional self-government was a milestone on the road to Independence, the Governments of the East and the West did not mark it with any extravagant celebrations. In the autumn the Queen sent her aunt, the Princess Royal, to greet the Regional Governments and convey to them Her Majesty's good wishes on the step that had been taken. This was a happy and successful visit, and H.R.H. appeared to enjoy her trip to various parts of Nigeria. The visit coincided with the centenary of the foundation of the Niger Mission of the Church Missionary Society and H.R.H. visited Onitsha, attended a service in the new Cathedral, and took part in a vast open-air gathering in a field near the cathedral where about 10,000 people gathered to give thanks for the work of the Mission. An evening occasion at Onitsha, when H.R.H. switched on the lights of the great new market, was remarkable for the swarms of yam beetles which, attracted by the lights, collected in vast numbers, getting into everyone's clothes and hair, and even down the backs of the ladies' dresses. The Princess took all this with great calm and looked forward to the story she would have to tell when she returned home and showed off a bottle filled with the bugs. She went to the North too and visited Kaduna, Zaria and Kano, but because of a slight indisposition, was unable to carry out all her programme. I had to take her place at the evening reception at Zaria, and was asked by the leading lady if I would agree that the ladies, who had been practising their curtseys for the Princess, should make them to me instead, so as not to waste all their careful preparations.

More obvious results of the conference were those affecting the

Federal Government. The chief difference was that there was now to be a Prime Minister and I, as Governor-General, had to appoint the member of the House of Representatives who seemed to me the most likely to command a majority in the House. The leader of the Northern party had the biggest following and at the same time was popular and respected by members of the other parties. I had been impressed by the way in which the Southern ministers during the previous two years had obviously looked up to him in our discussions in the Council of Ministers. So I appointed Alhaji Abu Bakar Tafawa Balewa Prime Minister, and the choice was accepted unanimously throughout the country as a good one.

The new Prime Minister had to submit the names of his ministers to me, and we had much discussion about the various possibilities and the best appointments for the various ministries. Abu Bakar was determined to have a cabinet representative of the whole country which would, as a national government, prepare for Independence. He therefore approached the Action Group, who had previously not been represented in the Council of Ministers, asking if they would join and take part in an all-party government to prepare for Independence. Chiefs Awolowo and Rotimi Williams agreed, and Chiefs Akintola* and Eyo Rosiji† were appointed ministers. The other ministers came from the N.C.N.C. and the N.P.C. and included most of those previously in the Government. The Prime Minister recommended Chief Festus Okotie-Eboh‡ to take over the important portfolio of Finance, and we had a long talk about his suitability. As it turned out, Festus – a flamboyant character – did pretty well in many ways; he got on well with big business tycoons and in his attendance at Commonwealth Finance Ministers' meetings he made friends with many of his fellow-members which was of considerable value to Nigeria financially. I always found him easy to deal with, and he was usually ready to take advice. But as the years passed he became something of a by-word for making money on the side, and when he was murdered in the coup of January 1966 it was apparently because he was supposed to have made large sums by taking bribes and salting them away in

* *Chief Akintola* – a Yoruba from Ogbomisha, Western Region. Barrister, Member House of Representatives 1954–9. Federal Minister 1957–9. Premier Western Region 1959–66. Assassinated 1966.

† *Chief Eyo Rosiji* – a Yoruba from Oshogbo. Member of Federal House of Assembly 1954–9. Minister Federal Government 1957–9. Left Nigeria 1962, now resident in U.K.

‡ *Chief Festus Okotie-Eboh* – an Ijekri from Warri where he had trading and educational interests. Member of N.C.N.C. and of House of Representatives 1954–66. Minister of Labour 1955–7. Minister of Finance Federal Government 1957–66. Assassinated 1966.

Switzerland. He was a cheerful rogue and one could not help liking him, though his loud voice and habit of shouting down his opponents in discussion sometimes made the Council of Ministers a rather un-edifying body, especially if he was arguing, as he often did, with Chief Akintola, another talkative minister with a high-pitched squeaky voice. At these meetings K. O. Mbadiwe, the senior N.C.N.C. minister, took the seat next to me at the council table and professed to be my legal adviser in the absence from the Council of the Attorney-General. I found him ready to please, and after arguments and obvious differences of opinion in the Council he customarily called on the Council to await the compromise which he saw the President composing; this often worked, and we would reach agreement on some formula which I had scribbled out. Another gambit I had when things seemed difficult, and the Council appeared to me to be going off the rails, was to raise my arm and look pointedly up my sleeve, for I had once amused the ministers by saying that that was where I kept my reserved powers. This usually provoked a laugh, and I have always found that if one can make people laugh one can get away with most things.

Abu Bakar, the Prime Minister, always sat directly opposite me, whether in the old council room next door to my office in the grounds of Government House, or later on in the new cabinet room which we built in the Prime Minister's office. The new venue was brought into use before Independence in order to emphasise the Prime Minister's coming responsibility for presiding over the Cabinet. Abu Bakar would listen quietly to the arguments on the various subjects on the agenda and not show his hand until almost all the other ministers had given their views. He would then sum up and usually his views were decisive. They were always sound and sensible, except on rare occasions when he had obviously not grasped the point at issue, and then he could be unbelievably determined and stubborn until he found that he had not understood what it was all about.

I had the greatest admiration for Abu Bakar, for he was a man of the highest integrity who was obviously serving his country in condi-tions which he found difficult, and would much rather have been at home looking after his family and his farm, or carrying on his earlier profession as a teacher. He was a most religious and sincere Muslim and was devoted to his family. He told me that when he was absent from home, in Lagos or elsewhere, he tried to telephone to Bauchi every evening to see if his family were all right. As Independence grew nearer in 1959 and 1960 I saw more of him, as he used to come in frequently in the evenings and talk about his problems and mine. Occasionally I made some excuse for not attending a Council meeting and asked the Prime Minister to deputise for me, and I never found that this created an awkward precedent or that he misused his opportunities.

I felt it was impossible to maintain the accepted constitutional position that foreign affairs and defence were to be kept entirely outside his orbit until Independence actually took place. It would have been most unfair to plunge the new Nigerian Government and its Prime Minister totally inexperienced into the cold, hard world. Consequently we discussed defence and foreign affairs, and I showed him all the British Government's papers that came to me about neighbouring countries and the trends of foreign affairs, although they were not supposed to be shown to the Nigerians. I never had the slightest fear that he would abuse my confidence. We even established embryonic Ministries of Foreign Affairs and Defence. We selected promising young men from the Civil Service throughout the country and with the assistance of the British authorities had them attached to British embassies and high commissions in various parts of the world for training in embassy work. Most of these trainees did well, and many of them now hold high posts in the Nigerian Foreign Service. Abu Bakar also asked me for help in forming a secret service, and here again we had invaluable assistance from the British authorities who helped us to pick suitable people and gave them some training. Abu Bakar was naïve about this, giving as his reason for having a secret service the fact that Dr. Nkrumah of Ghana had one and was snooping in Nigeria with it. Nkrumah was not one of Abu Bakar's favourites, for they were of totally different types: Nkrumah flamboyant and totally extrovert while Abu Bakar was reserved and much less of the demagogue, though he was a good speaker, with a splendid command of English, a resonant voice and a fund of common sense.

We became very close during these years and I appreciated the confidence he placed in me. There was little we could not discuss, from the troubles we had with the leader of his party – the Sardauna of Sokoto, Premier of the North – to his difficulties with the noisy, argumentative Southerners who seemed to take all their squabbles and troubles to him. I remember one occasion when Chief Festus was going off to some conference abroad, and Abu Bakar reported to me the guidance he had given him; then, with a twinkle in his eye, he added that Festus had spoken to him about his desire for a son and heir, and how he had only daughters. Did the Prime Minister not think that in his absence 'the Power of the North' might not be brought into play with Mrs. Festus? I asked him what he had replied and with another smile he said, 'I referred him to his friend, Mohamed Ribadu.'*

* *Mohamed Ribadu.* Member of N.P.C. in Federal House of Representatives. Minister for Lagos Affairs 1954, Minister of Defence 1961.

Ribadu was a Northerner from Ademowa and a shrewd, intelligent man, who was very much *persona grata* with the Northern Premier, and seemed to act as the Sardauna's representative in the Federal Cabinet, reporting to Kaduna about everything that happened. Abu Bakar's position was far from easy for, although he was Prime Minister, he had no party of his own and could not depend on the votes of the N.P.C. members in the House of Representatives in any policy which was not approved by the Premier of the North who led the party. This situation never became critical during my time in Nigeria. However, when in 1965 the Premier of the West, Chief Akintola, and the Premier of the North acted together, the Prime Minister was unable to intervene to deal with the disorders in the West, and it was this alliance which, I believe, led to the *coup d'état* in January 1966 and Abu Bakar's death.

The Sardauna relied a great deal on Abu Bakar to reconcile the growing class of educated Northerners with the Emirs and important tribal leaders who were the basis of the N.P.C. During talks Abu Bakar would often tell me of troubles in the North, of a row between the Sardauna and an Emir, or squabbles in the party, and would ask for leave to go to Kaduna, as well as for the loan of the Governor-General's aeroplane. He would then disappear and come back in two or three days, saying he had settled the difficulty.

Abu Bakar became interested in foreign affairs as Independence approached, and made one or two journeys abroad. He attended the celebrations for the Independence of Togoland and enjoyed meeting West African leaders there, especially the President of Togo, Sylvanus Olympio, whom he found congenial. He also had a conversation with Sekou Touré, the President of Guinea, and liked him. He pressed me hard to allow Nigerian troops to go as part of the United Nations forces in the Congo in 1960, but so long as Nigeria was a British colony this was impossible. Very soon after Independence he revived this idea, and Nigerian troops were sent to join the U.N. forces, and Nigerian police helped to maintain law and order in Leopoldville, where they received glowing reports.

Abu Bakar was always a modest man, who won his important position by sheer merit and reliability. Immediately after Independence it was necessary to send a delegation to the United Nations General Assembly in New York to apply for Nigeria to be admitted to the organisation. Abu Bakar came and discussed with me who should go on the mission, and I had great difficulty in persuading him that no one could do the job nearly as well as himself. It was with some reluctance that he went, and made a most successful and impressive speech in the Assembly after Nigeria's entry had been approved.

During the winter of 1957–8 the three commissions appointed by the Secretary of State as a result of the conference toured Nigeria. The Minorities Commission under the Chairmanship of Sir Henry Willink* was the most important and long drawn-out. It heard a great deal of evidence all over the country and eventually found difficulty in deciding how essential it was to have new states for the minority tribes. In all the disputed areas there was no large single group who feared being overshadowed in the existing states; rather there were numbers of small tribes, and the problems in the existing regions would only be repeated if the minority areas were separated. It seemed quite ridiculous to think of having separate states for some 200 tribal units both small and big. I also believed strongly that with Independence near it would cause a great deal of confusion and possibly trouble to create new states in 1958; I felt that this would be setting Nigeria off on its new independent future in very uncertain and disturbed conditions. I told Sir Henry Willink that in my view any new state should be recommended only in the most imperative circumstances. Politicians – African ones at any rate – have little regard for administration and seem to think that you can cut up a service and yet expect the different parts to function just as before. I suppose we administrators often put too much emphasis on the efficient working of the wheels and routines of government, but in my opinion many politicians have little idea how things are run and are quite ignorant about administration, especially the length of time it takes for a new organisation to find its feet and to function reasonably well. It seemed to me that the Nigerian minority leaders, who were asking for the whole system of government to be upset by the creation of new states, were making it necessary either to delay the Independence of the country, or ensuring that it became independent with its administration in chaos. Dr. Azikiwe and Chief Awolowo, who had previously been pressing for new states chiefly in order to break up the monolithic character of the Northern Region, became less insistent on this policy after they had taken over the administration of their own Regions.

Sir Jeremy Raisman† and his commission, who were dealing with the allocation of revenue, had a less argumentative if no easier task. The points at issue were so technical that few people really understood them, and it only concerned a few ministers and high officials in the

* *Sir Henry Willink*. Conservative M.P. 1940–8. Minister of Health 1943–5. Master of Magdalene College Cambridge 1948–66. Chairman of many committees of inquiry including Commission of Inquiry into problems of minorities in Nigeria 1957.

† *Sir Jeremy Raisman*. Indian Civil Service 1916–45. Finance member Government of India 1939–45. Chairman Nigeria Fiscal commission 1957–8.

various governments who know their respective requirements for the development of their services. Naturally each government, whether Federal or Regional, wanted as big a share of the cake as it could obtain. It must be remembered too that in 1957–8, though oil had been discovered at Oloiberi and Afam in Eastern Nigeria, no one yet had any idea of the rich oilfields capable of giving substantial revenues to the country which were to be opened up within the next ten years.

Lord Merthyr's* commission dealing with constituency boundaries had the easiest task of the three, and although there were a few complaints in individual instances, the exercise was speedily and effectively carried out and there was little or no bother.

In the autumn of 1957 I repaid a visit to Lagos by the Governor-General of Spanish Guinea by going to Fernando Poo. The Governor-General, Don Faustino Ruiz del Gonzales, was a portly, cheerful little man who had enjoyed his visit to Lagos, and was very pressing that I should go and see him at Santa Isabel. I wished to go to see how the Nigerian labourers in the cocoa and palm plantations were being treated, as there had been complaints at Enugu by the Eastern Regional Government that their people were not always accorded a straight deal by the Spanish authorities. There were some thousands of Eastern Nigerians in Fernando Poo most winters, and it seemed to me that the reports of ill-treatment had been much exaggerated because so many went back year after year. No doubt there were some bad plantation managers and there were also some Nigerians who did not appreciate the rules of a more authoritarian administration than that of the British. I visited two or three estates and saw numbers of the Nigerians, including the Federal Government's representative, and satisfied myself that the situation was reasonably satisfactory. We had some gargantuan meals and parties and were hospitably welcomed, with a pleasant house allotted to us. Here my personal servant, Stephen, let us down by over-indulgence in Spanish brandy just on the evening when I was holding a reception to repay the hospitality we had received. The result of this visit was the preparation of new contracts of service for Nigerians in Fernando Poo, which were accepted by both the Federal and Eastern Regional Governments of Nigeria and by the Spanish Government.

While I was at Fernando Poo, the Governor-General wanted me to go to Rio Muni, a small Spanish colony on the mainland to the south of the Cameroons. We spent a few hours at its capital, Bata, but were not greatly impressed. The hospital was a fine building with European

* *Lord Merthyr.* Chairman of Committees and Deputy Speaker House of Lords 1957–65. Chairman Constituency Delineation Commission 1957–8.

doctors, surgeons and nurses and excellent equipment, but it was remarkably empty of patients. We had lunch with the local Governor and were enjoying an excellent meal, when the door opened and an official announced '*Tornado approchara*' and that we must return to the aircraft and get back to Santa Isabel. So, leaving our host and the excellent meal, we rushed out to the airport, and were soon in the air on our way back, duly arriving at Fernando Poo before the storm. This was lucky as the landing ground was uneven and sloped downwards to the sea, and a landing in a strong wind might well have been unpleasant. It was on this trip, before reaching Santa Isabel on my first arrival, that I had to don my ceremonial uniform in the aircraft. The only way I could get my sword into its scabbard, which was fixed to my trousers, was to lie on the floor of the aircraft and have it slipped in along the floor. There was not enough height if I stood up. It was as well that Don Faustino did not see his guest getting ready.

There was a mishap with Don Faustino over national anthems. At Lagos we gave him a state dinner, with all the ministers and high officials, and at the end, after drinking the Queen's health, I proposed that of the Governor-General and of Spain, and the army band struck up what they thought was the Spanish national anthem. Most of us knew no better, but Don Faustino was taken aback and his staff seemed agitated. Later on it was discovered that the army band's book of national anthems was very old, and they had played *Hymno del Republico*, the anthem of Franco's enemies and opponents. I of course apologised to Don Faustino who took it very well. Next evening we omitted anthems and had a cinema show, and Don Faustino then called for dancing; his staff provided music, with '*Harmonica y guitara*', and my staff somehow produced lady partners and we had a gay evening. On my arrival at Santa Isabel the British anthem was played, and then what I took to be the Spanish anthem, while the guard of honour presented arms; but the Spanish anthem didn't stop and I stood at the salute for a long time feeling rather foolish, until Don Faustino led me along the guard while the band played on. Presumably it had not been the Spanish national anthem at all but incidental music for the inspection of the guard.

Following the conference in 1956 the Governments of the Eastern and Western Regions appeared to be managing fairly smoothly, but the North was going through a difficult transitional period which posed a number of problems. The creation of a ministerial system of government cut right across the administrative organisation which had existed since Lord Lugard's time. This was especially the case with the large emirates of the far North which Lord Lugard had conquered and then retained as the basis of his administration with its clearly-defined ladder of responsibility. The village chief was responsible to a district head, who in turn was responsible to the emir. The administration of the emirate was supervised by a British Resident and his District Officers, and the Resident himself was directly responsible to the Governor of the Region. Although the Resident and his officers were required to work through the Emir and the district heads, in the early years they undoubtedly exercised considerable direct control throughout an emirate, especially over taxation and expenditure, and in the last resort recalcitrant or oppressive native authorities were removed. It seemed to me, after a few tours in the North, that the authority of the Resident and his District Officers was becoming much less effective than it had been. The Emirs and their subordinate officials were in such close touch with the Premier and ministers at the Regional capital that the Resident's reports to the Governor did not have their previous validity, and it seemed to me that the Resident and the District Officers were often by-passed.

On the one hand the transfer of power to Nigerian ministers was bound to reduce the authority of the Resident and lessen his ability to control the work of the native administrations, but on the other hand not all the Emirs were glad to accept the innovation of ministerial power. It was one thing to be ruled by foreigners and another to have as rulers men of one's own race who were perhaps of less ancient lineage, or came from other emirates which only a few decades before had been their bitter enemies. This perhaps was not so noticeable with the aristocratic Sardauna of Sokoto as Premier, as many of his ministers also came from princely families; but with democratic elections and the spread of education the time might soon come when educated nobodies held political power. The Emirs were certainly afraid of rapid steps in democratising their institutions, and indeed it was reported that the sudden decision of the North in 1957 to agree to self-government and Independence in 1959 was due to the determination of the Emirs to get Independence before democracy had spread too far. This view of the situation was certainly supported by a Sudanese *kadi* in the school of Islamic Law at Kano whom I knew well. When I asked him what he thought would happen in the North when Nigeria became independent, he answered in a flash, 'The Emir will rebuild the walls of the city', and when I asked why, he replied 'to keep out democracy and limit the power of politicians'. In a note written at this time, I wrote: 'The Emirs are worried about the increasing power of the politicians and feel that the tenure of their offices may be undermined. I tried to persuade some of them that by broadening the basis of their councils, and by devolving power to lower councils, they would be able to continue guiding the affairs of their Emirates for a consider-able time yet. But there is bound to be a drive against their authority, when the results of the expansion in education begin to tell.'

The fact that the Premier of the North, the Sardauna, had a strong, energetic personality and belonged to the family of the Sultan of Sokoto, the leader of the Muslims in Northern Nigeria, gave him great prestige, and even before the Region became self-governing in 1959 he exercised considerable powers. In his autobiography his complete absorption with Northern Nigeria is made abundantly clear: he disclaimed any intention of interfering in Federal matters, and indeed went as far as to say: 'What happens in Lagos is not of great consequence here in the North.' I never understood how far the Sardauna, as head of the N.P.C., influenced the actions of the Prime Minister, but I do not think, that he interfered much, although in one or two cases the Northern ministers reacted strongly against decisions of the Federal Government, notably when Chief Festus succeeded in obtaining a loan of £3,000,000 from Israel. The Sardauna himself always assured me that he took no share in the decisions of the Federal Government, but the fact that his party held half the seats in the Federal House certainly restricted the freedom of the Prime Minister, who could not expect the support of the party members if the head of the party and his ministers in the North disagreed with Federal policy. On the other hand, as I have mentioned before, the Prime Minister too had great influence with the party, especially with the younger educated members, and was frequently required to go up to Kaduna and straighten out party differences or pacify those with whom the Sardauna had quarrelled.

With the tension growing between the politicians and the Emirs and the danger of too much centralisation of power in the hands of the political leaders in Kaduna, it was thought by the Governor and his British advisers that if provincial authorities could be evolved to supervise and encourage local government authorities, and also to provide a provincial forum where proposals for educational and econo-mic development could be discussed and hammered out, this would stimulate a sense of local identity and development which might become effective antidotes to political domination from the centre. With the help of Mr. R. S. Hudson* of the Colonial Office, a scheme was worked out and was approved in 1957 by the Regional Houses of Assembly and House of Chiefs.

It struck me from my discussions on my Northern tours that the proposals were much more likely to be effective in the provinces where

* *R. S. Hudson.* Colonial Service 1918–49. Commissioner provincial devolution, Northern Nigeria 1965. Head of African Studies Branch, Colonial Office 1949–61.

there were a number of small native authorities than in those where one authority predominated. It also seemed unlikely that the most powerful Emirs – Sokoto, Kano and Bornu – would willingly allow any of the powers exercised by them to be handed over to the province councils. Sir Bryan Sharwood-Smith worked very hard on these proposals, and was able to persuade his ministers to sponsor them in the Northern Parliament, but after he left Nigeria the Sardauna's enthusiasm waned, and nothing of any serious value came of them.

The Northern people, with 1,000 years of Islamic civilisation behind them and their religious links with the Middle East (in 1959 we celebrated the millennium of Kano City with a festival), were conservative and satisfied with their cultural heritage. They therefore did not absorb Western education, technical skills or civilisation, brought in from the coast by the British, with the same enthusiasm as did the Southern people in Eastern and Western Nigeria. With few exceptions the schools and colleges provided by the Government in the Northern Islamic provinces were seldom filled; I found in 1955 that the secondary schools at Kano and Sokoto had little more than half the pupils they could have coped with. The result was a dearth of young educated Northerners to fill the cadres of the civil service or take up employment either in trade or in the lower grades of the railways, post office, police and other Federal services. This led, by the middle 1950s, to a barely disguised dislike of the Southerners who had come north to fill all these subordinate posts, and to the Northern ministers making it a point of policy to prefer expatriate British officials to Southerners. It also resulted in strenuous efforts to train young Northern men by crash courses to take on the work which non-Northerners were doing. Effectively it was not 'Africanisation' but 'Northernisation' which was taking place, and within reason it seemed a sensible policy. But I felt it was unjust when Northerners appeared hostile to educated Southerners, simply because the latter had been quicker to prepare for new employment opportunities.

I did not see much evidence that the dislike of the Northerners for the Southerners was based upon religion. The Prime Minister of the Federation, the Premier of the North and many of the Northern ministers were devout practising Muslims, but they always seemed to have a tolerant attitude towards Christians. In later years after Independence the Sardauna undoubtedly used his position as Premier to spread Islam in the pagan parts of the Region, but I had no suspicion of this happening in the years before Independence. It is, however, a widely held belief that throughout history Muslim peoples have never co-operated with non-Muslims, and certainly in the Sudan the contempt of the Muslim Northerner for the Southern pagan was little disguised, and for a Northern Arab marriage with a Southern woman was in my time almost impossible, although concubinage was of course frequent. How far this feeling existed in Northern Nigeria I do not know, but I imagine it was present in some degree. One or two unguarded remarks by the Sardauna and others occasionally gave away their real feelings. On the other hand, in Western Nigeria and Lagos itself there was a large Muslim population, between 40 and 50 per cent in some places, and there always appeared to me a wonderfully tolerant attitude to these religious differences. A single family might contain Christians, Muslims and pagans among its members and yet they succeeded in living together in amity.

A more potent cause of ill-feeling was the difference in ordinary custom and behaviour between the dignified, polite, rather aloof Northerner and the uninhibited, vociferous Southerner who noisily showed his disagreement in Council or Parliament without good manners or restraint. The Northern leaders in conversation constantly reverted to the way in which they had been insulted and pilloried by the Southern politicians and street crowds in Lagos after their opposition to a motion for speedy self-government in the House of Representatives in 1953. The Sardauna wrote: 'We went out into the screams and insults of the large crowds of Lagos thugs waiting for us in the courtyard . . . we were all very glad to get into our special train that evening and head for the high hills and plains of the North.' There was then strong feeling that the North should secede from the Federation and give up the attempt to work with the Southerners. This agitation died down, but the ill-feeling engendered by these weeks of conflict was not speedily overcome, and was always latent until Independence and certainly lay behind the bitter reaction of the Northerner people to the military coup at the start of January 1966, when Ibo officers murdered Northern and Western politicians and army officers and for some months were the rulers of Nigeria. When the reaction came, thousands of Ibos in the North were killed, often in the most brutal manner. The deep latent hatred boiled over.

A note of mine written in December 1956 is relevant here. 'The general outlook of the people is so different from that of those in Southern Nigeria as to give them practically nothing in common. There is less difference between an Englishman and Italian, both of whom have a common civilisation based on Greek and Roman foundations and on Christianity, than between a Muslim villager in Sokoto, Kano or Karsina, and an Ibo, an Ijaw or a Kalabari. How can any feeling of common purpose or nationality be built up between people whose culture, religion and mode of living is so completely different? In Churchill's first volume of his history of the *English-Speaking Peoples* he tells how various races and stocks combine to make our present-day population after a thousand or twelve hundred years. But here in Nigeria we are only at the beginning and the process of coalescence has barely begun. There is common interest in communications and access to the sea, and mutual advantage in peaceful trading, but what else? When the British go, what will keep these diverse peoples together within the artificial boundaries drawn on the maps in the 1880s and 1890s?'

I could only try and influence the situation through the Federal Government and the Regional Governors. In this latter respect I was lucky to have Sir Gawain Bell* in the Northern Province to replace Sir Bryan Sharwood-Smith who retired in September 1957. Sir Gawain had worked with me in the Civil Secretary's Office in Khartoum in 1951–3 and I knew him well. He spoke excellent Arabic and seemed an ideal choice for Northern Nigeria, with his experience of the transitional period leading to independence in the Sudan. As it turned out he and the Northern Premier got on extremely well, and his success in adapting himself to the change between being the executive colonial governor and the constitutional head of a self-governing Region was proved by the readiness of the Northern ministers to retain him as Governor until his term of appointment ended in 1962.

The constitutional conference had laid the foundations of regional self-government and eventual Independence, but there was still some way to go before that final goal was achieved. In September 1958 the conference was re-opened in London with the reports of the commissions as the main subject for consideration. The report of Sir Jeremy Raisman's commission into the alteration of revenues evoked some criticism but was generally accepted as reasonable. The Regions considered that the Federal Government was very generously treated, and it may be that Lagos, as the capital city, absorbed too much of the revenue with its educational and building programmes. But the division recommended was accepted and was not altered for several years. The Delineation of Electoral Boundaries Commission was unanimously thought to have carried out its task 'in a very reasonable way', as the Sardauna said, though of course it was not possible to have absolute equality of numbers in the various constituencies. Some had appreciably more electors than others as a result of the administrative boundaries of provinces and divisions, which the Commission had been instructed

* *Sir Gawain Bell*. Sudan Political Service 1931–55. Seconded to Palestine 1938. Military service Middle East 1941–5. Assistant Civil Secretary and Deputy Civil Secretary 1951–4. Permanent Under-Secretary Minister of the Interior 1954–5. Governor Northern Nigeria 1957–62.

to keep in view. The Minorities Commission under the Chairmanship of Sir Henry Willink had had the most difficult task. It did not recommend the creation of any new Regions, chiefly I think because it was not proved that minorities were being seriously prejudiced under the existing arrangements, though of course the protagonists of fragmentation alleged that they were. In addition, as I have already pointed out, any new Regions would almost certainly have been composed of several tribal units causing the same accusations to be repeated, while any reorganisation would have created administrative difficulties. The commission recommended the creation of a board to undertake the development of the Niger delta, a proposal which was accepted by the conference with little enthusiasm except by the representative of the Rivers peoples, Mr. Birieye,* and which I later found difficult to implement. There were also some minor recommendations to ameliorate the conditions of minorities, but the major problem was in fact shelved.

The resumed conference also agreed that the Northern Region should become self-governing in March 1959, and the provisions which had been applied to the East and West in 1957 were adopted for the Northern constitution.

The British Government, pressed to fix a date for Independence, agreed that if the Federal Parliament due to be elected late in 1959 passed a resolution asking for Independence, it would be granted as soon as the necessary legal instruments could be prepared and a Bill passed by the British Parliament. It was not thought that this could well be done by 2 April 1960, the date which the Nigerian delegates unanimously proposed, and they eventually accepted 1 October 1960 as proposed by Her Majesty's Government.

The Conference also dealt with a number of other less important matters. I agreed to chair a further conference in Nigeria to formulate electoral rules and regulations and later to appoint an electoral commission to ensure that the general election took place in a peaceful and orderly manner. The question of a defence agreement between Great Britain and Nigeria was also raised, and Duncan Sandys† discussed it with leading Nigerian representatives. They were unhappy about it but eventually initialled an agreement which was not destined to be ratified after Independence.

This was the last important conference before Independence, though we did have a final smaller meeting in London in May 1960,

* *Harold Birieye*. Representative of Rivers States at Nigeria Constitutional Conferences 1957 and 1958.

† *Duncan Sandys*. Conservative M.P. 1935–45 and from 1950. Held various ministerial posts including Minister of Defence 1957–9.

when the Independence constitution was submitted to the leading Nigerian delegates and accepted by them as being a true record of what they agreed to. This was a much shorter meeting than previous ones and was far less emotional. We had a new chairman: Iain Macleod* had become Colonial Secretary in place of Alan Lennox-Boyd. We were all sorry that he had resigned for he was on friendly terms with all the Nigerian leaders, who admired him and found him approachable. They had known him for several years and under his guidance the two big conferences had gone so well that Mr. Macleod had little to do.

Northern Nigeria became self-governing in March 1959, and as it was Ramadan and the Muslims were fasting, the actual transfer of authority from the Governor to the Premier and his Council was done very quietly and without celebration; but later, in May, the Northern Region staged an official celebration at which the Duke and Duchess of Gloucester were Her Majesty's representatives. My wife and I flew to Kano to welcome Their Royal Highnesses and the Secretary of State Mr. Lennox-Boyd, and we attended the durbar which the Region staged at Kaduna. This was a repeat performance of that arranged for the Queen and the Duke of Edinburgh three years earlier, and was a magnificent spectacle. Some 4,000 horsemen and 900 men on foot, gaily dressed in all the colours of the rainbow, marched past the royal pavilion and stands on the green polo ground in a seemingly never-ending column. Each provincial contingent was headed by the local chiefs and their retainers, who were of course the brightest and gayest, with many of the horses outdoing their riders in the brilliance of their trappings. There were some in chainmail, others were dancing and the entertainers sometimes dallied in front of the pavilion holding up the parade. At the end of the march-past the finale consisted of massed horsemen charging at full tilt up to the pavilion, shouting and cheering at the tops of their voices, and waving their swords and spears. Many participants had come hundreds of miles, and the whole exercise was a great feat of organisation.

The royal party carried out the usual tour of Nigeria and came to us in Lagos for four or five days. The weather was very hot and the Duke felt the heat badly, so the programme was not very strenuous. The 'state dinner' was awkward as several things went wrong. There was a contretemps when we sat down as the servants had forgotten to put salt in the salt-cellars on the table. In humid climates like Lagos, salt must only be put out in the salt-cellars just before the dinner

* *Iain Macleod.* Conservative M.P. 1950–70. Colonial Secretary 1959–61. Died 1970.

begins, and this had been forgotten. Instead of telling one waiter to go round and fill all the salt-cellars on the table, the head waiter had them all taken away and filled in the pantry, while we all waited for the first course, trying to make conversation until the exercise was completed. We had no fans in our dining room, but there was an eight-armed punkah pulled by one of the gardeners who sat outside the room. This evening the rope which pulled the punkah broke between numbers four and five; which meant that Their Royal Highnesses and we ourselves at the head of the table were without the pleasantly cool movement of air. The Duke said, 'Robertson, it's getting bloody hot' – and I told the servants to bring in some of our moveable fans. However, before they could arrive my private secretary, John Bongard,* stood up on the table and joined up the broken rope, and the punkah began to work again. My wife and I were far from happy as he did this, for the table was not very strong in the middle, and we feared a far worse catastrophe if it collapsed, and china, cutlery and table ornaments slid on to the floor. But fortunately the table supported his weight. The Duke was diligent in visiting army units, inspecting a Boy Scout parade and taking a parade of troops and police on the racecourse. The Duchess for her part visited hospitals and museums and inspected Ben Enwonwu's† statue of the Queen outside the Parliament building. She was a charming guest. We had a number of evening parties for them, and after these were over and the Duke had said good-bye to the guests and taken the Duchess away to their rooms, he usually returned and sat gossiping with me for an hour or two over our whiskies. He was very easy to talk to and obviously was intensely interested in the army and knew a great deal about it. I was not well up in army matters, nor did I know many of the senior officers whom His Royal Highness talked about, but he was wrapped up in army affairs, and one felt sorry that he had not been able to enjoy a full military career.

In July 1959 my wife and I paid state visits as Governor-General of Nigeria to Liberia and Sierra Leone. It was a bad time of year to make this trip as it was the height of the rainy season, and when we landed at Robertsfield airport in Liberia it was misty and drizzling. The guard of honour waiting to greet me was wet and dishevelled and its turn-out accordingly was not very good. I had the impression that my Nigerian A.D.C., Captain Ralph Shodendi,‡ was rather ashamed

* *John Bongard.* Northern Nigerian administrative officer seconded to act as Private Secretary to Governor-General 1959.

† *Ben Enwonwu.* Artist and sculptor from Onitsha, Eastern Nigeria. Sculptor of statue of Queen Elizabeth II erected outside House of Representatives, Lagos.

‡ *Ralph Shodendi* – a Yoruba from Abeokuta, at this time a captain in the Queen's Own Nigerian Regiment and A.D.C. to the Governor-General. Later Commandant of army training school, Kaduna, where he was assassinated 1966.

of this African army. We were taken into Monrovia in large cars, which travelled very fast with sirens booming, to a state reception by President Tubman.* Speeches, drinks and presentations took some time and my wife and I were very hungry as it was hours since breakfast. We were accommodated in the President's rest house and were most comfortable, though we wondered why there should always be a posse of people outside our bedroom door. Later we were told these were security personnel to protect us from any possible danger. My private secretary told me that the lady member of the guard was carrying a revolver under her arm, and we wondered how he had discovered this.

In the evening the President gave a dinner and a dance in our honour, and a good time was had by all, though it was somehow not exactly what we had expected. I had no idea what to give the President as a present, but someone told me he enjoyed Johnnie Walker Black Label whisky. So I brought two cases of this with me and sent them to him with a little note saying I hoped he would enjoy 'the wine of my country'. I received a charming note thanking me, and saying he certainly enjoyed the wine of my country as it was both 'stimulating and sedative'. Next morning I had to lay a wreath on the Founding Fathers' memorial. The rain was still pouring down and the guard of honour was soaked to the skin, while the wreath I was to lay was so weighed down by water that I could not lift it myself and had to be helped by my A.D.C. and the British Ambassador. That afternoon I visited the new port which had just begun to function, and went up-country to see a mine where iron ore was being excavated. We stopped on the way back to Monrovia and I was installed as paramount chief of a tribe.

We did not have long enough to make any useful assessment of Liberia's progress. There were some good buildings in Monrovia and the élite, composed of the descendants of the original ex-slaves from the United States of America who settled there in the first half of the nineteenth century, were well educated. But there seemed little contact between them and the indigenous population, though by all accounts there had been much more in recent years than previously. Some of the sophisticated equipment in a girls' secondary school surprised us, as it seemed unlikely that the girls in their own homes would find the expensive electric cookers, dish-washers and laundry equipment which they were being taught to use at school. The big Firestone rubber estates at Robertsfield were impressive in themselves, but the colony of American engineers and agriculturalists seemed to have little contact with the native population, and to be a little *imperium in*

* *W. V. S. Tubman.* President of Liberia from 1944 until his death in 1971. Leader of True Whig Party.

*imperio*. It was also interesting to learn that the leading Creoles, from the President downwards, had extensive plantations farmed by hired labour, whose production was processed by the Firestone people and from which the absentee owners drew large profits. The President was leader of the True Whig Party which had been in power for several generations, he himself having been first elected President in 1944. He held office up to his death in 1971 and undoubtedly did much for his country. He came to Lagos to return my visit in 1960.

We flew on to Sierra Leone and were met at the airport by the Governor, Sir Maurice Dorman,* whom I had previously met in 1954 in Trinidad. The airport was across the harbour, and our journey back to Freetown was made in a deluge of rain. A welcoming crowd of Nigerians on the quay at Freetown were very wet but enthusiastic, and I saw more of them later when I attended a Nigerian gathering. At this time Sierra Leone was in a transitional stage between colonial government and Independence; its Premier was Sir Milton Margai – a charming man who for years had practised as a doctor in Newcastle-on-Tyne.

Sir Maurice and Lady Dorman were excellent hosts and arranged several parties in our honour at which we were able to meet and talk to many of Sierra Leone's leading people. Sir Maurice also took me up-country as far as Bo, where I was enlightened about the diamond problems and saw something of the interior. The integration of the freed slaves of Freetown with the indigenous inhabitants of the country had progressed further here than in Liberia, though it still seemed to be the fact that the Creoles of Freetown were disinclined to share political power with the local people, although Sir Milton Margai – and later his brother Sir Albert – made brave efforts to break down the barriers. Fourah Bay University College was interesting; it was associated with Durham University, and quite a large percentage of its students came from Nigeria. A number of Sierra Leoneans had filled senior positions in Nigeria and even in the late 1950s there were still several in senior government positions.

After an interesting break we returned to Nigeria and its problems. The staffing of the civil service remained a worry, for the lack of adequately trained Nigerians made it necessary to persuade the governments of the need to retain some expatriates after Independence. It was also essential to make conditions palatable for those who stayed, both in financial terms and in the conditions of service. Experience and merit should not be endangered by nationalistic desire to push up less efficient and less able Nigerians to the detriment of the

* *Sir Maurice Dorman*. See above, page 174.

expatriate. But while it was possible to avoid such preferential treat-
ment so long as the Governor-General had the final say in personnel
matters, once Independence was achieved there would be no long-stop
to protect the expatriate. But the end of 1959 it was clear that, judging
by the experience of the Eastern and Western Regions, about 30 per
cent of the expatriate staff would leave in the first two years of self-
government, and there seemed no reason why a similar exodus would
not occur in the Federal and Northern Region services.

The Colonial Office had initiated schemes to assist the official and
to see that he was not left unprotected in the rapid transfer of power.
It was agreed with the Nigerian Government that when the Federal
Council of Ministers and the Regional Executive Councils were denu-
ded of their expatriate members – and it could be held that the careers
of expatriate officials had been interrupted by a 'change of masters' –
they should be entitled to retire on the pensions they had earned by
their length of service plus a lump sum compensation for the loss of
career. The compensation was graduated and reached its maximum at
about the age of forty-one, it being held that before that age the official
could no doubt find another occupation fairly easily and his loss of career
was the less the younger he was. Above that age the compensation fell
away until it disappeared at normal retiring age, when it could not be
held that the official was losing any part of his career. The maximum
payment was £9,000. It was likely, therefore, that men in the late
thirties, the post-Second War intake, would wish to go at about forty-
one when they would get the maximum, while men approaching the
end of their service might soldier on without feeling they were losing
anything. But of course every case was different depending on factors
such as the individual's health, whether he was married and had
children, and whether he and his wife liked the service and the
Nigerians.

There was a danger that just about the time of Independence a
great proportion of expatriate officers would decide to take their
'lumpers' and leave the country with a seriously weakened civil service.
The British Government therefore introduced two special schemes,
A and B, which gave the officials some inducement to stay on. There
was much correspondence between London and Lagos about the
schemes before they were introduced, and in the event they were only
partly successful. Shortly before Independence a further proposal was
made by Her Majesty's Government that it would supplement the
salaries of expatriate officers to bring them up to higher levels to corres-
pond with the rise in the cost of living. I tried to persuade the Nigerian
ministers to accept this suggestion but was not successful. A majority
of them held that the proposal was insulting to Nigeria for they could

pay their officials what was necessary, and if such an arrangement was made, the officials would have a divided loyalty. The situation in the Federal service was therefore uncertain at the time of Independence.

In addition to the feeling of insecurity of tenure and worry about the growing cost of living, the actual conditions of work in the last few years were becoming unsatisfactory. After the post of Chief Secretary had been abolished in 1957 there was no definite head of the service. As Governor-General (assisted and advised by the Public Service Commission), I had an ultimate responsibility, in matters of appointments and promotions, but the Establishments Department was moved about from one ministry to another and ultimately was formed into a separate ministry of its own, and officers therefore had no responsible leader. Furthermore, as men retired and suitable replacements were not usually obtainable, there were frequent transfers from post to post, as the Establishments Branch tried to stop the important gaps. This led to lack of interest and intimate knowledge of the problems facing the ministers. Political interference in the service was another reason for doubts and malaise among officials, and attacks by back-bench members of the House of Representatives on named individuals were far too common. With all the difficulties which the civil service faced at this time it was remarkable that the machine continued to function as well as it did, and this I was sure was due to the many senior officers, who had a pride in their work and a devotion to duty.

CHAPTER XII

# LAST STEPS TO INDEPENDENCE

Under the Federal constitution of 1954, the House of Representatives sat for a term of five years. It first met in January 1955, so a general election had to be held in December 1959 and for some months preparations had been under way. As instructed by the constitutional conference, I convened a meeting of the political parties to work out rules for electoral procedure, registration of electors, voting and other matters, and we sat for two or three days discussing the many points that arose. I was surprised at the variety of possible electoral malpractices, but the Nigerians were well aware of all sorts which would never have occurred to me. However, we achieved unity of purpose and the rules and regulations were eventually agreed. It was decided that we should have an electoral commission to organise the elections throughout the whole country, but it was of course necessary to cooperate with regional administrative authorities to carry out the work, as the Federal Government had no administrative staff in the regions. I was fortunate to find in R. E. Wraith, a don at Ibadan University who had made a study of local government, an eminently suitable chairman for the Electoral Commission and he and his Nigerian colleagues did fine work in organising the exercise throughout the country despite many difficulties, complaints, disputes and squabbles.

There was anxiety about the maintenance of law and order, and the Inspector-General of Police and his regional commissioners had a big task arranging for the adequate policing of hundreds of polling stations throughout the country and for keeping order during the excitement of canvassing before the actual voting. At the constitutional conference the question had been asked 'who will be responsible for seeing that the election is conducted in peace?' There was quite a pause before I said that it seemed to be my responsibility as Governor-General; and the party political leaders accepted my undertaking. I was therefore closely interested personally in all the arrangements made both by the Electoral Commission and the Inspector-General. In order to avoid risks we decided to bring in the army too and have units of the Nigerian Regiment distributed around the country to support the police – ostensibly on manoeuvres and exercises, but posted in the areas where we thought trouble might arise.

Chief Awolowo and the Action Group realised that they had little hope of winning many seats in the Eastern Region, and that if they were to have a chance of a majority, they would have to make a big impression in the North where half the constituencies were situated. The party therefore appointed electoral agents in the North, and Chief Awolowo did some vigorous campaigning there. He caused considerable ill-feeling by employing a helicopter and flying in it over the Northern cities, thereby leading to accusations of infringing the purdah of the Northern ladies in their homes as leaflets and pamphlets were showered from the air. Chief Awolowo's electoral meetings in the North were sometimes rowdy and his line of attack on the N.P.C. was mainly against the feudal Emirate system and emphasised his party's intention of democratising the regime should it be returned to power. The Northern Premier and ministers were perturbed by this and were loud in their allegations that the Action Group were sending thugs and corner boys to the North to create trouble. There were a few incidents; some people were killed in rioting in the Igala area, and there were other rowdy meetings with some fighting. I therefore sent for Chief Awolowo to come down from Kano by air. He, of course, denied that his agents were at all provocative; according to him they were not thugs but electoral agents sent to help the Northerners, who had had little previous experience of elections, to understand the procedure and explain to them the standpoints of their party. He reminded me of my undertaking to see that everyone had a fair deal, and complained that his meetings were being broken up by noisy N.P.C. groups, and that at Bida a herd of cattle had been driven through an open-air meeting. He seemed very optimistic of success in the North and, as far as I could see, had been grievously misinformed by his agents, who had exaggerated their success in influencing Northern voters and had thereby succeeded in getting money, bicycles, radio sets and other weapons of war from the party headquarters – greatly to their own personal gain. At the end of our talk I took Chief Awolowo to the top of the staircase and bade him good-bye; half-way down the stairs he turned and with a beaming smile said, 'I shall be coming up and down these stairs very often when I am your Prime Minister.'

There was a reasonably good turn-out of voters on the actual day and not much trouble at the polling booths. I visited several in Lagos and was relieved to find long queues of voters, chatting and laughing happily together in a relaxed atmosphere. Then came the counting of the votes and the gradual notification of results. Before all the counting had finished, rumours began to circulate that the N.C.N.C. and the Action Group were getting together, and might form a coalition;

there was no doubt that Dr. Azikiwe and Chief Awolowo were in close touch through various go-betweens. It seemed clear that although there were a number of seats still to be declared, the state of the parties would finally be approximately N.P.C. 140, N.C.N.C. 90 and Action Group 75, and if the Action Group and N.C.N.C. formed a coalition they would have a majority in the House of Representatives. I believed that this could be very dangerous for Nigeria's future as, from all I had learned of the Sardauna and the Northerners, they might well decide to leave the Federation for they would not readily accept a national government of the Southern parties. Even if this did not happen, there was bound to be a serious political situation. This view is supported by the Sardauna in his autobiography where he wrote: 'A sudden grouping of the Eastern and Western parties (with a few members from the North opposed to our party) might take power and so endanger the North. This would of course be utterly disastrous. It might set back our programme of development seriously; it would therefore force us to take measures to avert the need.'

Under the constitution the Governor-General was enjoined to appoint as Prime Minister the person who seemed to him most likely to command a majority in the House of Representatives, and it seemed to me that if Abu Bakar could persuade some of the Southern members to support him, he could command a majority. At the same time there were reports that several N.C.N.C. members from the Mid-West, like Chief Festus Okotie-Eboh and his friends, were not ready to join in a coalition with the Action Group on account of their long local rivalries. I invited Abu Bakar to come and discuss the position with me and we went over these various points. He thought that he might well be able to find some support in the South. I finally asked him to advise me whether I should ask him to form a government at once or wait a little longer until the situation clarified. Abu Bakar replied that I should invite him to form a government immediately and I did so on the grounds that the leader of the party with the greatest number of seats was surely the most likely to be able to form a government which would win the support of the House. As far as I remember now, I took this action entirely on my own and did not consult the Secretary of State, for the matter was urgent and could not wait.

Abu Bakar went away and a few days later I heard rumours that the N.C.N.C. and N.P.C. had come to an agreement to form a coalition and had decided on a share-out of offices. Abu Bakar rang up and asked if he, the Sardauna and Dr. Azikiwe could come to see me, and when they arrived at my office he presented me with a paper containing their proposals for the various appointments. Dr. Azikiwe was to leave his Premiership of the Eastern Region and become President of the newly formed Senate; it had also been agreed that when I retired, the Prime Minister would advise the Queen to appoint Dr. Azikiwe Governor-General. The Council of Ministers would be composed of N.P.C. and N.C.N.C. members, almost equally divided, with most of my old ministers reinstated and a few additions, to take the place of the Action Group members who would go into opposition. Dr. Azikiwe and the Sardauna both expressed themselves satisfied with the proposals, although earlier 'Zik' had criticised my action in asking Abu Bakar to form a ministry as 'premature and inept'. He had, I think, hoped that with a Southern coalition he would be Prime Minister, and he was not altogether satisfied with the Presidency of the Senate and future Governor-Generalship. These two offices would give him little or no political power, though of course the Governor-Generalship had considerable prestige and influence.

The new parliament was opened in January 1960, when I read the Speech from the Throne, and one of its first actions was to pass a resolution asking the British Government to give Nigeria Independence on 2 April 1960. This gave too little time for the constitutional drafting to be finished, and for the preparation for adequate celebrations of such a memorable event, so 1 October was eventually agreed on by all parties.

I wondered what I should do myself, as Abu Bakar had been pressing me to agree to stay for some time after independence. He mentioned two years as a suitable period, but I felt that this was far too long. I agreed with him that it would be better for continuity that I should not disappear immediately on Independence Day, but I felt strongly that it would be wrong psychologically for the same white face to appear for too long in Government House after Independence. I also thought that to be Governor-General after Independence, with no executive power, would lay me open to be blamed for any mistakes my ministers might make without my having any authority to prevent such unfortunate happenings. Furthermore, the fact that Dr. Azikiwe had been led to believe that he would succeed me made it all the more necessary not to delay my going. But Abu Bakar's desire for me to stay made it awkward as I did not wish to fail him. Fortunately, when Mr. Harold Macmillan, the British Prime Minister, came to Lagos in January 1960 on his African tour, I was able to discuss the matter with him, and when he agreed with me, he was good enough to persuade Abu Bakar that my decision was the right one. So it was arranged that I should stay on for a month or two after Independence until things settled down and the new constitution had begun to work.

The months before Independence were busy ones, as there was much to do and many visitors to Nigeria, most of whom called at Government House and many of whom requested interviews with me. The ordinary routine of government had to be carried on and there were the usual almost weekly meetings of the Council of Ministers. I also presided over the Defence Council and the National Economic Council which held two meetings, one at Enugu and the other at Lagos. In March I unofficially and unconstitutionally asked the Prime Minister to take over active control of the police and the armed forces, for which I was, of course, constitutionally responsible until Nigeria became independent. I retained the right to be informed of his decisions and to intervene, if I thought it necessary. Needless to say Sir Abu Bakar – he was knighted on 1 January 1960 – carried out his side of the bargain meticulously and I never had any cause to regret my action, especially as it seemed essential to me that he should be completely *au fait* with this side of government work when the country became independent. Mr. Iain Macleod chaired a final constitutional conference in London in May to approve the draft constitution for the independent Nigeria. This was not controversial and the Nigerian parties were represented by only a few of the leaders.

On his visit to us Mr. Harold Macmillan was accompanied by a large staff including Sir Norman Brook, Secretary to the Cabinet. My wife and I were delighted that he brought with him our son James* as representative of the Colonial Office – his thoughtfulness over this we greatly appreciated. Mr. Macmillan was such a stickler for correct protocol that I found it most embarrassing whenever we met, for he greeted me as the Queen's representative with the courtesy bow normally made only to royalty.

I was to open a new session of Parliament on 13 January and read the speech from the throne, which had been approved by the Council of Ministers a few days before. As this ceremony coincided with Mr. Macmillan's visit, it was arranged that, after I had left the House, the Nigerian Prime Minister would welcome him and he would address the members. From Lagos he visited Ibadan and Kaduna, and finally left Ikeja airport for Salisbury and South Africa on 18 January. How much his experience in Ghana and Nigeria influenced him in preparing his famous 'Wind of Change' speech in South Africa is of course something one cannot know, but his visit to the Nigerian Parliament, where African members were in a vast majority and few white faces were to be seen, must have seemed a tremendous contrast to the parliament in South Africa.

Abu Bakar and I had long interviews with Mr. Macmillan about

* *J. H. Robertson.* Colonial Office 1953–65. Joined C.E.I.R. Later Director, Inter-Banking Research Organisation.

the future of the country, but my chief concern was to put to him the complicated position regarding the Southern Cameroons. For this we called in Mr. John Field,* the Commissioner, and Mr. Foncha,† the Premier of the Southern Cameroons Government. As I explained earlier, the British Cameroons were part of the old German colony which had been occupied by the British and French armies in the 1914–18 war. It had then been divided up, the French taking the lion's share and the British a slice on the western edge of the country. Nigeria had administered this on behalf of Her Majesty's Government, the Northern area being treated as an integral part of the Northern Region, while in the later years the Southern section had been made a separate region of the Federation with its own administration and, eventually, its own assembly and executive council. With the approach of Nigerian independence the future of these two mandated territories had to be decided. They were not, like Nigeria, purely British responsibilities, and it seemed clear that some arrangement had to be made to consult their people about the future. Obviously the United Nations, whose wards they were, would have to be satisfied that their future status was in accordance with their wishes.

Some form of plebiscite would have to be held, and one of my problems was to see that satisfactory arrangements for this were made. In the interval between Nigerian independence and the holding of the plebiscite, the Nigerian Government could not continue to be responsible for the administration of the territory, and Her Majesty's Government would have to be directly in charge through the Commissioner for the Cameroons, who would no longer work through the Governor-General, but would be directly responsible to the Colonial Office. The British Government would have to find the financial support which Nigeria had previously given to the Cameroons, and would also have to provide troops which had previously come from the Queen's Own Nigeria Regiment.

The problem was intensified by the situation just over the border in the French Cameroons where a rebellion had been going on against the Government for several years. As early as 1956 we had been worried about security along the frontier, and in 1957 I had met the French Governor, M. Torré, in Lagos to discuss the situation. He complained that rebel bands found security in the British Cameroons and from their bases there raided the French territory and created what amounted almost to a civil war. We tried to patrol the frontier

* *Sir John Field.* Colonial Administrative Service Nigeria 1936. Commissioner for the Cameroons 1956–61. Later Governor St. Helena.

† *J.N. Foncha*, Premier of Southern Cameroons after 1959 election. Favoured unity with French Cameroons and after 1961 plebiscite became deputy to President Ahidjo.

with our rather inadequate police force, but M. Torré was not satisfied and for quite a time I had stationed units of the Queen's Own Nigeria Regiment along the frontier opposite the troubled areas to try and prevent the rebels taking refuge in our territory.

The Nigerian Council of Ministers was not prepared to permit Nigerian troops or police to be used for this purpose after Independence and it was necessary to find other means. The Prime Minister was also opposed to using Nigerian police in the Cameroons at all after Independence, and was not happy about arrangements which I had approved for training Cameroonian recruits in a new police school near Tiko staffed by Nigerian police N.C.O.s. However, he was very reasonable, and we managed to work out mutually agreeable arrangements, whereby Nigeria lent staff to the Western Cameroons on an agency basis to be paid for by the Cameroons budget. The civil service was also a problem; the great majority of the more senior staff in all services belonged to the Federal civil service and many of them were British or Nigerian. The Nigerians did not look forward to remaining under a Cameroonian administration as they feared discrimination against them in favour of Cameroonians, the great majority of whom were junior and less experienced. The British enjoyed their work in the Cameroons and were ready enough to work on so long as their prospects and careers were safeguarded. Eventually, by dint of much correspondence and discussion, reasonably satisfactory arrangements were concluded. Those Nigerians who would not continue to serve were brought back to posts in Nigeria; a number of the British agreed to continue their service with supplementary financial benefit; Cameroonians were pushed forward; and numbers of additional expatriates were recruited, so that when Nigeria became independent there was the nucleus of a Cameroonian service to carry on the administration until the plebiscites took place in April 1961. The British Government undertook to provide a British battalion to take the place of the Nigerian troops who had been guarding the frontier, and on my farewell visit to Buea in the middle of September 1960 I found units of the Border Regiment.

Arrangements for the plebiscites were also put in hand. Sir John Dring,* previously of the Indian Political Service, was appointed as adviser to the Governor-General and to the Governor of the Northern Region on the running of the plebiscite, and he spent some months in the area working out arrangements with local officials. As it transpired, the arrangements made were reasonably successful; there was no dislocation of law and order, and the wheels of government turned

* *Sir John Dring.* Indian Army and Political Service 1923–52. Adviser to Governor-General for the Northern and Southern Cameroon plebiscites in 1959–61.

steadily if perhaps a little more slowly. The plebiscite took place in a peaceful atmosphere, with the Southern Cameroons voting overwhelmingly to join the new Cameroons state, while the Northern area equally decisively determined to continue its association with Northern Nigeria. President Ahidjo of the French Cameroons considered that too much pressure had been put on the Northerners by the Regional Government, but his protests were not endorsed by the United Nations supervisors and the results of the plebiscites were accepted.

Once the question of the Cameroons had been decided, it was possible to proceed with the arrangements for Independence Day. An elaborate programme of celebrations had been planned – at perhaps too great an expense – but, as someone said, such an occasion could only happen once in a nation's history and the Federal ministers quite naturally wished to make an impact on the world. My wife and I were to be hosts to H.R.H. Princess Alexandra, who was coming to represent the Queen at the celebrations, and I had also invited Lord Kilmuir,* the Lord Chancellor, and Lady Kilmuir to stay with us in Government House – he had been a friend of mine at Balliol in 1919 and we had subsequently met from time to time, so I was glad that the British Government had chosen him as their representative. We also had to prepare for the entertainment of other guests at dinners and luncheons, as well as a garden party and an evening reception. And, of course, besides all this I had to satisfy myself that preparations for the important public functions were being properly handled.

I presided over the Council of Ministers for the last time on 23 September, for after Independence the Prime Minister would preside over cabinet meetings, and I should become the representative of the Queen as constitutional Head of State. I took the opportunity of this last meeting to address the Council, and I append a record of what was said. (See Appendix A.) It was at once a sad and happy occasion and for me marked the end of a long, friendly association. The next morning I received a charming letter from Senator Majekodunmi, one of the Council, in which he said:

'May I say how happy I was at the sincere and, if I may say so with respect, courageous advice you gave to Council this morning. I have not been privileged to have worked with you for as long as some of my colleagues, but in the few months in which I have served in Council I have constantly admired your efforts to promote the unity of our country to ensure objectivity in our approach to our many problems.

* *Lord Kilmuir* (formerly Sir David Maxwell-Fyfe). Conservative M.P. Home Secretary. Later Lord Chancellor. Died 1967.

'There can be no doubt that our success and the greatness of our country will depend in no small degree on how much we have benefited from the advice you gave us in so forthright a manner. We shall miss you and your wife very much when you depart; our consolation is that we know that you will both continue to keep a lively interest in our fortunes and we know that you wish us well.'

Princess Alexandra arrived in Lagos on 26 September and began a series of engagements which culminated on the evening of 30 September, and the morning of 1 October. It would be tedious to describe them all, but our garden party on the 28th was unforgettable. No sooner had Her Royal Highness appeared on the steps leading from the house to the lawn and a fanfare of trumpets had sounded than the heavens opened and a downpour ensued. Many of the guests were soaked and new hats and dresses were ruined. A certain number of guests had been warned that they would be presented to H.R.H. and they stood their ground in the rain. So H.R.H. sallied out in the deluge and the presentations were made. I tried to hold an umbrella over her head but she got very wet and so did I.

On the evening of the 30th the Government gave a formal dinner party for Nigerian leaders and overseas guests at the new Federal Palace Hotel and thereafter we made our way to the Racecourse, where a floodlit tattoo had been arranged. This culminated at midnight with the lowering of the Union Jack and hoisting of the new Nigerian flag. For this ceremony the Prime Minister and I – in my full regalia – stood on a dais near the flag-pole in the floodlit arena. The Union Jack was illuminated; the guards of honour from the Nigerian army, police and navy, as well as the British navy and army and a Rhodesian contingent presented arms; and the bands played 'God save the Queen'. Then the lights all went out, a minute passed and when they were switched on again the new Nigerian flag waved out in the breeze on the mast. After another salute by the guards of honour, and after the new Nigerian national anthem* had been played, I turned to congratulate the Prime Minister and shake his hand, to find that he was emotionally overcome and that tears were coursing down his cheeks. It was the culmination for him and many Nigerians of years of effort. I did not myself find this rather formal parade as emotional as the small ceremony that I had arranged earlier at six o'clock that evening when the Union Jack which flew at Government House on a tall flag-pole was lowered

---

* Nigerian National Anthem. Shortly before Independence a competition was held and the entries were played to the Council of Ministers for their adjudication. The ministers had no knowledge of the authors and composers and were disappointed to discover that the entry they chose was the work of expatriates.

for the last time. My staff and I felt we were watching the end of an era as the flag had flown there for over sixty years. The tattoo ended with a wonderful firework display.

Next morning came the final ceremony of the transfer of power. My wife and I drove to the Racecourse where, in front of Federal and Regional ministers on a large dais in the middle of the vast arena of crowded stands, I took the oath of allegiance to Her Majesty as Governor-General of the independent Federation of Nigeria. The oath was administered by the Chief Justice of the Federation, Sir Adetokunbo Ademola,* and I then spoke to the gathering.

When this part of the proceedings was over, Princess Alexandra arrived in procession with an escort of mounted police provided by native administrative units from the Northern Region. She addressed the company and read a message from H.M. the Queen. She then handed a copy of the Act of the British Parliament which granted independence to Nigeria to the Prime Minister, Sir Abu Bakar Tafawa Balewa, who made an excellent speech in reply, which I append to this Chapter. (See Appendix B.) That evening the Federal Government held a State Ball which was a wonderful occasion, attended as it was by all the leading Nigerians and by the representatives of the many foreign governments who were attending the birth of the new nation.

And so the celebration came to an end and H.R.H. set out on a tour round the Regions. I attended her on her visit to the University College at Ibadan where she received a wonderful welcome from the hundreds of young Nigerian students, and a day or two later I flew to Port Harcourt where she visited the port installations and performed a number of other engagements. Her tour ended with a rapid three-day visit to the North, ending at Kano, where I bade her farewell on her return journey to London. She was a popular and charming envoy and her interest and sympathetic approach to everyone she met made her beloved by all who had the good fortune to meet her.

After she had gone I went on from Kano to Katsina to bid farewell to the Emir and his Council. The Emir Ngogo was a charming man, a great lover of horses and a first-class polo player. He had accompanied me in 1957 to the Ghana independence celebrations and had stayed on other occasions in Government House at Lagos, when he came bathing with us at Lighthouse Beach: his secretary had never seen the sea before. I had met the Emir more than twenty years before in the Sudan when he had come with his father on the pilgrimage and spent a night at En Nahud in Western Kordofan. I always thought that the Sardauna

* *Sir Adetokunbo Ademola.* Son of the Alake of Abeokuta. Barrister of the Middle Temple. Practised in Nigeria 1934–49. Became a judge in 1949 and Chief Justice of Western Nigeria 1955–8. Chief Justice of the Federation 1958–69.

of Sokoto as Premier did not make enough use of his talents and was rather jealous of him. On my return to Kano I was able to attend the opening by the Sardauna of the Arabic School at Ahmadu Bello University, a very Muslim and very Northern occasion.

I returned to Lagos with barely a month left before I was to leave Nigeria, and I wished to pay farewell visits to the Regional capitals and say good-bye to the Premiers and their ministers. These visits were friendly occasions, and the Premiers all made eulogistic speeches about my wife and myself and presented us with mementos from their Governments.

'Your Excellency,
'It has become a tradition in Eastern Nigeria that we receive our honoured guests in this Stadium. I am, I think, correct in saying that among the first to be so received was your distinguished predecessor and countryman, Sir John Macpherson. Then, as now, a retiring Governor-General had come to bid us farewell.

'This could be a sad occasion; but we hope that it will rather be one of happiness and an afternoon that you will remember with pleasure in your English – or, should I say Scottish – home.

'Your Excellency, when you arrived in Nigeria five years ago, there those amongst us who were apprehensive. We wondered, notwithstanding your long and distinguished career on the other side of Africa, how you would accommodate yourself to the restless and uneasy Nigeria to which you had come. A nation was being born; and birth is neither an easy nor a painless process.

'We need not have worried. It soon became apparent that our new Governor-General was a man ideally suited, both by temperament and training, to the difficult and onerous duties of his office. You were imperturbable – and this was just as well, for there were ample grounds for perturbation in those days. You were liberal in outlook. You appreciated, sooner than most, the tremendous pace of the change sweeping across Africa and the powerful surge of national pride which bore that change along.

'Above all, Sir, you were wise in Council. Our ship of state was guided at all times truly and well; and when in the fullness of time you handed over the helm you did so calmly and with dignity.

'During your tenure of office you have travelled widely throughout Nigeria. You have met, not only our leaders in the Council of Ministers, in the Legislature and in conferences in London and in Lagos, but also the people of Nigeria in their homes, on their farms and their places of work. In this way you have become known and respected by large members of our citizens in every walk of life; and you have contributed, in a way both personal and effective to the growth of Nigerian unity in diversity which is the great hope of our independent nation.

'Your Excellency, it is a measure of the importance which Nigerians attach to your high office that the person chosen as your successor is someone who, above all others, embodies the very spirit of Nigerian nationalism.

'Not the least of your successes is that, in this significant year, the relations between Nigeria and the United Kingdom, between the ambitious and promising young man and his former guardian, if I may use this simile, have never been more cordial. This has been amply proved by the joyful atmosphere on which our Independence was celebrated, by the great success of the visit of Her Royal Highness Princess Alexandra, and by the numbers of former administrators, missionaries and others who have travelled from Britain at our invitation to join in our rejoicing.

'Surely nowhere has the achievement of Independence been accompanied by such spontaneous manifestations of mutual goodwill and friendship. This need not have been so. That it was so is due in no small measure to your own strenuous endeavours.

'Sir, you have served Nigeria well, Our purpose today is to show our sincere appreciation for all that you have done in five long years of service. We assure you that here in Eastern Nigeria you will not soon be forgotten.

'As a token of our esteem it is now my privilege to present to you, Sir, an elephant's tusk – a symbol of wise authority which no one more justly merits – and a finely woven Akwette cloth – a reminder of Eastern Nigeria and of the friendship of her people.

'Your Excellency, may your retirement be a happy one and enjoyable reward for your years of toil and may God's blessing go with you.'

Equally pleasant things were said at Kaduna, where the Sardauna presided over an immense reception at the State House, and by Chief Akintola at an evening party on the lawns outside the Regional Parliament building in Ibadan. It was consoling on the eve of departure to find that our administrative efforts had been appreciated: one felt that it could not all be mere flattery or politeness, though I realised that when these pleasant things were said to me, they stemmed from the relationship which had grown up between the Nigerians and the British over many years, and while I was the recipient they were really addressed to the British Government and the many hundreds of British people who had lived in Nigeria over the years of our rule and had made themselves much loved by the Nigerians.

At Lagos it was much the same. There were too many parties and farewells, but a happy occasion was when the Prime Minister brought the Council of Ministers to bid us farewell. He made a charming little speech and produced a beautiful inscribed rose bowl from beneath his robes.

I

We embarked on the Elder Dempster liner *Aureol* on 15 November at the Apapa Quays. We had a wonderful send-off: the Marina, all along the harbour, was crowded with thousands of ordinary people who waved and cheered as we crossed the harbour in the launch. At Apapa there were crowds too, including the Prime Minister and the Council, and Dr. Azikiwe, who next day was to take over the Governor-Generalship from me, as well as other leading personalities. The police band was on parade and a guard of honour mounted. As the ship moved away from the quayside the band played 'Will ye no come back again' and I said to my wife, 'They'd be upset if we did!' And so we sailed down the harbour, escorted by H.M.N.S. *Nigeria* and pursued by the haunting notes of the 'Hausa Farewell' – played by the buglers of the Nigeria police.

And so home. What a wonderful experience it had all been and yet there was also a sense of achievement in that the transfer of power had been so smooth and happy; and we left assured that the British name and reputation were respected in Nigeria. The Prime Minister, Sir Abu Bakar, telegraphed to the ship: 'The Governments and people of Nigeria are most grateful to you for the valuable services you have rendered. Your contribution to Nigeria Independence will never be forgotten and we shall always owe you a debt of gratitude. We were happy that you completed your term of office with such success, and that when you left it was with the goodwill of all in Nigeria.'

### Appendix A : The President's Farewell Speech to the Council of Ministers and the Prime Minister's Reply

The PRESIDENT said that it was the last meeting of the Council of Ministers which he would attend and that it marked the end of an era, starting from 1922 when Sir Hugh Clifford established the Old Legislative Council, ever since which time the Governor or, later on, the Governor-General, had presided over the Council. By the Independence Constitution, which would come into force in eight days' time, the Council would be presided over by the Prime Minister in future. The President said that he would like to take the opportunity of thanking the Prime Minister and all the other Ministers for the never-failing courtesy and goodwill which thay had shown towards him as President. Sometimes he had been a bit sharp and rather unsympathetic but, by and large, since he first presided over the Council in 1955, he thought that he and the Ministers had got on very well together and there had always been a real spirit of co-operation. Any success which he might have had as Governor-General during those years had been due to the splendid support and backing which he had always had from the Council.

The President said that he had had an easy assignment in Nigeria because he had never had any doubt about the goal at which he was aiming, which was to assist Nigeria to obtain Independence as soon as was possible, consistent with the maintenance of good government, and to promote a real spirit of unity in the country. In carrying out that task he had been greatly helped by the Council. He also believed that the spirit of compromise and mutual respect shown by all the delegations at the various conferences in which he and the Ministers had taken part had had much to do with the successful conclusion which they had now reached.

The President said that he had felt personally very much complimented by the Prime Minister's invitation to him to remain as Governor-General in the independent Nigeria for six weeks after Independence; he would look forward to receiving the Memoranda and Conclusions of the Council during that time. He understood that a constitutional head of state was entitled to be informed of what was happening, to encourage his Ministers and, if he wished, to advise them. He hoped that in that way he might be of further use to the Council and perhaps begin to establish precedents for the future.

The President said that when he first came to Nigeria he knew little about the country and his affections lay more in the Anglo-Egyptian Sudan, where he had served for so long. But now he felt that Nigeria held just as big a place in his heart as the Sudan did and he had got to love it and its people very sincerely. He was sure that when he retired to his own country, his interest in affairs here would always remain very great and he would eagerly await news of how the new independent Nigeria was progressing. Nigeria had many advantages: she had Ministers who were trained and experienced in policy-making and in administration; she had also a virile and active population, diverse economy and was a potentially rich country. There seemed no reason why Nigeria should not flourish in the future if the country had some luck and members of the Council were statesmanlike. It would be a tremendous joy to all Europeans who had worked here with Nigerians if the country made a real success of its Independence and moved forward to take its rightful place in Africa and among the nations of the world. The President felt very confident that the country would do so.

The President then said that he would like to take advantage of his position as an old friend to give three pieces of advice. First, he said that he had continually, since his first speech when he had been sworn in on 15 June 1955, harped almost wearisomely on the need for unity – unity of purpose and unity of heart. He thought the country was more united now than it was when he had first come to Nigeria and it might be that he had done something to help. But it was imperative that the Federal Government and Ministers should be apostles of that unity, especially now when the British Governor-General and Governors were going and were not there behind the scenes to help keep the governments acting in unison. Secondly, the President said that he would like to advise statesmanship in the Federal Government's dealings with Western Regional Government: that latter

Government was made up from an opposing political party which was much disliked for quite good reasons by the two parties forming the Government of the Federation. He understood there were some who wished the Federal Government to take the initiative in carving up the Western Region by setting up a Mid-West State and by annexing areas of the Western Region to the Federal territory of Lagos. Of course, it would by pleasant to get some revenge on the Action Group, and it might be that the two proposals in themselves had something to be said for them. But the question which should be asked was whether those proposals would do Nigeria any good and whether such action would make for a more united country or would rather weaken the country in the early days when it should be strong. Thirdly, the President advised that each Minister who went abroad should speak on his own subject; and that applied to Regional as well as Federal Ministers. At present, too many people in Ministerial positions toured the world and spoke on Nigerian policies on which they were not entitled to speak publicly. That especially, of course, referred to foreign policy, and when Nigeria became independent and had a Federal Minister for Foreign Affairs and Commonwealth Relations, it would be terribly important that only that Minister and the Prime Minister should speak in Foreign Affairs. Otherwise no one would know what Nigeria's policy was and great confusion would ensue. The President suggested that once Independence was achieved, the Minister for Foreign Affairs should make that abundantly clear to his colleagues and to the Regional Governments. He felt sure that after Independence the Federal Government must exert itself to deal solely in respect of matters in the exclusive list, and Regional Governments should be dissuaded from interference. Only in that way could Nigeria speak with one voice, and carry out a foreign policy discussed and decided by the Council of Ministers.

The President reiterated his thanks to Ministers for the assistance they had given him in carrying on the work of government; for assisting him in his policy for a gradual friendly and constructive transfer of power; and for all the kindness and friendship which Ministers had shown him. He said that his wife and himself would never forget Nigeria and they would watch the future with immense interest, feeling that they had a share in the country which they had been proud to serve.

The PRIME MINISTER said that all the Ministers in the Council had valued very much the time they had spent in the Council under the President's guidance. Ministers had been very lucky to have worked with the President. The Prime Minister said that he had been working more closely with the President than any other member of the Council, and he could not remember a single occasion when the President had refused to accept his advice. The President had always given him wise and mature advice. The Prime Minister said that any time the President was due to go on leave he, the Prime Minister himself, had always felt as if part of him were going away. He knew the President very closely and knew what his intentions were for Nigeria. The President had guided the affairs of the Federation with unparalleled wisdom.

The Prime Minister said that all the Regions in the Federation had accepted the President as a father; they had tremendous confidence in him and his wise advice.

The Prime Minister expressed deep regret that the President was leaving the country; he had thought that it would be possible for him to stay on much longer, but there were circumstances which made things work in the opposite direction.

The Prime Minister then referred to the three pieces of advice which had been given by the President and said that the Ministers would always remember them and that they, on their part, would try to live up to the President's expectation and the expectation of others who had helped the country. It was a difficult time because the face of Africa was changing rapidly. The Prime Minister said that he felt that Nigeria had a special responsibility to the whole of Africa and he expressed the hope that the country would surmount all its difficulties and, at the same time, assist other countries to stand on their feet.

The Prime Minister recalled that in January 1960 he overheard the President when he was talking to Mr. Macmillan, Prime Minister of the United Kingdom, and said, 'Nowadays, people can only trust in God and do their best'. The Prime Minister said that he would never forget that statement and it had been one of his guiding principles ever since. It would be the duty of all the Ministers to put away selfish interest and work for a united Nigeria.

The Prime Minister next referred to the President's advice about the opposing political party which was running the Government of one of the Regions. He said the President knew his views on that matter. Since 1954 his views had been that though some political parties were not represented in the Council of Ministers, that Council should regard itself as the guardian, not only of the parties represented in the Council, but of all the political parties in the country and of the country as a whole. He said that as a Muslim, he believed that if he condemned others because they did not share his political beliefs, he would be accountable to God for such actions. He believed that the Council of Ministers should strive after the best interest of the country as a whole.

The Prime Minister said that there would still be another occasion when he would be able to speak at length, publicly, to acknowledge his indebtedness to the President and the country's gratitude to him. He hoped that between now and the time of departure of the President from the country he would continue to receive the President's advice and assistance.

The Prime Minister said that he and his colleagues in the Council of Ministers would always remember the President's generosity. There were many people who like to cling to power but the President was always ready to surrender power. He wanted Ministers to know that since 1957, when he became the Prime Minister, the President, as Governor-General, had given him full responsibility over the affairs of the Government of the Federation. The Prime Minister said that last March the President, on his own initiative, handed over to him control over the army and the police, and he could say with every confidence that for the last two years the country had been technically independent. He expressed his gratitude to the President for the opportunity which had been afforded him and his colleagues to learn and benefit from the President's wide and mature experience.

The MINISTER OF FINANCE said that although there were two political parties represented in the Council of Ministers, the views which had been expressed by the Prime Minister represented the views of the whole of the Ministers in the Council and, on behalf of the Ministers, he associated himself with those views.

Ministers closely associated themselves with the views expressed by the Prime Minister and the Minister of Finance.

## Appendix B. Independence Day: The Prime Minister's Speech

Today is Independence Day. The first of October 1960 is a date to which for two years every Nigerian has been eagerly looking forward. At last our great day had arrived, and Nigeria is now indeed an independent sovereign nation.

Words cannot adequately express my joy and pride at being the Nigerian citizen privileged to accept from her Her Royal Highness these Constitutional Instruments which are symbols of Nigeria's Independence. It is a unique privilege which I shall remember for ever, and it gives me strength and courage as I dedicate my life to the service of our country.

This is a wonderful day, and it is all the more wonderful because we have awaited it with increasing impatience, compelled to watch one country after another overtaking us on the road when we had so nearly reached our goal. But now we have acquired our rightful status, and I feel sure that history will show that the building of our nation proceeded at the wisest pace: it has been thorough, and Nigerian now stands well-built upon firm foundations.

Today's ceremony marks the culmination of a process which began fifteen years ago and has now reached a happy and successful conclusion. It is with justifiable pride that we claim the achievement of our Independence to be unparalleled in the annals of history. Each step of our constitutional advance has been purposefully and peacefully planned with full and open consultation, not only between representatives of all the various interests in Nigeria but in harmonious co-operation with administering power which has today relinquished its authority.

At the time when our constitutional development entered upon its final phase, the emphasis was largely upon self-government. We, the elected representatives of the people of Nigeria, concentrated on proving that we were fully capable of managing our own affairs both internally and as a nation. However, we were not to be allowed the selfish luxury of focusing our interest on our own homes. In these days of rapid communications we cannot live in isolation, apart from the rest of the world, even if we wished to do so. All too soon it has become evident that for us Independence implies a great deal more than self-government. This great country, which has now emerged without bitterness or bloodshed, finds that she must at once be ready to deal with grave international issues.

This fact has of recent months been unhappily emphasised by the startling events which have occurred in this continent. I shall not labour the point but it would be unrealistic not to draw attention first to the awe-inspiring task confronting us at the very start of our nationhood. When this day in October 1960 was chosen for our Independence it seemed that we were destined to move with quiet dignity to our place on the world stage. Recent events have changed the scene beyond recognition, so that we find ourselves today being tested to the utmost. We are called upon immediately to show that our claims to responsible government are well-founded, and having been accepted as an independent state we must at once play an active part in maintaining the peace of the world and in preserving civilisation. I promise you, we shall not fail for want of determination.

And we come to this task better equipped than many. For this I pay tribute to the manner in which successive British Governments have gradually transferred the burden of responsibility to our shoulders. The assistance and unfailing encouragement which we have received from each Secretary of State for the Colonies and their intense personal interest in our development has immeasurably lightened that burden.

All our friends in the Colonial Office must today be proud of their handiwork and in the knowledge that they have helped to lay the foundations of a lasting friendship between our two nations. I have indeed every confidence that, based on the happy experience of a successful partnership, our future relations with the United Kingdom will be more cordial than ever, bound together, as we shall be in the Commonwealth, by a common allegiance to Her Majesty Queen Elizabeth, whom today we proudly acclaim as Queen of Nigeria and Head of the Commonwealth.

Time will not permit the individual mention of all those friends, many of them Nigerians, whose selfless labours have contributed to our Independence. Some have not lived to see the fulfilment of their hopes – on them be peace – but nevertheless they are remembered here, and the names of buildings and streets and roads and bridges throughout the country recall to out minds their achievements, some of them on a national scale. Others confined, perhaps, to a small area in one Division, are more humble but of equal value in the sum-total.

Today we have with us representatives of those who have made Nigeria: Representatives of the Regional Governments, of former Central Governments, of the Missionary Societies, and of the Banking and Commercial enterprises, and members, both past and present, of the Public Service. We welcome you, and we rejoice that you have been able to come and share in our celebrations. We wish that it could have been possible for all of those whom you represent to be here today. Many, I know, will be disappointed to be absent, but if they are listening to me now, I say to them: 'Thank you on behalf of my countrymen. Thank you for your devoted service which helped to build up Nigeria into a nation. Today we are reaping the harvest which you sowed, and the quality of the harvest is equalled only by our gratitude to you. May God bless you all.'

This an occasion when our hearts are filled with conflicting emotions: we are, indeed, proud to have achieved our Independence, and proud that our efforts should have contributed to this happy event. But do not mistake our pride for arrogance. It is tempered by feelings of sincere gratitude to all who have shared in the task of developing Nigeria politically, socially and economically. We are grateful to the British officers whom we have known, first as masters, and then as leaders, and finally as partners, but always as friends. And there have been countless missionaries who have laboured unceasingly in the cause of education and to whom we owe many of our medical services. We are grateful to those who have brought modern methods of banking and of commerce, and new industries: I wish to pay tribute to all of these people and to declare our everlasting admiration to their devotion to duty.

And finally, I must express our gratitude to Her Royal Highness the Princess Alexandra of Kent for personally bringing to us these symbols of our freedom, and especially for delivering the gracious message from Her Majesty The Queen. And so, with the words 'God Save Our Queen', I open a new chapter in the history of Nigeria, and of the Commonwealth, and indeed of the world.

# CHAPTER XIII

# REFLECTIONS

My years in Africa were ones of immense and rapid change both in that continent and in the world at large. Critics of our colonial history usually seem to forget how primitive the African territories were when we took them over, how tenuous a growth was law and order, how poor were communications and how exiguous was education, yet all developed and contributed to the transition to Independence, which came much sooner than we envisaged when I arrived in the Sudan in 1922. The changes were not achieved without very great effort by a relatively small number of men, although it appears currently unfashionable to recognise their work. Economic development, which in early days we had thought of as the way of bringing more prosperous living to the colonial people, was termed 'exploitation', though I have never been able to understand how our critics thought the dependent territories could be developed without the injection of capital from abroad and the gradual training of the people in the skills and techniques required for economic progress. Our problem often seemed to be one not of excess capital but of trying to find financial resources. The British Government until 1942 made little attempt to assist the colonies financially; each territory had to pay its own way, and Treasury aid, given only to a few impecunious territories which could not balance their budgets, was pruned to the last halfpenny. The two great world wars also held up development through lack of manpower and materials, and this continued for some years afterwards while the world climbed slowly back to normality. There was also the economic blizzard of the early 1930s. Nigeria, the Sudan, Kenya and Uganda – countries I knew something of – all had the same problems, though of these the Sudan was much the poorest in its national potential. The Sudan too, as a Condominium, was less eligible for British assistance than colonial territories, though the British Government did assist the Sudan by guaranteeing a loan raised in Britain in the early twenties to build the Sennar dam and develop the Gezira scheme, and in 1946 the Attlee Government made a grant of £2 million as a repayment of the Sudan's wartime assistance to Britain.

The constant problems of finance made economic development

difficult, but international changes occurred much faster and altered the African situation markedly. The economic crisis of the early 1930s and the Second World War altered the British situation, so that by 1960 the world was a very different place from what it had been in 1922. Britain was no longer the leading world power; her place had been taken by two super-powers, the United States and Russia, and we had felt the changes in Africa. In the Sudan we had always been aware of world affairs, partly because being a Condominium the Sudan Government was under the control of the Foreign rather than the Colonial Office. We sometimes felt in the Sudan that in matters affecting Egypt the Foreign Office was too much swayed by the British Embassy in Cairo, and that the need for good relations with Egypt sometimes led to the welfare of the Sudan being sacrificed. However, in the end the Sudanese obtained the right of self-determination, which was what we worked for, though, as I have described, some of the terms of the 1953 Anglo–Egyptian Agreement unfortunately led to the tragic developments in the Southern Sudan.

Being under the Foreign Office also affected the Sudan in other ways. We suffered from the Foreign Office's lack of interest in internal administration and consequently there was a lack of authoritative advice readily available to us when we came to establish parliamentary institutions. The Colonial Office had much experience and expertise which we could only obtain in private and personal ways, although sometimes in Nigeria I thought that it wished to be too much in the picture and demanded a great deal of detailed information about matters which should have been dealt with on the spot. In some ways the Sudan's virtual independence was an advantage, and made possible more rapid Africanisation than I found in Nigeria, as well as contributing to the efficiency and beneficence of our administration.

But it was not only in the Sudan that the effects of the changing world situation were felt. American pre-conceived ideas on colonial rule led to pressure by the United States and by the U.N.O. to hasten the hand-over of power; presumably on the assumption that British rule in African territories was comparable with our dominion in America in the 1770s. The manifest difference between the less advanced African communities and the America of Washington, Franklin, Adams and Jefferson was not always appreciated by the average American. Furthermore, liberal opinions in the United Kingdom, combined with Britain's loss of wealth and power as a result of the two great wars, left the British Government only too ready to get rid of their colonial responsibilities as soon as they could, without considering too closely whether such hasty action was to the ultimate benefit either of the colonial people or of British interests. This policy was intensified around 1960 with Macmillan's 'Wind of change' speech and Iain Macleod's colonial secretaryship. Ironically, it is commonplace now to criticise the British Government and those of us who were in positions of authority in the colonial territories for going ahead with independence too soon, before the peoples concerned were ready for it. Americans have asked me: 'Why did you leave so soon before the colonial territories were ready to rule themselves?' and when I have replied, 'Partly, I am sure, because of your pressure on us to go', have answered that they did not know then what they now know, and that we should have resisted their pressure.

However, developments within the territories themselves played a more important part than international pressure in ending colonial rule. I had always believed that it should be possible for the ruling colonial power to achieve a friendly and orderly hand-over to an independent government of the indigenous people when the latter were ready, that is when a reasonable proportion of them were educated and an adequate number had received some training under our guidance in the business of ruling the country; also when a form of democratic government had been evolved and was functioning satisfactorily. As time passed and I saw more of the transitional period, this ideal of a carefully graduated approach to self-government until the time for Independence arrived began to seem less likely ever to be achieved. The snags were too many: the education of the masses proceeded far less speedily than the advancement of a small élite, and as this élite grew in number and experience, it became more and more evident that it would not wait until the mass of the population acquired the sophistication and experience required for the basis of a democratic society. Outside forces had also impinged on the élite, as the Egyptians did in the Sudan. Furthermore, democracy as we know it requires the existence of many societies and organisations which can influence the policies of the government. In the United Kingdom the churches, trade unions, professional associations and numerous other interest groups represent the opinions and views of various sections of the community. In the new African countries such influential bodies did not exist. Furthermore, the training of a civil service in any new territory begins slowly, and for perhaps a generation the indigenous civil servants could not aspire to fill all the top posts. But there came a time when they started knocking at the door, and although their inexperience, lack of wide outlook and sometimes inadequate education seemed to make most of them unable to fill the high-level posts, their pressure and the political agitation which accompanied it gradually undermined the confidence of the expatriate officers. This led to the early retirement of key personnel and the impossibility of recruiting replacements from the old, well-tried sources.

A further difficulty was that colonial political leaders did not always agree that they should walk for some time before they started to run. In British Guiana, the Waddington Commission had recommended a fairly advanced form of constitution which, while giving considerable power to the Guyanese ministers, yet contained reasonable checks and balances until they had gained some experience. But Cheddi Jagan and his ministers did not wish to co-operate, and sabotaged the whole scheme by their refusal to take one step at a time. In the Sudan half the politically interested élite similarly refused to co-operate with the efforts made by the Sudan Government to train and educate the Sudanese in the techniques of administration and government, and thereby partly frustrated the efforts made by the British to prepare the Sudan for self-government. It was always humiliating and depressing to have one's sincere efforts to prepare the country and its political leaders for self-government and independence ridiculed and attacked as imperialistic manoeuvres. It was my good fortune in Nigeria to benefit from the trust which the Nigerian leaders felt in the two Colonial Secretaries, Oliver Lyttelton and Alan Lennox-Boyd, leading to their acceptance of Britain's promise to give them Independence soon, even if there were delays and apparent hesitations. By 1958 and 1959 the British Government was fully committed to the liquidation of the colonial empire, and it was obvious that delays would lead at least to discontent and ill-feeling and at worst to serious disorder and unrest. Had such events occurred they might well have necessitated the use of force, and in Nigeria we had no British troops or British police and relied on African N.C.O.s and other ranks, with some British officers. Her Majesty's Government had no troops to give us and, if it had been able to provide them, the British people in the late 1950s would not have agreed to their use to delay the handover of power.

This criticism of undue haste in handing over power is based on hindsight and on the difficulties which have arisen since Independence rather than on the situation at the time. Clearly it was in our best interests to leave before discontent and agitation had eroded the good relations which existed between the British and the Sudanese and Nigerians. There also appeared to be positive advantages in saving the existing good relations; we should make it more feasible for some of our expatriate officials to remain in the service of the new countries; the new governments might value the links with Britain and the advice and assistance which they could receive from the British; and our trading interests might be maintained. All these results might well be lost if we stayed too long and finally left after fighting and bloodshed in an atmosphere of hatred and suspicion.

Unfortunately, events showed that our early departure left many problems to be resolved by the successor governments. In the Sudan, North–South integration had not been achieved, and the newly-empowered politicians tactlessly, but no doubt unintentionally, exacerbated the divisions. In Nigeria, similarly, we had not resolved the difference between the Northerners and Southerners. We could only hope that the unity which we had enforced on the country had become sufficiently well established to persist after we had gone. I must admit to having been wrong in both these instances, but who can assert that, had we waited until what we regarded as more satisfactory solutions had been found, things would not have been worse rather than better?

Another frequent criticism made now is that our attempt to found democratic states based on the Westminster model was a mistaken policy. However, it is not easy to see what other policy we could have followed. Most of the leading politicians in our African territories had absorbed British ideas of democratic rule from their education, both in the schools at home and in university education abroad, or in reading for the United Kingdom bar examination. In Nigeria there were several hundred young men who had been called to the Bar in London. I was astonished in 1956, when the Queen held a reception at the Law Courts in Lagos, to see some 400 Nigerian barristers in wigs and gowns march in procession into the hall where the ceremony was to be held. All had been educated in the United Kingdom and been called to the Bar there. Moreover the European officials who for two generations had administered these countries had been brought up to believe that democracy was the best form of government; many of them had fought to preserve it in two world wars, and they naturally sympathised with the policy of attempting to leave their proven democratic form of government behind when they had to leave.

It has also been said in the last few years with regard to Nigeria that the colonial administration *imposed* a Federal form of government upon the country. This is entirely untrue. The Federal constitution of 1954 was the result of the 1953 and 1954 conferences, when the Nigerian political leaders who attended insisted upon a Federal set-up as being what *they* wanted. The Prime Minister Abu Bakar Tafawa Balewa described this very clearly in a speech which he made in the Nigerian Parliament in September 1957: 'But to me the most important result of the constitutional changes in 1954 was the introduction of a Federal form of Government for Nigeria – a system which I had advocated as far back as 1948 in the old Legislative Council. I am pleased to see that we are all now agreed that the federal system is, under present conditions, the only sure basis on which Nigeria can remain united. We must recognise our diversity and the peculiar conditions under which the different tribal communities live in this country. To us in Nigeria, therefore, unity in diversity is a source of great strength, and we must do all in our power to see that this federal system of government is strengthened and maintained.'

The constitution was the result of long, free discussions, in which the Nigerians had considered and confirmed every word and every sentence. Similarly, in the conferences between 1954 and the achievement of Independence in 1960, they were apparently in complete agreement with all that was decided. Admittedly, the actual drafting of the constitutional instruments was done by legal draftsmen in the Colonial Office, but these drafts interpreted the conference decisions, and on completion were examined and accepted by the Nigerians. The only exception was the abortive defence agreement between Nigeria and the United Kingdom, which was prepared in 1958 as a result of talks between the Nigerians and the Minister of Defence, Duncan Sandys. The Nigerian political leaders were not happy about this proposal, and I and the Regional Governors considered the proposal unhappy. But they eventually initialled it at the time on the understanding that they would reconsider the question and come to final decisions as soon as Nigeria became independent. The Federal Government then repudiated it. The Prime Minister told me that they initialled originally because they feared that Her Majesty's Government would delay their Independence if they did not accept. Thus the Federal constitution itself, as brought into force on 1 October 1960, was freely negotiated and accepted by all the political party leaders.

Why then did it fail? Partly, I am sure, because the force of tribalism was greater than anyone had estimated; partly because many of the politicians were corrupt and aimed at their own enrichment rather than the good of their people; and partly because the Prime Minister, Sir Abu Bakar, in later 1965 and in January 1966, was prevented from taking strong action in the Western Region. This resulted from his inability to carry his party and its leader, the Sardauna, with him, when the Sardauna had agreed to support the Western Premier Akintola against the opposition in the Western Region. If Sir Abu Bakar had been sure of majority support in the House of Representatives, I have no doubt that he would have acted in January 1966 as he did in 1962 when he suspended the Western constitution and installed a Federal commissioner to restore law and order and good government. As he said in the Federal parliament in

May 1962, 'No responsible Government of the Federation could allow an explosive situation such as that which now exists in Western Nigeria to continue without taking adequate measures to ensure that their is an early return to the Region of peace, order and good government.' But in December 1965 and January 1966 his party, the N.P.C., was not of the same mind, and Sir Abu Bakar had not the power to intervene.

Looking back now, perhaps the mistake lay not in supporting federation, but in the failure to divide the vast Northern Region into smaller states, as from time to time recommended by Dr. Azikiwe and Chief Awolowo. But it is also obvious that this would have been bitterly opposed by the Sardauna and the Northern Regional Government, as the Sardauna made very clear in his book *My Life*. As it was, the vast proportion of Northern constituencies in the Federal House of Representatives made it almost impossible for any one party, except the N.P.C., to be in power in the Federal Government, and it was probably the frustration caused by this situation which led to the plot in 1962 by some Action Group leaders to overthrow Sir Abu Bakar's Government and which set in train the events leading to the fatal developments of January 1966.

The question 'How much of the legacy we bequeathed to these territories is likely to remain?' is often asked but is very difficult to answer. The personal friendships between individual British officials and the Africans they ruled are bound to fade as the years pass, and people on short-term educational, technical and commercial contracts seem unlikely to develop the same close links. The ties of language and culture, however, remain and there seems no falling-off in the numbers of Africans coming to Britain for further education and training. It is likely, therefore, that future friendships will be forged much more in Britain than in Africa, and this will throw much of the responsibility on to the British public.

While there are great numbers of individuals ready and waiting to help, it cannot be said that the British public as a whole was ever greatly interested in what we were trying to do in Africa. Few appeared to understand our purpose, and the great majority did not even have much knowledge of the continent's geography. 'Oh, you're working in the Sudan. Do you know my cousin in Johannesburg?' was the kind of comment one received. It can only be hoped that in future the British people will feel a need to help, and there is perhaps a growing awareness of the poverty of Africa and other parts of the 'Third World'.

In the Sudan and in Nigeria since Independence there have been tragic events – notably the conflict between Southerners and Northerners in the Sudan and the war in Nigeria to prevent the break-away of the Eastern Region, which came to be known as Biafra. I trust that nothing in the policies with which I was associated in my overseas service exacerbated the tensions which led to these events: it is, of course, a constant personal feeling that with more wisdom one might have ordered things better and thereby averted them. But there is some consolation in the way both the Sudan and Nigeria have returned to peace and are settling down under the enlightened leadership of Generals Nimeiry and Gowon respectively. Reconciliation and a determination to forget the past have been successful, and the auguries for the future are brighter than ever before. Perhaps this spirit carries on the tradition of the former rule. It is pleasant to think so.

9. The last full meeting of the Executive Council, Sudan Government, March 1953. In the chair Sir Robert Howe, Governor-General. Members of the Council (l. to r., round table): El-Sayed Abd el-Majed Ahmad, Under-Secretary for Economics and Trade; (hidden) El-Sayed Ibrahim Ahmad, Councillor without Portfolio; El Ferik R. L. Scoones Pasha, *Kaid el-'Amm*; Sir Charles Cumings, Legal Secretary; El-Sayed 'Abd el-Rahman Ali Taha, Minister of Education; El-Sayed Mirslai Abdulla Bey Khalil, Minister of Agriculture; the Author; El-Sayed Dr. Ali-Bedri, Minister of Health; Sir Louis Chick, Financial Secretary; R. C. Wakefield, Councillor without Portfolio; El-Sayed Mohamed Ahmed Abu Sin, Councillor without Portfolio; El-Sayed Abdel Rahman Abdoon, Under-Secretary for Irrigation; (standing) H. Colville Stewart, Secretary.

10. The Author with the Regional Premiers outside Government House, Lagos, on the day of his arrival in Nigeria. L. to r.: Dr. Azikiwe, Chief Awolowo, the Author, the Sardauna of Sokoto.

11. Group at Benin, Mid-western Nigeria, August 1958: the Author and Lady Robertson, his niece Elizabeth Crowther, the Oba of Benin, and Benin chiefs and notables.

12. The Author and Lady Robertson with Alhaji Sir
Abu Bakar Tafawa Balewa, the Prime Minister of the
Federation of Nigeria, who had come to meet them at
Ikeja airport on their arrival from home leave.

13. The Author with the Prime Minister at Ikeja airport waiting to receive Princess Alexandra, September
1960.

# INDEX

ABA, 185, 201
Abdel Gader, leader of Hassania tribe, 31–2
Abdel Magid scheme, 26, 28–9, 32, 33
Abdel Rahman el Mahdi, Sayed, Sudanese politician, 20–1, 92, 95, 97, 98, 113, 123, 139, 141, 149; agricultural activities, 33–4; domination of Legislative Assembly, 115; fear of Egyptian infiltration, 153; urged to stage coup, 147
Abdel Rahman Ali Taha, educationalist and politician, 35, 115, 118, 140
Abdel Salam el Khalifa, politician, 121, 136
Abdulla Bey Khalil, leader of the Legislative Assembly, 115, 117–19, 141, 147; disquiet over Southern situation, 151; and labour legislation, 126
Abu Bakar Tafawa Balewa, Alhaji Sir, Federal Prime Minister of Nigeria, xiii, 205, 213, 216, 235, 241, 243, 244, 246–8, 255–6, 257; assessment, 214–15; forms government, 234–5; Independence Day speech, 248–50; knighthood, 236; reasons for overthrow, 256–7
Abu Bakr el Meleik, Sheikh, 15–16
Abu Bukr Ali el Tayeb, Sudanese official, 138
Abu Hamed, 7
Abu Shenina, 64
Abu Simbel, 6
Abu Zabad, 44, 46, 53
Abyad, Lake, 49
Abyei, 46, 50
Acholi tribe, 106
Action Group, 187, 188, 207, 234, 246, 247; election campaign, 233; joins Federal administration, 213
Adelabu, Nigerian politician, 188

Ademola, Sir Adetokunbo, Chief Justice of Nigeria, 241
administration, division of functions in Nigeria, 192
Administrative Conference, 102–3, 105; Sudanisation, 94; report on local government, 127
administrative service, Sudanisation, 83–4
Advisory Council, proposed for Southern Sudan, 106–7
Advisory Council for Northern Sudan, 85–6, 92, 94, 99, 102
Afam, 218
AFLOC scheme, 87
Africa, effect of world changes, 252–3
African Continental Bank, 198–9
Africanisation see Nigerianisation, Sudanisation
Agaira people, 52
*agawid*, panel of elders, 30
Agricultural Department research station, Shambat, 7
agriculture, 5, 137; auctions, 54; Gezira scheme, 128–9; mechanical crop production scheme, 124, 138; Southern development plan, 110–11; Western Kordofan, 42; White Nile, 25
Ahidjo, President of French Cameroons, 239
Ahmadu Bello, see Sokoto, Sardauna of,
Ahmadu Bello University, 242
Ahmed Atia, see Atia, Ahmed
Ahmed el Garoad, litigant, 20
Ahmed el Tahir, Sheikh, Grand Kadi, 100
Ahmed el Tai, Sheikh, 28
Ahmed Mustafa Abu Rennat, Sheikh, 46
Ahmed Yousef Hashim, politician, 120
*El Ahram*, newspaper, 145

259

Gezira Province, 67; and the War, 68, 76

Gezira scheme, 9, 11, 25–6, 67, 81, 86, 124, 128–30, 251

Ghana, independence, 203–4

Ghibeish, 43

Gibb, Professor H. A. R. (later Sir Hamilton), 4

Gibbons, Brigadier E. J., Commissioner for Southern Cameroons, 186

giraffe, 50, 62

Gloucester, Duke and Duchess of, tour of Nigeria, 226–7

Gold Coast, independence, 203–4

gold production, Sudan, 60, 76

Gordon (Bill), 177

Gordon, General Charles, 8, 103

Gordon Memorial College, 20, 105

Governor-General, Nigeria, powers modified, 209–10

Governor-General's Commission, 154–155

Gowon, General, 258

Goz Abu Kelab, 39

Graduates' Congress, 41, 94; dispute with Sudan Government, 83

grain crops, 26, 42; taxes, 17–19

Grand Kadi, 99–100

Greeks, conscription in Sudan, 87

Grey, Ralph, Chief Secretary Nigeria, 194

Griffiths, V. G., educationalist, 34

Gubba, 60

gubbas (tombs), 17

gum arabic, 5

Gumuz tribe, 57

Guyana Industrial Workers' Association, 173

Gwynne, Bishop, 66

HABBANI see Idris Habbani

Hadendowa people, 138

Halawin tribe, 22

Hamar tribe, 44, 48; gatherings, 49

Hamza see Mirghani Hamza

Hanafi Ali, mamur, 17, 23

Hancock, G. M., Deputy Civil secretary, Sudan, 110

Hantoub, school, 131

el Hag Agbar, Sheikh, 52

Hashim see Ahmed Yousef Hashim

Hassab el Rasul wad Bedr, Sheikh, 17

Hassaheissa, 12, 22

Hassan see Khogali Hassan

Hassan Mamoun, Sheikh, Grand Kadi, 100

Hassan Sid Ahmed, sub-mamur, 58

Hassania tribe, 31

Hausa people, 187

Hawkesworth, Geoffrey, Governor Kordofan, 167

Haselden, E. C., Sudan Agent in Cairo, 113

Hemeida Khamis, Sheikh, 52

Henderson, K. D. D., Governor Darfur, 156

herds, taxes, 18

Herbert, Lieutenant-General Sir Otway, G.O.C.-in-C West Africa, 191

Hibbert, Denys, Director of Education Southern Provinces, 135

Highland Light Infantry, 74

Hillali Pasha, Egyptian Prime Minister, 149

Hillalia, 20

Hillard, R. J., head of Sudan Railways, 115

hippopotamus hunting, 51

Holford, Charles, Judge Blue Nile Province, Sudan, 16, 63

Hope Waddell Institute, 185

hospitals, Berber, 137; Equatoria Province, 136; Ibadan, 182

Howe, Sir Robert, Governor-General of the Sudan, 133, 146, 150, 152, 154, 157; appointment, 102; assessment, 160–1

Howe, Lady, 102

Huddleston, Arthur, Governor Blue Nile Province, 11–12, 26, 39

Huddleston, Sir Hubert, 83, 90, 95, 96, 99, 102, 160; appointed Governor-General of the Sudan, 68; assessment, 100–1; presses for Sudanese self-determination 97–8

Huddleston, Lady, 89

Huddleston, May, 39

Hudson, R. S., Commissioner Provincial Devolution Northern Nigeria, 221

Humphry, J. M., Governor Kassala Province, Sudan, 83–4

Humr people, 42, 48, 51

Hussein Sirry Pasha, Egyptian Prime Minister, 149